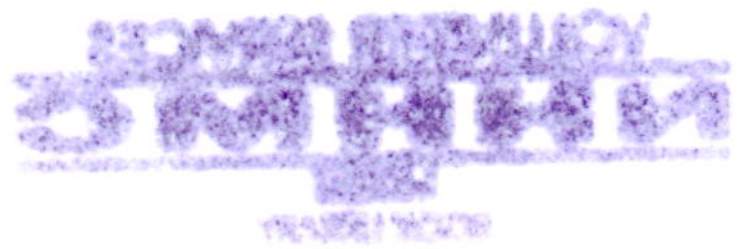

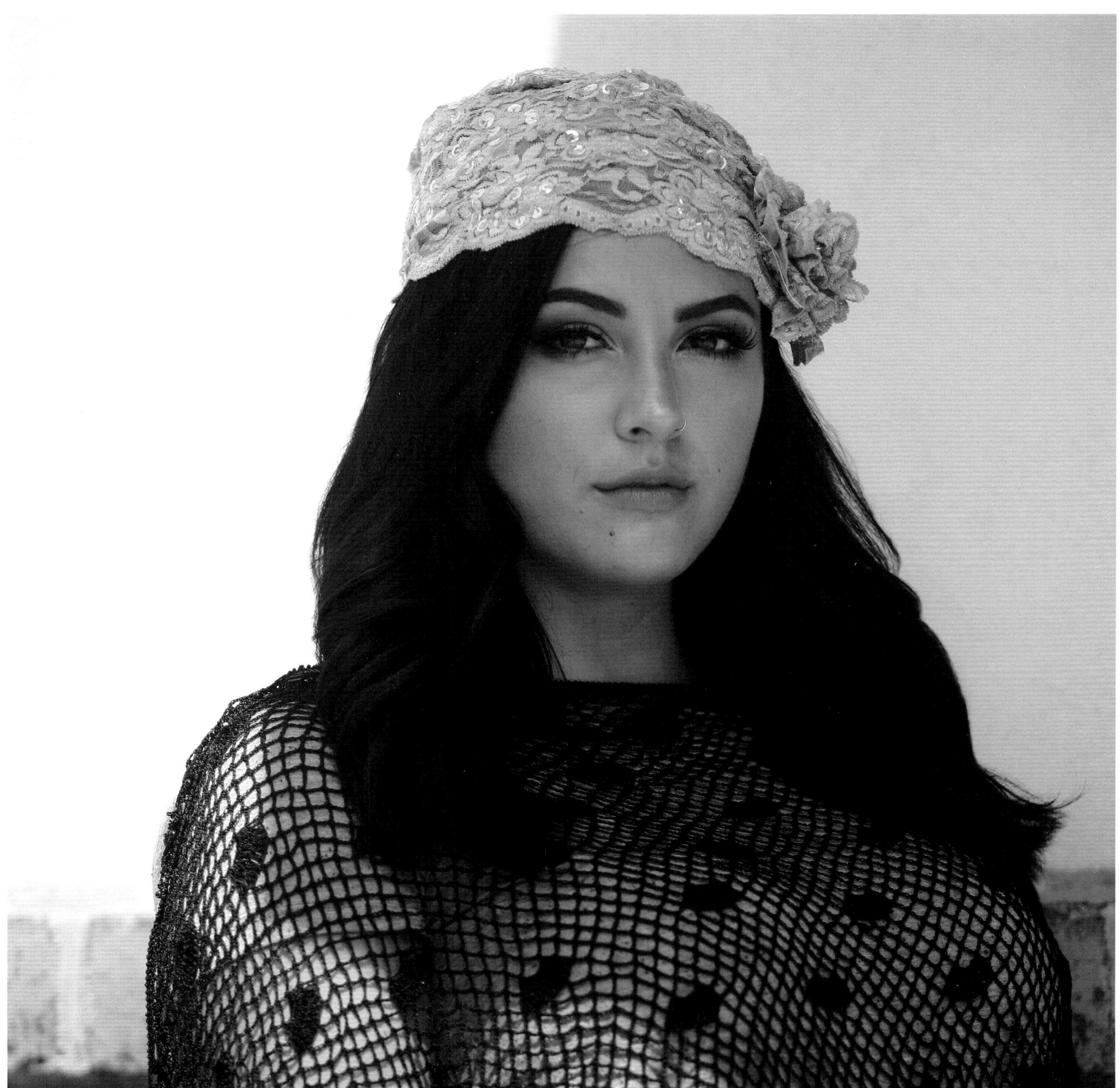

Samantha Stone

SOLO

A Celebration of Women on Their Own

PORTRAITS & PROFILES *of*
NEVER MARRIED, DIVORCED & WIDOWED

by Kathleen Fitzgerald

Solo

Published in the United States of America by

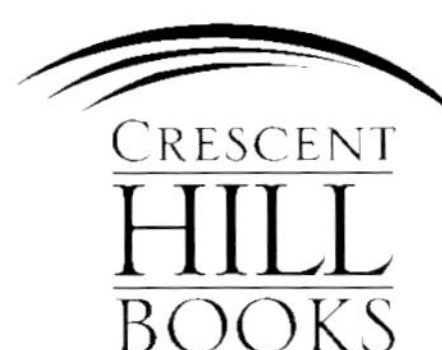

2410 Frankfort Avenue
Louisville, KY 40206
www.crescenthillbooks.com

Solo is a creation of CELB, LLC.

For information about the creation of Solo: *A Celebration of Women on Their Own,* please contact the author at KathFitz.com

All names, images, and life stories in this book have been used with written permission from the women on the following pages.

Printed in China.

Text and Cover Design by Gail Spring and Kathy Davis.

Library of Congress Cataloging-in-Publication Data

Library of Congress Control Number: 2018960710

Solo: A Celebration of Women on Their Own / by Kathleen Fitzgerald

1. Photography of Women. 2. Women - Social conditions.

ISBN: 978-1-889937-36-6

First edition.

ACKNOWLEDGMENTS

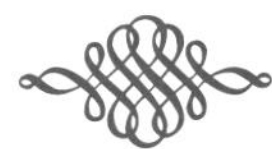

Although this book is titled *Solo,* I surely could not have done it alone! I am grateful for the assistance in finding just the right women to feature in this volume. Many thanks to the ladies who helped me find them: Gail Fisher, Joan Powers, Stephanie Counts, Dianne Ridgeway Cross, Cathy Brunges, Ina Chadwick, Susan Mahan, Eileen Winnick, Ellen Lontz, Ginger Propper, Gloria Fitzgerald, Carol Scoggins, Rebecca White, Eileen Logan, Ann Hughes Pratt, Courtney Seiter, Edgar Tello, Angie Jacoby, Lauren Cole Vertlander, Tara Hauk and Joan Gradus.

I am thankful to my editors, Meg Lemore and Jane Tanner. To my graphic designers, Kathy Davis of IdeaSwirl and Gail Spring of Duncan-Parnell, for creating a beautiful layout that features the women and their stories with taste and harmony. In addition, thank you to Lisa Jewel, my creative partner who brought clarity and texture to every page. Her sharp instinct enabled me to clarify my vision and bring these stories to life.

To Andre Brandon in San Francisco for his retouching skills and the team at Dalmatian Black and White photo labs in Greensboro, NC, for outstanding printing work. To Lorraine Fico-White of Magnifico Manuscripts for proofreading.

To my photo assistants: Grannie Gimenez, Rayhanna Baguadatu, Kathy Kuhner Henry, and Krishna Puppala.

Lastly, but really firstly—to my husband, John. He has encouraged me for years and has made it possible for this dream to come true.

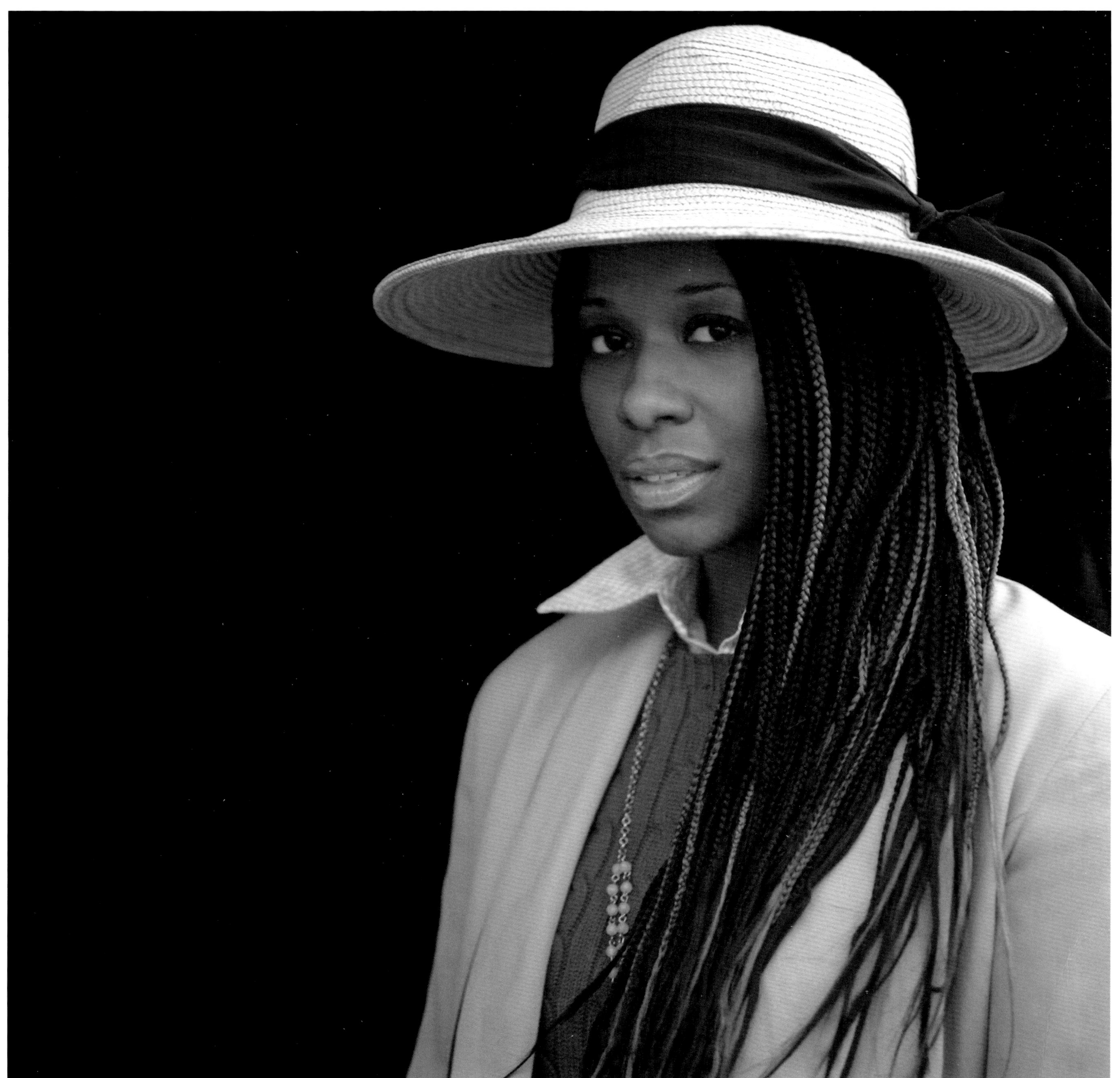

Kim Evans

DEDICATION

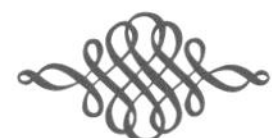

I opened up this book with the faces of younger women whose lives are just unfolding. These stories are for them, and for women of all ages, who are facing the inevitable joys, choices and challenges that life will bring.

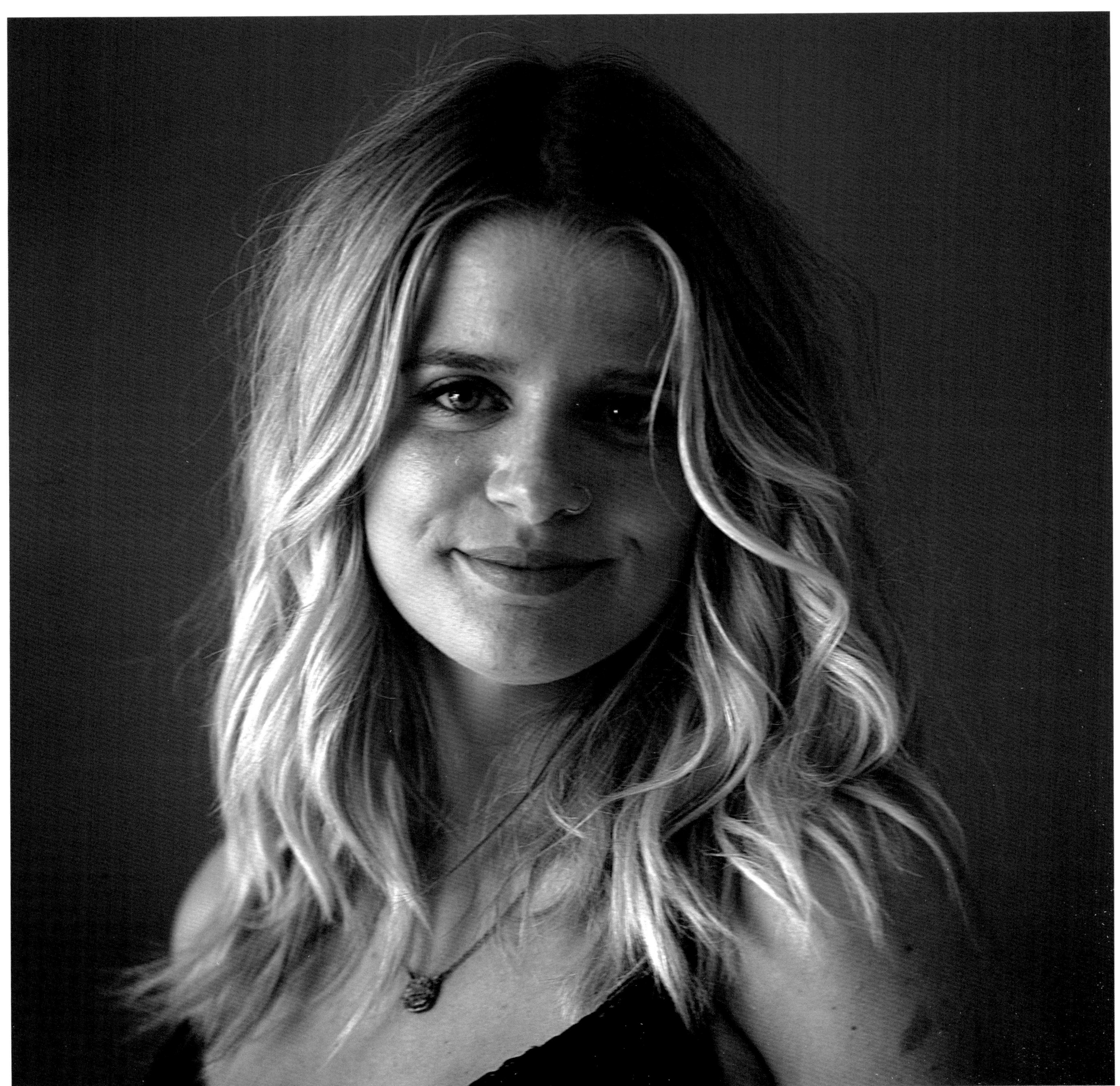

Lauren Doolittle

INTRODUCTION

This collection of portraits and profiles celebrates the ability of women to evolve and grow as they navigate the challenges of life. These women have experienced diverse life paths: some never married, while others are divorced or widowed. For many of these ladies, the word "solo" is simply a moment in time, while for others it's a destination.

Like fairy tales, their stories have villains, heroes and seemingly insurmountable obstacles, often turned magically into blessings. There are no victims in these pages but many victories celebrated in these life stories. Collectively, they demonstrate the personal growth achieved during periods of accomplishment and adversity.

Some of these women would still love to find Prince Charming; others would happily show him the door. Some met the love of their lives and cherish the memories and families that often followed. Many have interesting careers and ascended the ladder of professional success. A few of them were groundbreakers as the first women in their fields. Having a man by their side was not a prerequisite. All of these women have acquired an education, either by degree or determination.

In many cases, I was impressed by the bold decisions they made to find happiness and contentment. Some found the courage to end broken marriages. Others came to accept that the man of their dreams hadn't shown up and the clock had struck midnight. The widows, many who found themselves alone for the first time, deeply grieved the loss of their beloved husband. In each situation, the women reflected, then acted, and invariably headed out in new directions.

As I listened to their stories, I marveled at their flexibility, tenacity and deep introspection. Over and over, I heard about the importance of letting go of regret, and accepting to play the hand dealt, in order to move forward both spiritually and emotionally. I recognized in their responses that you can't get positive results from negative thoughts. In other words, worry is imagination going in the wrong direction. It was obvious that with persistence, tiny steps often led to enormous leaps. It was often voiced that solitude was undervalued and a great place to visit if you wanted to know yourself better. Another theme that prevailed was not to allow the voices of others to overpower your own beliefs and intuition. Finally, what was consistently mentioned was the power of female friendships, and how maternal women are to one another when the chips are down.

Today, more women are living alone than with partners. One trend driving this statistic is that many younger women are delaying marriage to finish higher education or to start a career. As the mores have changed, so have the rules regarding living together and choosing not to marry. At the same time, divorced women are living longer and delaying remarriage or not remarrying at all. One of the biggest influences over the past fifty years is the economic freedom many women now enjoy. "Saying Yes to the Dress" is not disappearing, but being single no longer carries the stigma it once did. Today, unmarried women adorn the covers of *Vogue*, *Glamour*, *Vanity Fair*, exhibiting accomplishments that have nothing to do with their marital status. They have personal narratives and style that millions of women envy.

It took six years for me to complete this project. The result is a lush, colorful bouquet of unique personalities from all across our country. It was a joy to meet these ladies and hear their stories told with such honesty, wit and candor.

This project could be infinitely larger because women such as these are pervasive in our diverse society. Only a few decades ago, it would have been uncommon to see women police officers, pilots, doctors and other career and life paths this generation sees as commonplace. Today, a woman adopting a child alone is admired, and women entrepreneurs are on the playing fields hitting home runs. All over our country, women continue to forge ahead, weaving the fabric of the world into a new and interesting pattern—all while embracing being solo.

SOLO

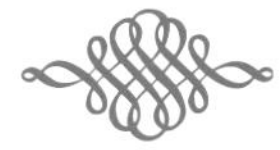

A Celebration of Women on Their Own

PORTRAITS & PROFILES *of*
NEVER MARRIED, DIVORCED & WIDOWED

Lauren McNally

I was the youngest in a big Irish Catholic family. My siblings married early, and I was happy taking care of my nieces and nephews. I was the little girl who loved playing house. You could call me a baby person. I would endlessly play with my dolls, envisioning the time I would have children of my own.

In my twenties, I was not into the bar scene the way my friends were. I dated on and off, but I couldn't imagine spending the rest of my life with anyone I met. For someone who desperately wanted a family, this was not a good thing.

At thirty-four, I made the decision to go the fertility route with an anonymous donor. I tried several times, but it didn't work. In all honesty, I didn't have the finances to continue.

I started researching countries from which I might want to adopt. The biggest criterion was a country that would consider a single woman. I was drawn to Ethiopia. I got on a waiting list and prepared myself for a long wait. I then heard that they would soon be cutting off any single women from adopting. I immediately wrote a letter asking for two children, stipulating that I did not care if they were boys or girls. I knew I wanted two children from the same country, as this made sense to me logistically. Who knew that my writing that letter, at that moment, catapulted me to the top of the waiting list. Little did I know, a young girl was about to give birth to boy-girl twins.

Once they were born, I got on a plane immediately to meet the family. To this day, I keep the family informed. I send them photos. One day I will explain everything to my children, before taking them to meet their biological mother.

Now I have a new second family. I've met other parents who adopted from the same country. We have twice-yearly events held in different places. I belong to another adoption group, closer to home, and we see one another often.

I come from hard-working, middle-class people. I am teaching my children those values. I work hard, so they go to daycare like most of my friends' children. I just bought my own house. They know we are a family without a traditional father and see my dad as their father.

During all my years of trying to meet the right man and get pregnant with in vitro, I kept feeling that I was wasting my time. Now I can look back and see the reason for all the heartbreaking disappointments. It all had to happen to put me in the time and place to have my children. I used to become furious when people said that everything happens for a reason. Now that is what I'm saying!

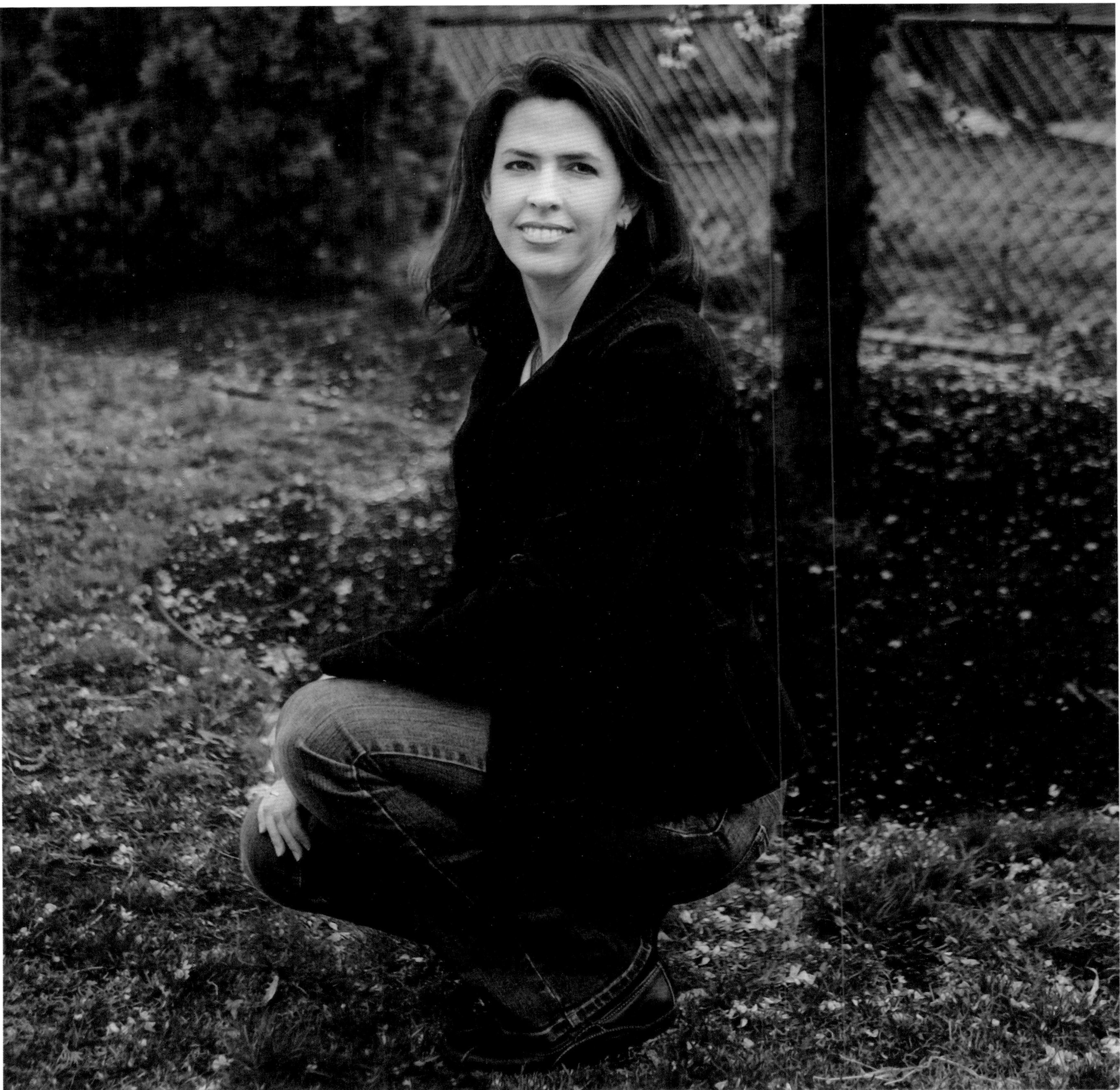

Shirin Behzadi

I was one of five outspoken, active children. My father was my idol. His example of hard work and integrity, along with a loving disposition, shaped me from my earliest years. In 2009, I was diagnosed with a brain tumor. It was lodged between my optic nerves and was wrapped around my major artery. It was considered terminal.

After a very short period of sadness, I began researching and interviewing doctors. I learned that I only had one option: removal of the tumor. It was quite possible that I would wake up blind. I told my two children what was happening in the non-scariest way I could. I told a few friends and I continued working. I wondered how I could work if I ended up blind.

This particular surgery only had been performed five hundred times in the world. My surgery lasted nine hours. I went into that operating room not knowing whether I would wake up or whether I would still have sight. The next thing I remember was the surgeon leaning in close to my face and asking, "Shirin, I think we got it all. Can you see? Can you see?"

I will never forget his face as I stared out eagerly at the world and said, "I can see! I can see!" The next few days were excruciatingly painful. Shortly after returning home, I was rushed back with pain that felt like death. They discovered that I had lost all the spinal fluid in my skull. I went back into surgery for five hours, followed by weeks of fever, severe anemia and liver failure. With persistent effort, I walked a little more every day and improved my physical strength. It would be two years before I felt physically like myself again.

The emotional trauma kicked in after the surgeries. I had kept it together from diagnosis all the way through surgery. I had battled all my health issues alone. I was married but alone, abandoned in my hour of need. I started tackling the core issues of my life, the biggest one being my marriage. I got rid of all my toxic relationships and enriched my life with loving, caring ones. I was a successful, educated, and athletic mother who had never learned to just "be." Slowly, I learned to focus on the beauty around me. Every experience was magnified, and I started seeing the details in life I had missed in my rush of "doing."

We are different people, with varying dispositions—but once you face a life threatening illness, you learn to fight—like it or not. I believe in God and a higher power. I have drawn strength when I thought I had none. I summoned courage when fearful and felt loved when I was lonely—all because of my faith.

Today, at work, I focus on elevating others to help them realize their natural talents and setting a good example. At home with my children, it's about being open and honest. I teach them how to bring out the best in themselves by focusing on integrity, self-esteem and how to create rewarding relationships. In social circles, it's about listening and valuing others' life experiences.

Since cancer, many dreams have come through for me: writing professionally, motivational speaking, and finding a wonderful new love. Today these are my priorities. The hole in my head ended up making me whole.

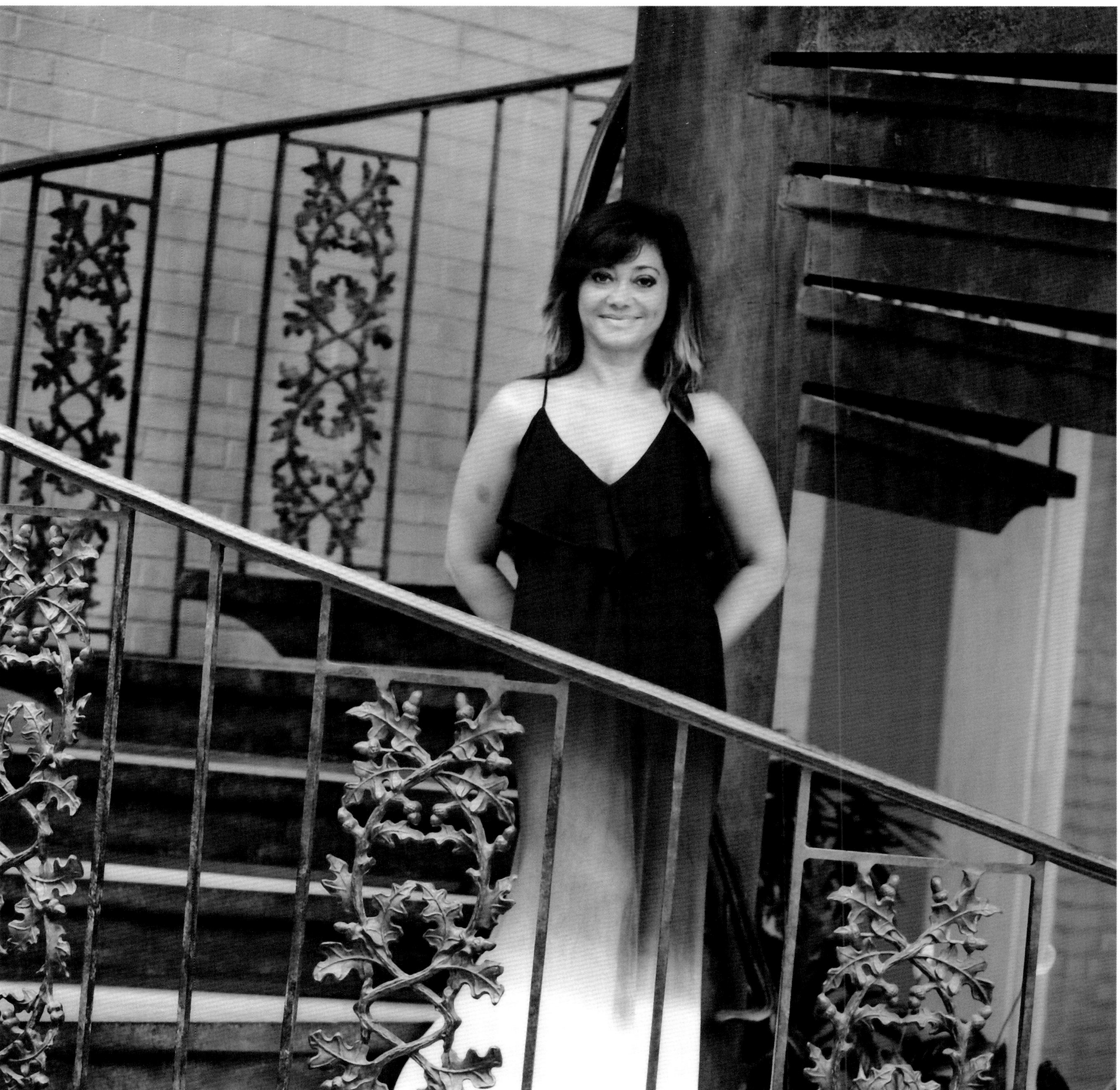

Mary Niepold

I grew up in a small Southern town. When I was in eighth grade, Marilyn Monroe and Audrey Hepburn were Hollywood's ideal women. I certainly didn't feel like I fit, and often walked into a dance or party feeling like a wallflower.

I realized eventually that instead of feeling sorry for myself, I could be kind or do something for someone else. That realization shaped my life. I was a young woman in the early 1970s, when the world was changing. I was a free spirit who had no problem challenging authority. I was an anti-war demonstrator in college and carried that mentality throughout my life. I fight for what I believe in.

I married and started a family. My years being a mother were extremely happy, but unfortunately I loved the idea of marriage more than the reality. I left without taking alimony because I felt that it was one more thing to make women dependent upon men. Since then, I have had a few great loves that did not lead to marriage. That said, there is not one man who has been part of my life that I would feel uncomfortable asking for a favor.

A few years ago, I was sitting in Barnes & Noble grading papers and sipping coffee, when a young man I'd never met asked if he could sit with me. Next thing I knew, he was telling me about his recent trip to Africa and about African grandmothers searching for their grandchildren because their mothers had died of AIDS. He told me about the challenges these women were facing and how they needed help. By the time he finished talking, I felt like a mule had kicked me.

I teach journalism at a large university and love my job. I have two terrific children and five grandchildren, who are the loves of my life. No one, including myself, would have believed that my life would change over a cup of coffee with a stranger. But I found myself unable to forget his words or the pictures he'd created in my mind. A few months later I flew to Africa and volunteered at an AIDS orphanage. I soon found out to my outrage that nothing was being done to help the grandmothers. I started putting together a plan.

After meeting with government officials and the grandmothers of those children, I set myself a goal to help them help themselves without any handouts. Most of them had second-grade educations, no husbands, and little hope. What they had, though, was plenty of love. We set up three cooperatives in Kenya where we taught business skills for vegetable sellers, productive sheep farming, and textile work. Today, we have started programs all over Africa, including a preschool program, and now the young children are teaching their grandmothers how to read.

I did not do this alone. I had help from many people and organizations. I have to give credit to the Creator for nudging me when I needed it. I thank my parents' genes for making sure that I didn't look like Marilyn Monroe or Audrey Hepburn.

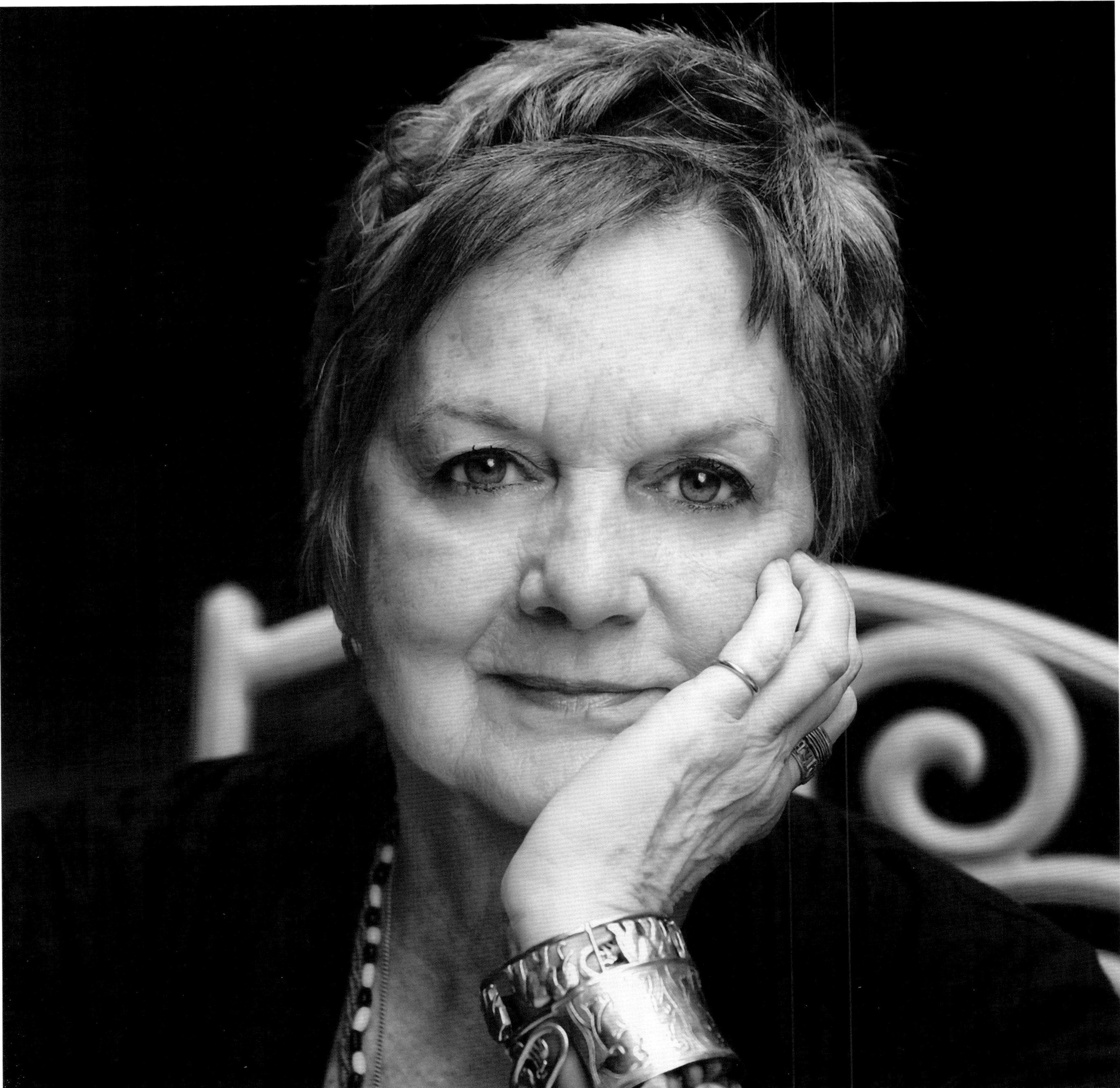

Marta Blades

My father was a scientist, my mother adored art and classical music. I was an only child in a house with servants. We had a pool in the backyard, and I would sit around with glass bottles I had collected and mix food coloring to create new colors. It was like magic to me. I would fall asleep thinking about what I might create the next day.

My adolescence was spent in Hungary during World War II, when the German occupation was a part of life. Toward the end of the war, when the army invaded and fighting was getting close, we had an hour to pack some belongings and depart. My father heard there were reports of soldiers doing the unmentionable to young girls. I was fourteen years old and it would be fifty years before I saw that house again. We escaped the fighting by going to the lovely hills of Württemberg, which were liberated by the American Army. I was educated at a convent school. I was enormously lucky to win a scholarship to study art at Marian University, in Indianapolis, Indiana. One of the things my parents instilled in me was that you truly own only what you have in your head. I married and had three beautiful children. After twenty years, my husband and I went our separate ways. After trying for a long time to make our relationship work, we decided to part wishing one another the best. We remained friends, and I have lived alone ever since.

Because I have spent so much of my life in the arts community as the director of an art gallery, I have many gay friends. I especially love gay men as they have the taste and wit I so admire. The problem is that my gay friends and I tend to fall in love with the same men! I respect all kinds of art and I did not attempt to become an artist myself until I retired. I do not take myself seriously, and I don't analyze everything. Recently, at one of my shows, a gentleman gave me the lovely compliment of saying that he gets lost while contemplating my canvases. At my age, I think that is far better than being lost in a conversation with me.

After receiving my second cancer diagnosis, my younger daughter and her husband invited me to move to North Carolina. I love it here. My one regret was that they did not want me to have the responsibility of a dog. After a few years, the cancer came back again and I refused surgery. My kids offered me everything they could think of and nothing worked until my final answer. "Yes, if you let me have a dog." So I do have a white furry male living with me, his name is Jack Smith IV, named after the doctor who treated me.

Everyone needs something to look forward to. Each year, I go to New York and see as many plays as I can in a week. It's my artistic marathon, with my best friend. If I get lucky enough to sell some paintings, I sometimes go twice.

I am not claiming to be Mother Teresa, but I have been conservative with men during my single life. I think I would have had a lot more fun if I had just a little more "tramp" in me.

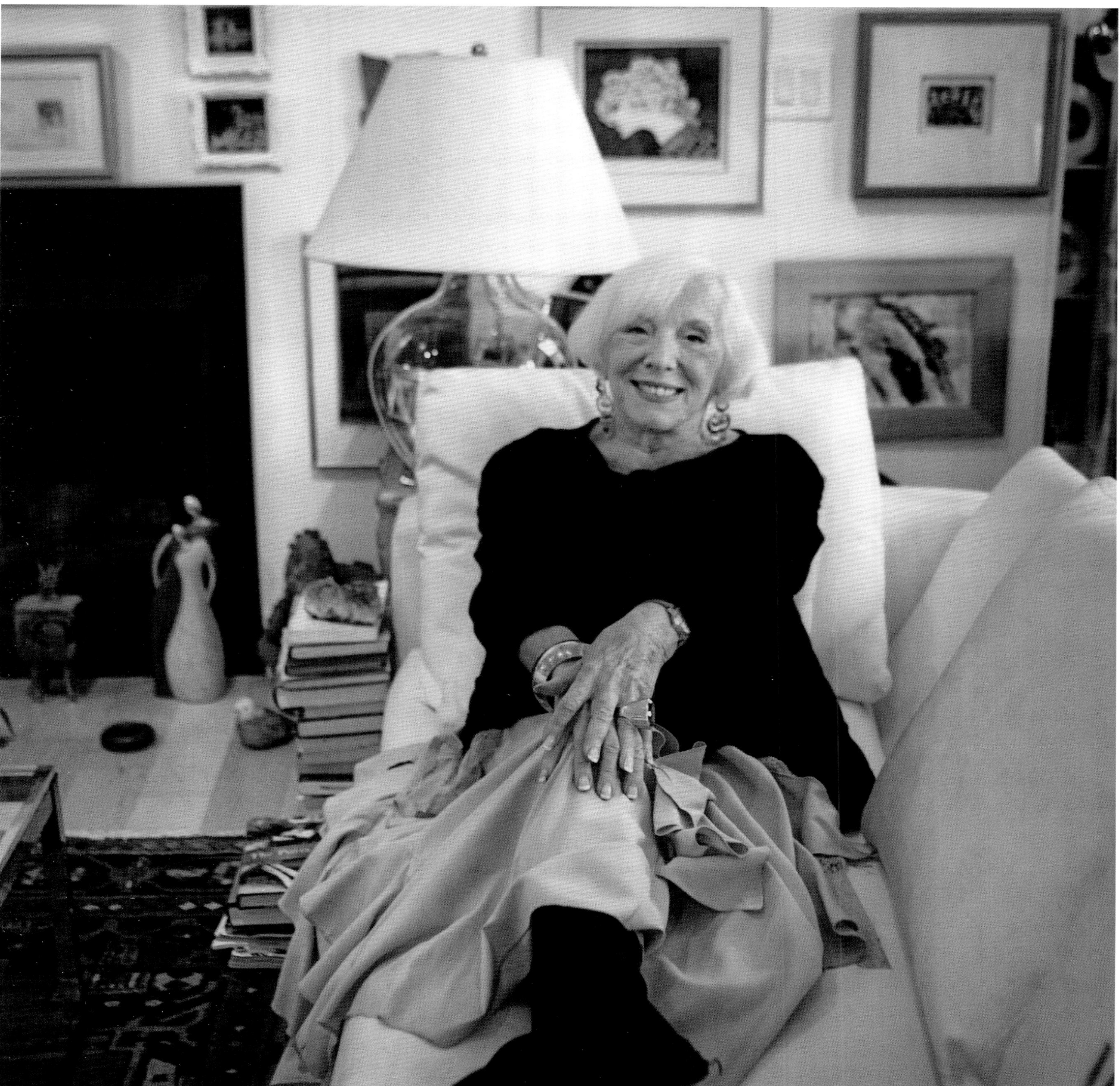

Bernadette Johnson

I have never married, but I have a daughter looking at colleges. When I became pregnant as a teenager, my boyfriend's parents persuaded us not to marry. They said to give the relationship the test of time! The test of time lasted five years. He was a great guy. We were just too immature.

Had we stayed together, I don't think I would've accomplished all that I have. Something I remember my mother saying early on was that if I was smart, my brains would carry me further than my looks. I went to beauty school and decided after graduating that I wanted my business and my home to be in the same place. I started searching and quickly found a place that was just good enough to raise my daughter and wonderful for business. My mother helped me out by co-signing for the loan. My home is upstairs and the salon is down below. The perfect morning commute.

One day, my front doorbell rang, and there were two white ladies looking for an appointment. I couldn't believe my eyes—white ladies at a black lady's salon! I tried telling them that it wasn't right, but the older one insisted. She said that they didn't have a car and lived only down the block. I finally said yes reluctantly, as I had to figure out what products to use. I noticed then that the younger woman was not right. She appeared to have the mentality of a child. The older woman was in charge. She had asked for a perm, which would have been okay, except for the texture of her hair, as it was not what I was used to. Finally though, I had it done and she was sitting under the dryer, while I trimmed the younger woman's hair.

When I went to check on the perm, the older lady's head was hanging down and something was clearly wrong. Her hand was cold, and before the scream could come out of my mouth, I remembered the younger woman. I went to the phone and quietly called the police. The ambulance arrived quickly and she was exactly as I thought—dead.

After a week of living at my house, the court took the younger woman and put her in a daycare program. I went to look at the place and didn't like what I saw, so I got them to let her come and live with me. That was when I went back to school at night to learn how to handle the situation. I ended up becoming a nurse's aide and observing psychosis patients. I do that a few nights a week. I also work at embalming in a funeral home. I was doing that before I went to beauty school. I know people who think what I do is awful, but what I couldn't do is work with people who are suffering.

It sounds like a lot, but I have tremendous energy and I want to focus in a positive direction. If I don't have a full inbox, I'm not happy. I love organization and setting priorities. I have done a great job with my daughter, who is respectful and gets good grades. She listens to me. Something I did with her that I wish my parents had done with me, is to do my best to explain "Why" when she asks a question, rather than just giving her a "Yes" or a "No" or a "Maybe" or a "Because I said so." A real answer. If I don't have it, I tell her I will think about it and let her know as soon as I can.

Recently, I started dating a man who friended me on Facebook. I knew him in high school, but he never looked in my direction. Turns out he is shy and had a crush on me for a long time. I have no idea if this is a small chapter in my life—or the start of an entire new book.

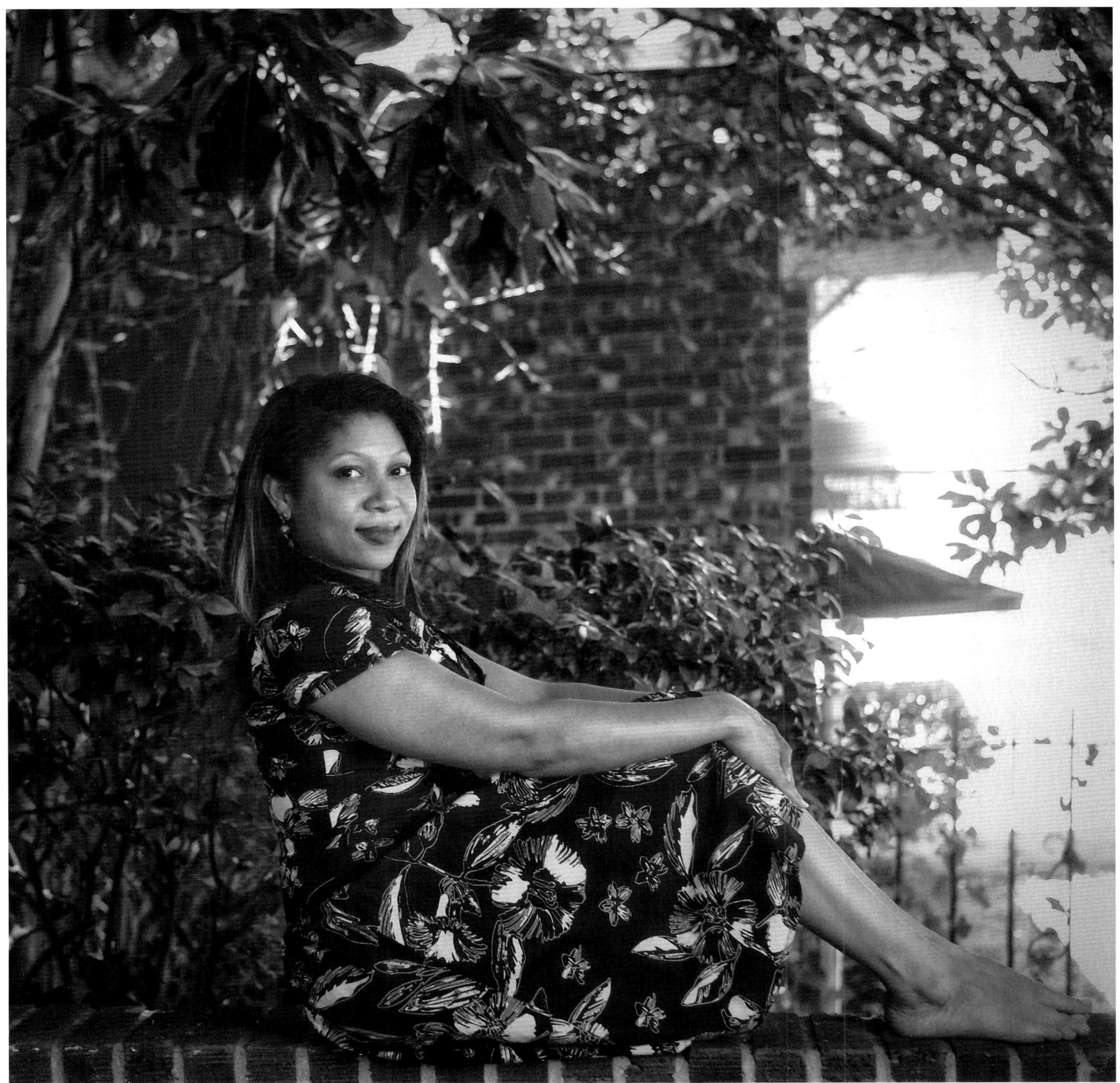

Karin Weston

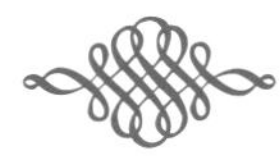

I was born in Germany near the end of World War II. The small town where I grew up in was poor and conservative. The town folks claimed to be religious, but I knew early on they were not kind. God was with them on Sunday but on vacation the rest of the week. Being born Catholic and out of wedlock in those years was scandalous. In spite of my birth, my widowed grandmother and my mother were able to enroll me into a Catholic school. The nuns, teachers and some of my classmates did not embrace me. It was blatant discrimination, but in those days, nobody came to my defense, including my own mother. That experience taught me early on not to set my hopes too high. I concentrated on my studies and imagined where I could escape to after the war.

In my early twenties, I met a young American Army officer. It was very romantic, just like that movie, *An Officer and a Gentleman*. He was very sweet, and I was thrilled when he proposed. Within months of getting married, he was shipped off to Vietnam. Six months into his tour, he was injured and evacuated to San Francisco. I had not traveled at all, so a trip to America was a big event. I was overwhelmed with the trip, but I was thankful to be reunited with my husband. He was in the hospital for quite some time. During this time, I learned to drive and studied to become an American citizen. The day I passed my exam, I was so excited! I wore red, white and blue during the naturalization ceremony. My life seemed to be getting back on track, but then my husband took another tour of Vietnam. I was pregnant when he left and gave birth to my daughter alone without any family or friends around to assist. Three years later our marriage ended in divorce. We had simply grown apart. Raising a child on your own by then was not a social taboo, as it was back in Germany. I had grown stronger, too, and could take care of myself and my precious girl.

I have a great work ethic and would take multiple jobs to make ends meet. I took jobs as an administrative assistant, weekend caterer and eventually I rose through the ranks to become VP of Sales for an electronic components manufacturer. I loved my job and being able to support us.

Eventually, I moved to Washington DC. There I met a doctor and we dated for five years. I did not want to be his girlfriend forever, and by this time my daughter was in college in California. I had a job offer in Los Angeles. When I told him I was just about to leave, he rather hastily proposed. The marriage lasted twelve years. Many of those years were happy, but eventually it ended in betrayal. I wanted to believe the best of him, but in hindsight I see his reluctance was a red flag.

As the years passed, I found myself living in the South. There I bought a new home, made friends, volunteered as a museum docent and took a job as a bookkeeper. My daughter was living in Los Angeles at the time and met a Jewish man. When they married, I began to learn a lot about the religion. When my granddaughter was born, I moved to LA, too. After getting to know the customs and traditions of Judaism from my son-in-law and his wonderful family, I found that the religion felt just right to me. I began the process of conversion. It was difficult and an enormous amount of study. I even became reacquainted with my first husband and his new wife and their family. We are all great friends now and spend holidays together. I had no idea that my life would turn out to have so many interesting paths. Now in my seventies, I have found myself enjoying life without a partner. I love being independent and have a great sense of fulfillment.

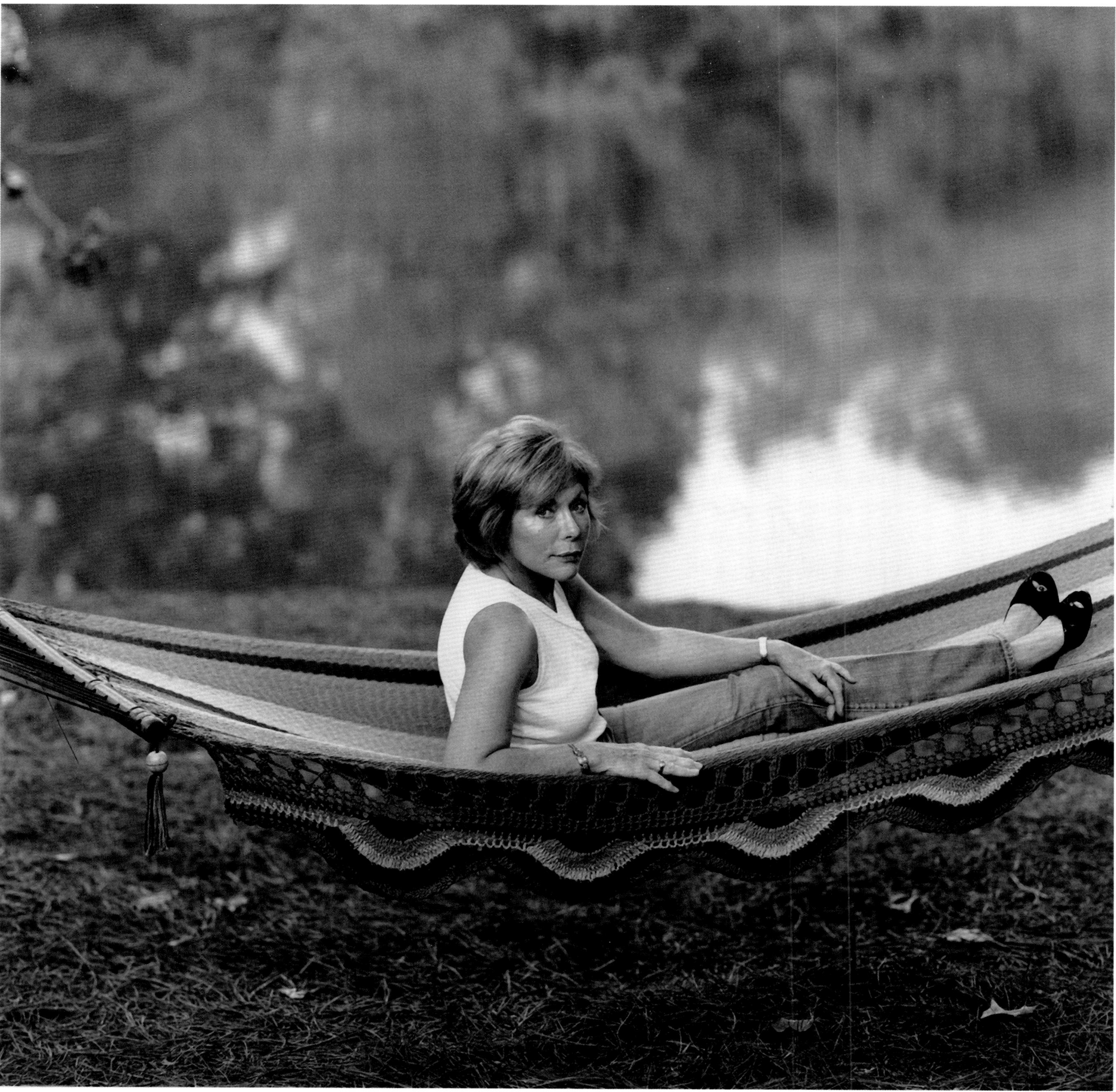

Clare Taylor

I always wanted children, but I married a man who didn't. I loved him and felt that I could put aside my wishes and have children in my life by teaching them.

My parents divorced when I was eight. Then I moved more times than I can count. It was an action-filled gypsy life that had some advantages, but not one I wanted for the rest of my life. The relationship I had with my father was all about doing. If we weren't sailing, we were skiing or camping. My self-esteem was low and my siblings had fun calling me "fatso." Today, I look at photos and am amazed that I looked completely normal.

In my twenties, I was raped at gunpoint and started to live in fear. Three months after that, someone broke into my house in the middle of the night and robbed me. Life was forcing me into counseling, since I could not get a peaceful night's sleep. The lessons I learned in therapy have stayed a part of my life. No one wants to say a rape was supposed to happen, or getting robbed was just fine, but if those things hadn't happened to me, I would not have developed the coping skills I have now.

For years, I thought I had a wonderful marriage. My husband acted as though he adored me and would embarrass me with compliments to anyone willing to listen. He traveled quite a bit but that was the nature of his career. I never complained. I was busy teaching and loved my job.

Eventually though, I became unhappy. I had a nagging feeling that something was not right, but couldn't put my finger on it. One morning my husband left for a trip overseas without his briefcase. I opened it, intending to call him and tell him what he had left behind but instead I was blindsided. There were photos of another woman in a new house and all the paperwork to go along with his secret life. Like most people, I had seen shows on *48 Hours* with stories like the one I was now living. I felt like I was in a science fiction movie. This couldn't be happening.

I confronted him with all the lies and the game was over. He left, and I was living in what felt like a living death. I ended my marriage within a week. I had to work to stay sane. I gave up television, got into a spiritual group, and reread all the journals I had kept for years, looking for the clues I'd missed.

Talking to women friends was great therapy and so was sports. When I'm sailing, I'm completely at peace. I learned to ask for help and share my needs. I found out how generous people can be when they know what you are going through. I have also learned that no one can read your mind. You have to speak up and say what you're feeling. I believe that if you are honest, people will pick up on your honesty. If you're dishonest, they pick up on that even more quickly. At the worst times of my life, many of my friends knew something was wrong, but did not want to rock my boat.

I am now a mother. I adopted my daughter as an infant from Vietnam. I named her Faith because faith had given me the will to live. I have never been happier.

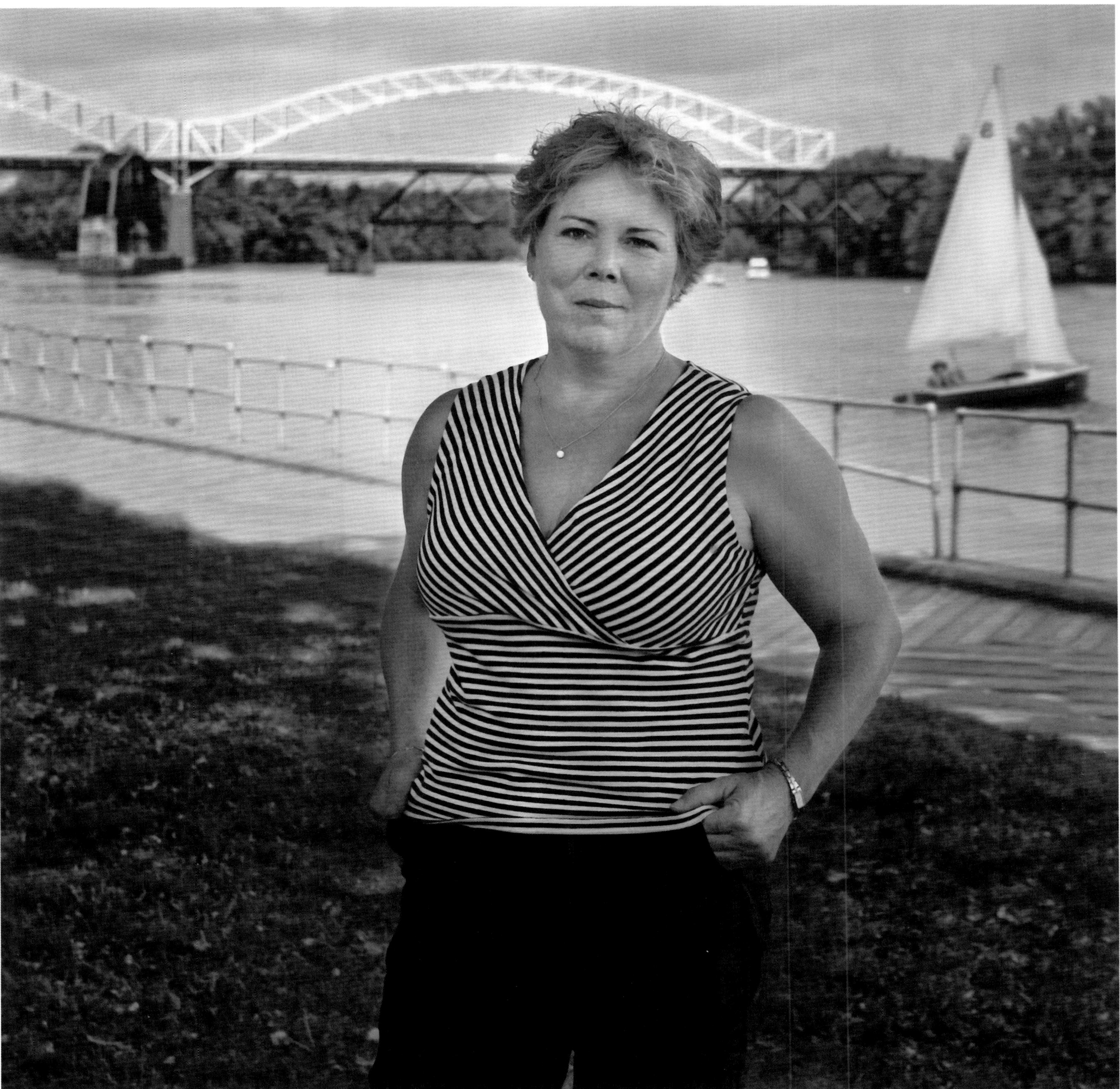

Sari Weatherwax

My parents made the best of everyday situations. As a family, we had long dinners with all of the children contributing to the conversation. My dad was enormously creative. For a long time he was the head art director at Leo Burnett advertising agency in Chicago. He was a sane man in the Mad Men era. At some point, he decided to open his own agency in Los Angeles.

We moved into a neighborhood that was like heaven for children. We played outside from sunup to sundown. We built underground forts and roamed the woods looking for deer and possum. It was an idyllic existence, as we were free to explore and use our imaginations.

As a young woman, I was invited to the racetrack with a friend. While there, he introduced me to another friend who was one of the thoroughbred owners. He was telling us that the jockey he was training had just quit. Without thinking, I jumped up and down, telling him that I could do it! My wild enthusiasm caught his attention and he tested me out on a wild Palomino. Despite being inexperienced—I nailed it. I did not know that I would work seven days a week, getting up at 4:30 a.m. every morning. I took horrible chances. I would ride at night without a whip and gladly ride the meanest horse in the stable. It became an addiction, as dangerous as heroin.

My parents were scared about my decision to become a jockey. They feared for my safety, but never let on how worried they were. When I mentioned to them that I might be interested in becoming a stewardess, they wholeheartedly approved. Back then, that career path was considered prestigious and many girls desperately wanted the opportunity. I passed the test and before I had too much time to think, I was hired. I moved from California to New England and flew domestically for many years until United bought Pan Am. Then I was offered the international route to Japan. During this period, I was having the time of my life. I was the person who knew how to live in the moment. I dated and had many proposals but was not ready to give up my independence.

I was a late bloomer, easygoing and innocent. I did fall madly in love once, with a man who was divorced. I thought it was my life-changing moment. After a year of dating, he reconciled with his wife and my heart was broken. Thankfully, my girlfriends provided a safety net under me. Talking with them in depth led to some serious introspection. I took a hard look at myself and realized that I had to stop just being a viewer of my life and become an active participant. I needed to pay more attention to what role I was playing in my relationships. I leaned into conversations learning to become more sympathetic to what people were saying. Despite the heartbreak, I grew tremendously from it.

That was all before Sept. 11, which changed my life forever. I lost sixteen close friends—people I had flown with for thirty-three years. After that, the senior people were asked to fly our troops to the Middle East conflict zones, 400 soldiers at a time. Military planes don't have the capacity of a 747, so commercial airlines were proud to provide flights. I was humbled and privileged to have taken our boys over.

Now, I am a docent at Ground Zero. My sensitivity and listening skills are being put to good use. I am a Presbyterian, yet I was given the honor of accompanying Pope Francis on his tour of Ground Zero. The experience is one of the highlights of my life. I felt the presence of God watching him bless the graves, with such love and compassion. His healing words were so filled with wisdom, and his explanation of the power of good over evil touched me profoundly.

I don't consider myself a feminist, even though I was one of the first woman jockeys. I think men should be allowed to have their own clubs and women should have the same option. Men and women are physically, biologically, and emotionally different. Why would any woman want to be like a man anyway?

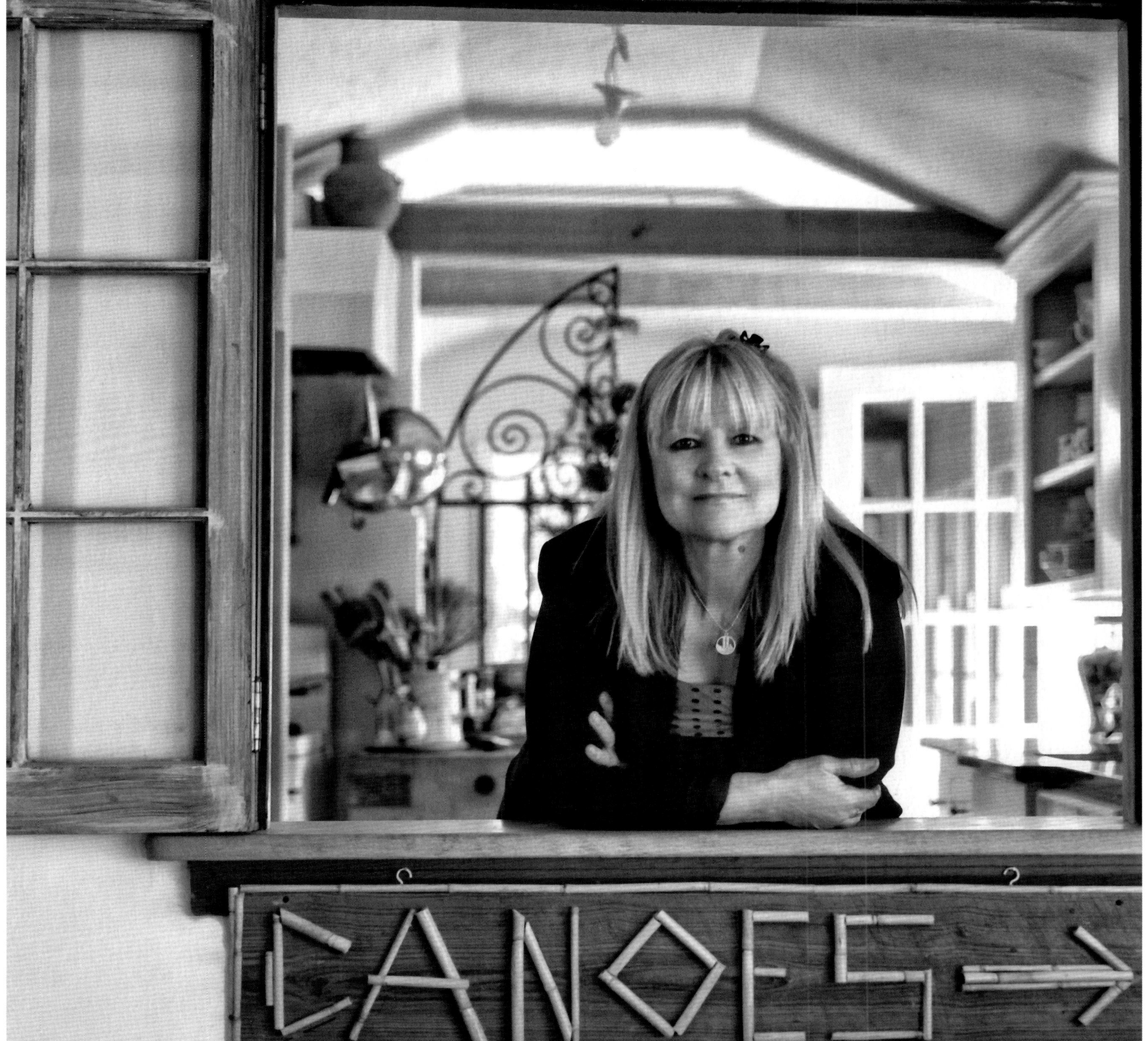
CANOES

Ros Ridgeway

I was the fourth child of seven. My father was a charismatic alcoholic. My mother died in childbirth. Back in those days, people did not know that alcoholism was a disease. They thought it was the result of a weak character and treated sufferers with disgust. Our family split up after my mother died. Some of us went to live with aunts and uncles. I went to live with my grandfather. He was a tremendous influence on my life. He was the most Christ-like person I have ever known.

I married at eighteen. In those days, it was not unusual to marry young. My husband was a marine, and we went from Ohio to North Carolina and eventually to Hawaii. I had my children during this time and also worked as a medical secretary. Once given the opportunity to take medical classes, I realized how much I loved learning. In time, my husband was sent to Guam and no dependents could go. I was back in Ohio, taking classes at the local community college while working at the veteran's hospital.

By the time my husband came home, I had changed, and so had he. He had medical problems and decided to move to Arizona. I filed for divorce when my children were in college. Then I moved to Boston, where I got my degree in public relations from Boston University.

There was another man in my life, who was a great love and mentor for twenty years. I never wanted to marry again because I saw no need to. I thought it best for my family if I stayed single.

For most of my life, I struggled with taking things people would do or say too personally. I'm sure it had something to do with the stigma of my early childhood. If I was at a party, for instance, and someone was talking with me and turned to talk to someone else, that would hurt me. As my self-esteem changed, I outgrew that problem, realizing these assumed slights had nothing to do with me at all. I gave up drinking. After having way too much to drink at my daughter's wedding, she told me I had embarrassed her. I knew I would never touch alcohol again. I also stopped smoking. I set a date, and that was that.

Another thing I have learned is how to be alone and happy in solitude. I did not set out to learn that lesson, but it was delivered to me when I lived in a rural setting and didn't know anyone. At first, I wanted to move. Then, as I would go for walks and be in nature, a side of me emerged that I hadn't known existed. I loved the sounds and changes in nature. Serenity became a gift.

I have been all over the world and have never had a "bad" trip. I have been to Russia three times, Antarctica, South America, and Asia. I have not missed out on many places. What I love the most is how traveling puts an end to misconceptions about people and places. People all want the same thing—a better world for their children and themselves. Some of the places I thought would be uncivilized happen to have the highest culture.

At this point in life, I'm enjoying being a docent at the Kennedy Center. I would love to get married again. That is, if George Clooney or a George Clooney look-alike rang my doorbell!

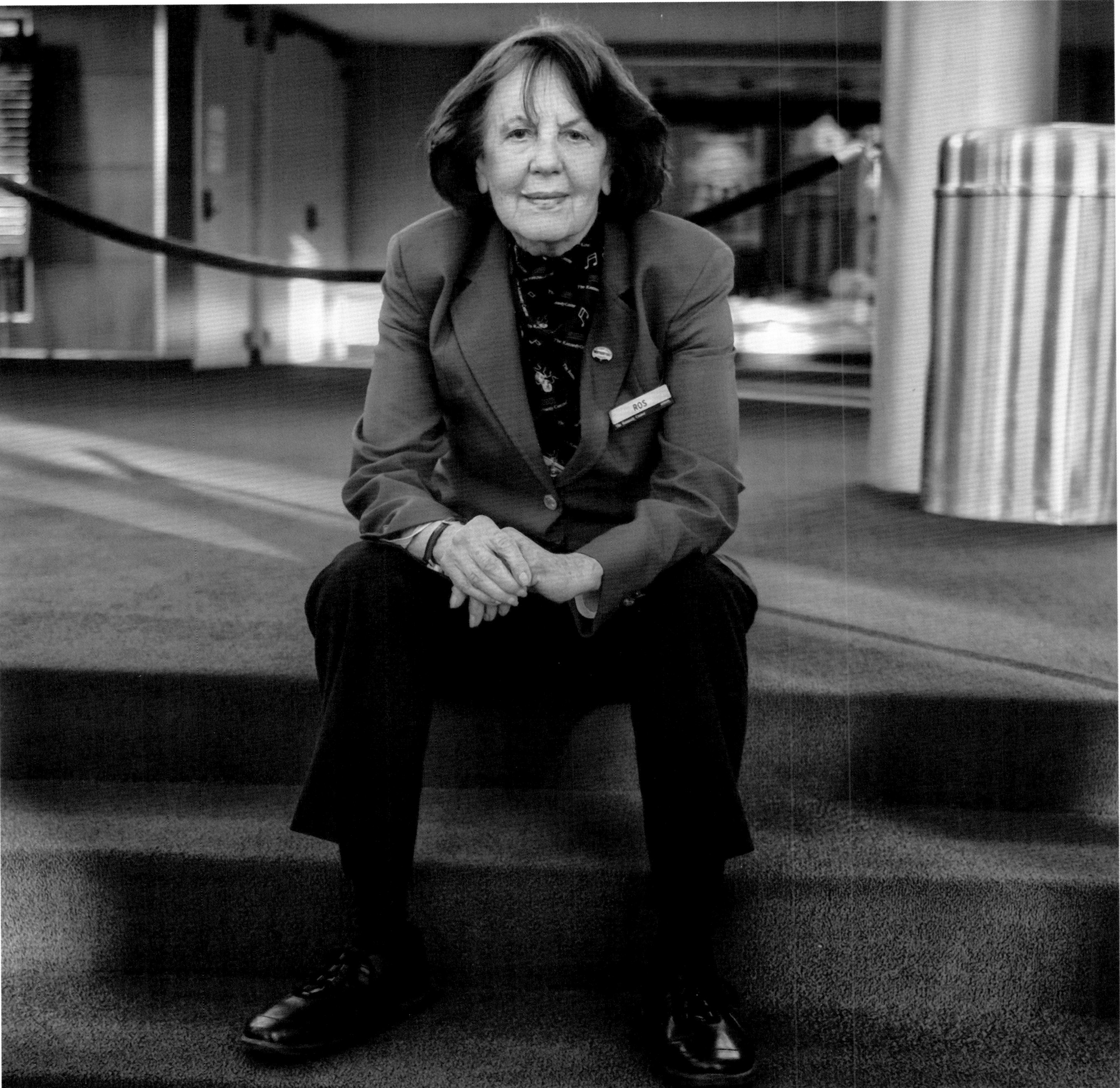
ROS

Jennifer Jones

I grew up in a single-parent household. My parents divorced when I was four. This was very rare in the 70s, and I was clueless that my situation was "different" than other children. My mom worked three jobs and my grandmother helped raise me and my siblings. My dad was a weekend dad.

My mother made sure we always had fun and were happy even though financial security was never guaranteed. I wore hand-me-down clothes and we struggled to make ends meet. I was taught early on that if I wanted things to happen, I had to work for them. The greatest lesson I learned from my mom was learning resourcefulness, independence and that sometimes deprivation is a blessing.

I did do a bit of modeling in high school, but I did not do any dating. I met my first love in college. It hit me like a ton of bricks. He was a handsome singer in a band and was completely wrong for me. He often criticized me and laughed when I was mad. He hated when I wore heels because I was taller than him. At the time, I thought his behavior was normal and that's just how men treated women. So, I made a lot of excuses for him. Things ended when I discovered he was cheating on me with a friend of mine. It was heartbreaking at the time, but it was huge blessing in disguise. Needless to say, I had trust issues with the boyfriends who came after him. Most of my relationships after that were short-lived.

Many years later, I moved for a new job and felt I had a bright future for love and life. That all changed after a routine, annual gynecological exam. I was diagnosed with the Big C. I was told even though it was just stage one, the only way to be sure the doctors could get it all was to have a radical hysterectomy.

I was in shock and immediately went into survival mode. I was terrified about my losing the ability to have kids and other repercussions to having a hysterectomy in my 30s. Most importantly, I had to focus on getting rid of the cancer inside of me. On the day of the surgery, a nurse casually asked me if I had children. She was just trying to make small talk, but it devastated me and I started to cry. My mother reminded me that God chooses only the most special people on Earth to adopt children and these circumstances proved that I was one of them. Best mom ever.

After the surgery, I was cancer-free, but I struggled with what I had lost for many years after. I would just cry at baby showers or anytime I saw a pregnant woman on TV. I couldn't talk about what I had been through or even admit that I was a cancer survivor. As time moved on, I knew I needed therapeutic help. Eventually, I tried therapy. The first few therapists were not a good fit, but I did find one I really liked. She didn't try and "fix" my problems. She just listened. She also recommended I try EMDR, a treatment commonly used for post-traumatic stress disorder. I was skeptical because I felt PTSD was much more serious than what I was experiencing. The treatment retrained my brain to file memories into a figurative filing cabinet. I was told to let myself feel the pain as best as I could. I did not expect all the emotion that erupted. I went five times, cried a lot, and never really knew if it was working. About a month later, I was talking to a group of people about the story and casually said, "when I had cancer…" without batting an eye. At that moment, I realized the EMDR worked! Today, I can recall what I went through without having to relive the trauma.

Today, I live in Charlotte, NC, and work as a creative director for an advertising agency. I love what I do and am surrounded by friends and even have a man in my life. He's a bit on the stocky side, snores and drools, but loves me unconditionally. His name is Winston and my faithful, four-legged friend completely fits the bill.

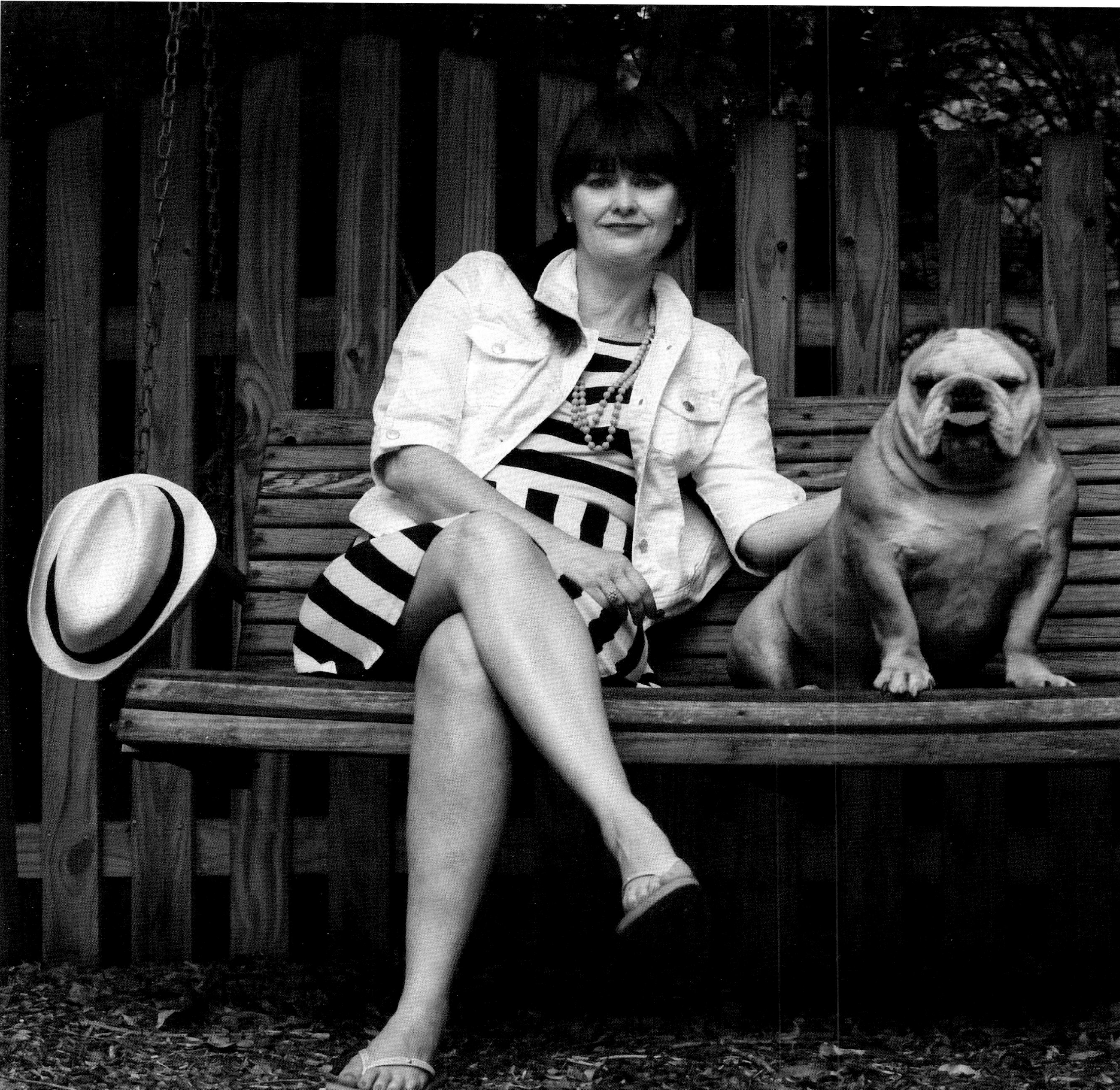

Marge Soznick

I grew up in New York in a Jewish household where nobody bit his or her tongue. I mean that in the best way! Never a dull moment—that was the motto of our house. Everyone interrupted everyone else, and we all laughed about it. My parents adored each other. I remember one night as we were going to sleep, my sister said, "Mom and Dad love one another so much that if there was a fire, they would save one another first." That kind of love terrified me.

When I was in my twenties, I met my husband in Florida through family friends. He was a born southerner who charmed the stockings off me. After we married, I found myself living on the other side of the Mason Dixon line. I'm an optimist and find the best in people, so learning to survive in a different environment wasn't hard for me. I learned early on that making friends is much easier than getting rid of them. I joined various cultural groups and generally found people to be enormously welcoming.

While raising my son and daughter, I started a career without knowing it. I volunteered for a charity affiliated with a local radio station. I had a great time and got some terrific write-ups. Eventually, I was offered my radio talk show, called "Marge at Large," and covered everything from wine tours in California to Fashion Week in New York. My husband was so proud of me. I had that show for thirty years.

We had a wonderful marriage and when he passed away after forty-two years, I was devastated. The worst was coming home from a trip to an empty house. It got so that I would arrange to have company over as soon as I walked through the door. His absent voice was the only sound I could hear.

I did not want my social life to end because I was no longer part of a couple. So, I did some smart things. I did not let a lot of time go by without having couple friends, as well as single friends over for dinner. I spoke about my husband as though he were sitting right next to me.

I kept myself informed about what was going on where I lived. I believe now, as I did then, that if you are an interested person, you will be interesting. I would go to parties and never arrive early or leave late. I embraced boundaries because I didn't want to be a pest or "Poor Marge." I insisted pretty quickly on paying for myself at dinner because I knew those invitations would dwindle if I didn't.

I adore politics. I'm a Democrat who has lots of Republican friends, mostly because I'm thrilled listening to a good argument. Over the years, I have been accused of being a facilitator. I love nothing more than introducing people with opposing views to one another, sitting back, and seeing what happens.

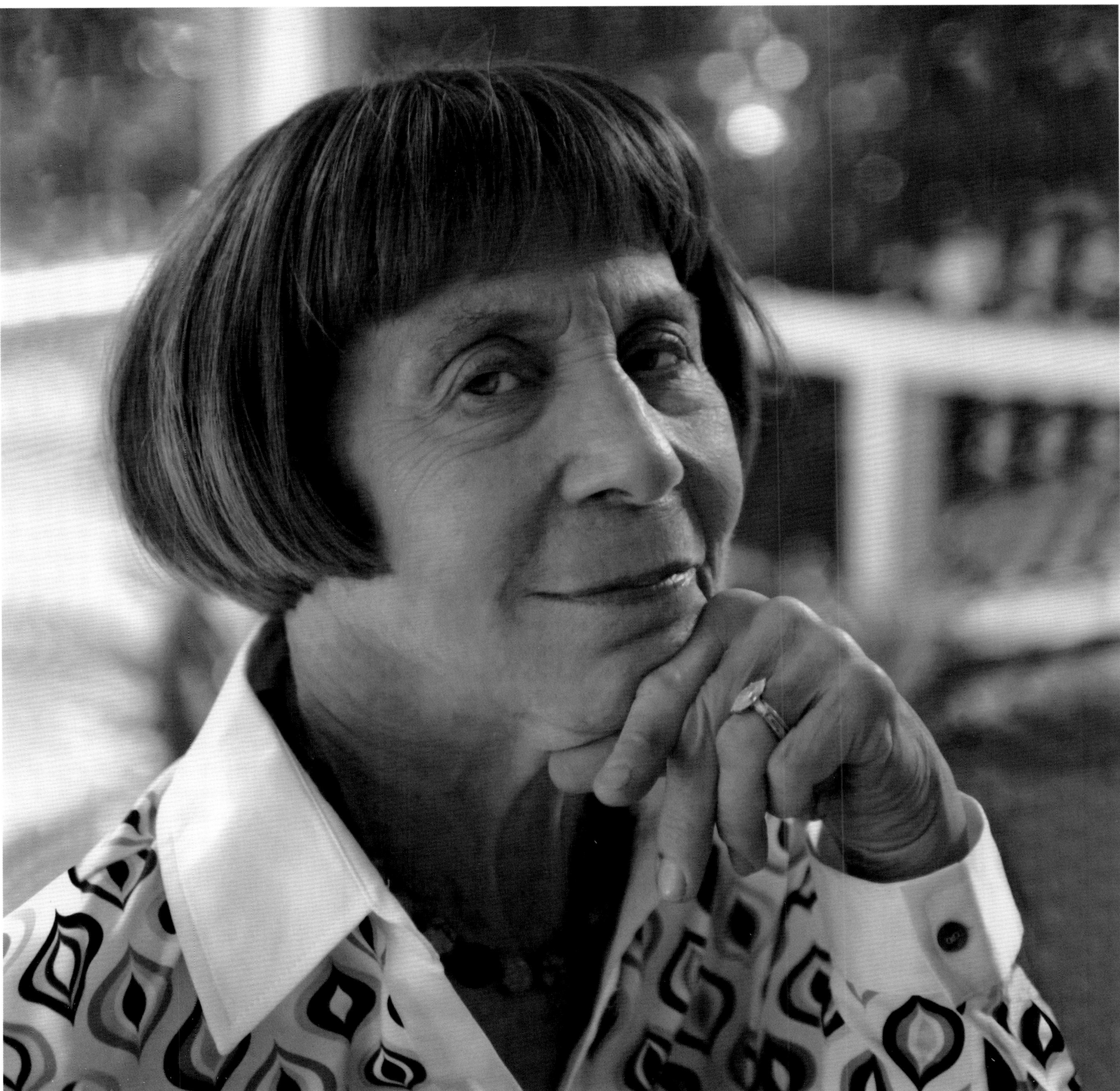

Bonnie Bowen

My mother brought me up to work. She never discussed my wedding dress or the adorable babies I would one day have. I knew I was expected to have a career and being the driven person I was, her expectations suited me. Life was easy because I never focused on the future. Every day I did my best to succeed at whatever I was doing. I did not come from money, so after high school I attended a state college, intending to become a psychologist.

I noticed that the people who had degrees in business were getting hired quickly into better-paying jobs than I would get with a psychology degree. Being the pragmatic person I was, I changed courses and eventually ended up at Columbia for my master's degree in business. The first time I met my future husband at school, it was that love at first sight, knock-your-socks-off feeling. We were married a year later. I got pregnant right away, just as planned.

I had a miscarriage, followed by several others. For seven years, I was obsessed with the desire to have a child. My life lessons up to that point taught me that if I tried harder, I could get what I wanted. The idea that I couldn't just pull myself up by the bootstraps and move on was a revelation. I went from doctor to doctor, and from procedure to procedure, until I was no doubt clinically depressed. I realized that I needed to stop trying so hard, to pause and reflect on what I was feeling, and perhaps to come to terms with the fact that I might have children in a different way than I had foreseen. I put my life problems on the shelf and went back to living as a wife and investment banker. During this time, I heard about a program called RAF at the university, which would allow me to become a donor recipient with my husband as the father. I was accepted and became pregnant quickly. I had my son at the age of forty-five. I thank God every day that I did not give up on my dream and fought for what has brought me unimaginable happiness.

The years after my son was born were magical. I was married to my best friend, and we were over-the-moon happy with our dream come true—at least that was what I believed. We had some business losses and I had some hormonal highs and lows. He had started traveling to China for business. Our sex life suffered during all the fertility problems, and I lost my self-confidence for a while. So there were some problems, but not once did I doubt our love for each other. We'd been married twenty-seven years, and I trusted him completely.

One day I received a phone call from a friend telling me that my husband was having an affair with a co-worker. I did not believe her, thinking that someone must have started a rumor, but when I confronted him, there was no denial. I was devastated beyond comprehension. She was Chinese and quite pretty, I always knew he loved Chinese food, but I never thought about his loving more than that.

I don't believe that absence makes the heart grow fonder. I think expectations are set about how wonderful the reunion will be and that often leads to disappointment. I think many marriages are a combination of both reality and fiction. In our own minds, we can make someone into whomever we want them to be. In my case, what I saw then was a figment of my imagination.

Today I live my life with honesty at the forefront. It is the kindest gift you can give someone. People look at other people the way they see themselves, and it's hard to imagine someone doing something you would find inconceivable. Not telling the truth out of kindness is unkind.

Today my son is a teenager, and my ex-husband and I co-parent successfully. He has remarried, and I have not. I went back to school, so that I can help women going through divorce with financial planning, estate planning, and tax planning. What I love the most is that I get to use my skills in psychology, as I help women learn to empower themselves.

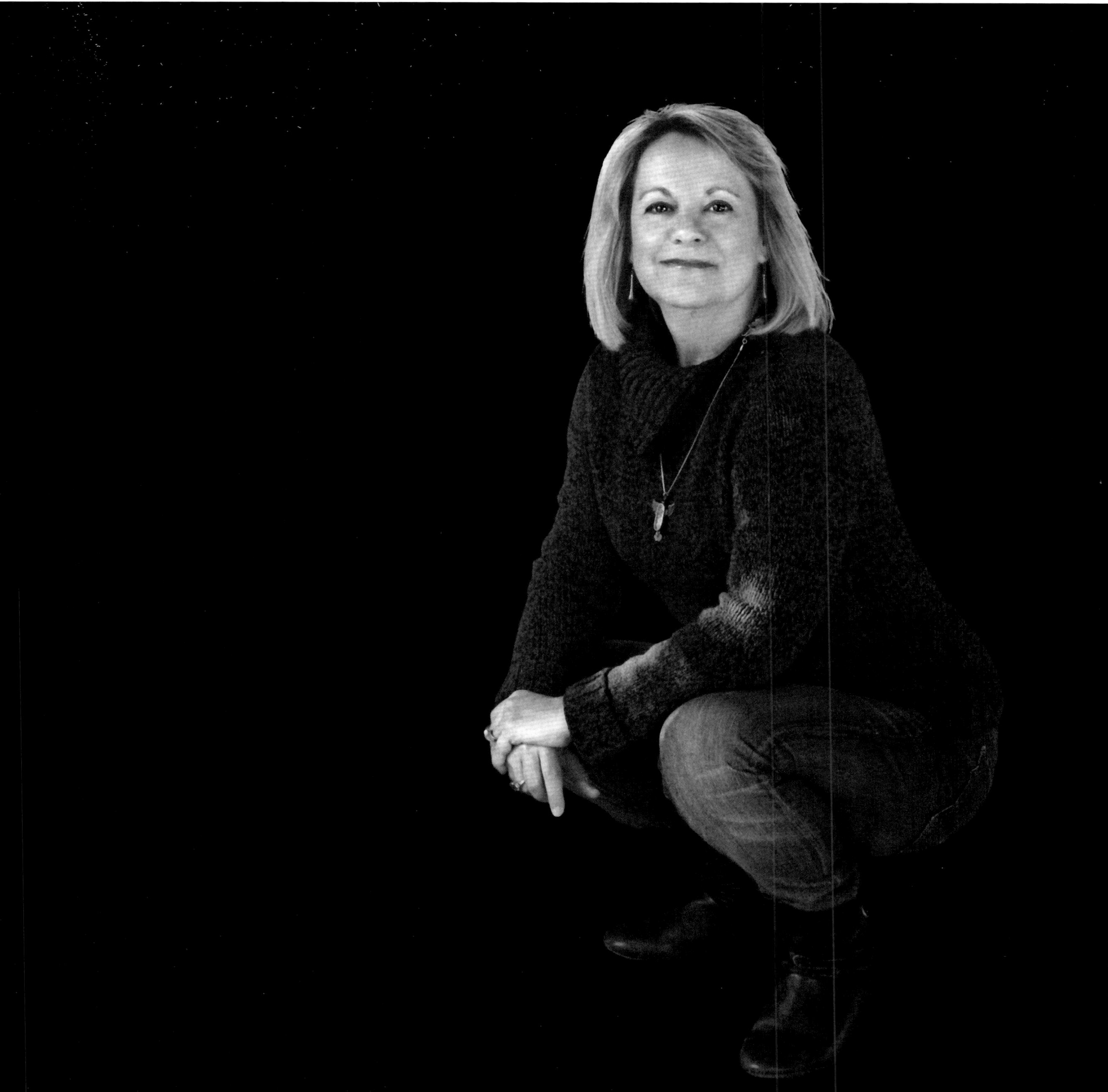

Kathy Posla

As a child, my life was like a fairy tale princess. I was born in Minnesota to adoring parents who loved one another. My dad worked with the United Nations and was adventurous. We traveled to Africa, South America, Central America, in all, thirty-two countries. My parents were originally from Italy. We eventually lived there for several years while going back and forth to Costa Rica. We quickly learned new languages and easily adapted to various cultures. It was an exciting gypsy existence and there was never a dull moment. I knew right from wrong in every culture and understood that we make our own choices. We alone are responsible for our decisions—good or bad.

I took getting married seriously and waited until I was thirty-three. The man I married was Italian and charming like my father. I loved his Italian roots and was sure I had walked into a romantic dream. Looking back, I realize I was too innocent to see his true nature. He was romantic with everyone. He even charmed the men! He took credit for my being alive, as if he were my father.

Eventually, I saw his dark side. I had horrible suspicions but did not tell anyone because I was expecting our second child. In spite of that, I investigated and discovered my worst nightmare was true. He was molesting our young daughter.

No divorce is easy, but mine was war. I had to move quickly to keep him away from my daughter. I had to have proof. I had to face evil to come out on the other side. I was afraid to face him but did. After the trial, he went to jail.

I took my daughters back to the United States. Here I am creative. My brain is never asleep. I wake up with all kinds of ideas. My grandmother taught me to sew when I was eleven. That is how I make my living now. I had a TV show and designed couture slipcovers for personal clients and companies.

Small gestures bring me joy. I see beauty in so many little things. I serve dinner to my daughters at a table set for queens. I might have one fresh flower as the star of the table for dinner or put rice and beans in a small adorable dish. Maybe I'll create gorgeous lining for the bread basket with matching napkins.

I expose my daughters to wonderful families. I want them to know there are many good men, even though I am picky and have not found one. So far they like good, kind boys. I hope it stays that way. I don't want to get married nor date. I like taking care of myself and my girls, without following anyone else's vision. I know for sure that money doesn't buy happiness and that instead, good pure relationships do.

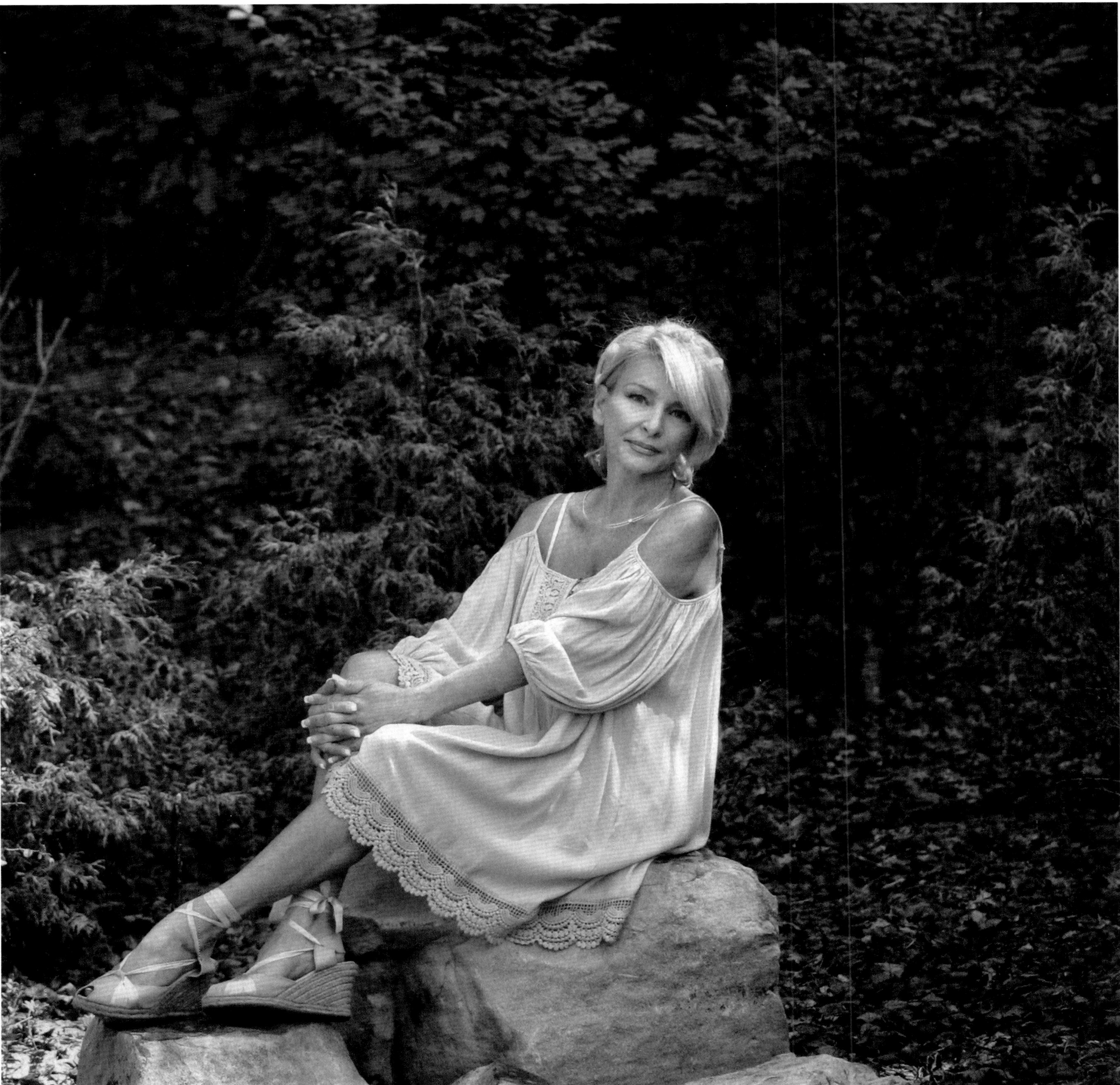

Maria Henson

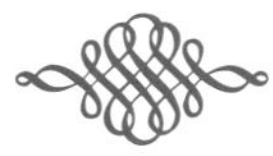

My parents were perfect role models. I expected to marry by thirty-three and have three children. I am in my fifties and have not married yet.

Early on, in about second grade, my mother realized that I was quite good at writing. She also recognized that I was marked down for writing outside the lines. She encouraged my creativity despite the push for conformity in schools. I have always loved art and started college with the idea of becoming an art major. I quickly realized that I did not have the patience for it. My father tried to persuade me to major in business. I did not take his advice but went with my gut instinct and became an English major.

My first job was as a reporter, working for a newspaper in Arkansas. I ended up going to Washington, DC, and covering Bill Clinton for them. After that, I went to Kentucky and covered a seventeen-hour hostage crisis that involved an abused woman. That led me to write editorials about how women fall through the cracks. The result was "To Have and to Harm," which focused on the abuse of women. I won the Pulitzer Prize for it. All of my work was in Kentucky but could have been anywhere in New York or Los Angeles. This reporting demonstrated the power of the press to initiate new legislation. I edited a series of editorials on the Hetch Hetchy Valley water system in California which also won a Pulitzer Prize.

I am a lifelong adventurer. So far I have traveled to forty-one countries. For me, traveling is my oxygen and collecting art is my passion. I have found out that some of the richest values are in the poorest places and that many "other" people have a lot to teach us.

I am never lonely, not even a little bit. I have friends all over the world, and today with advances in technology, I can be connected to Botswana in a few seconds. I spent a year there volunteering at an after-school program for children.

One of the best things that I have learned in life is that you may not be great at something, but you can try. I was never the kid picked for kickball or track, but I have become an athlete on my own terms. I can climb a mountain, and though I might be the last one to the top, I can do it. I swam from one side of Alcatraz to the other so slowly that the coach might have thought I'd drowned. But I did it.

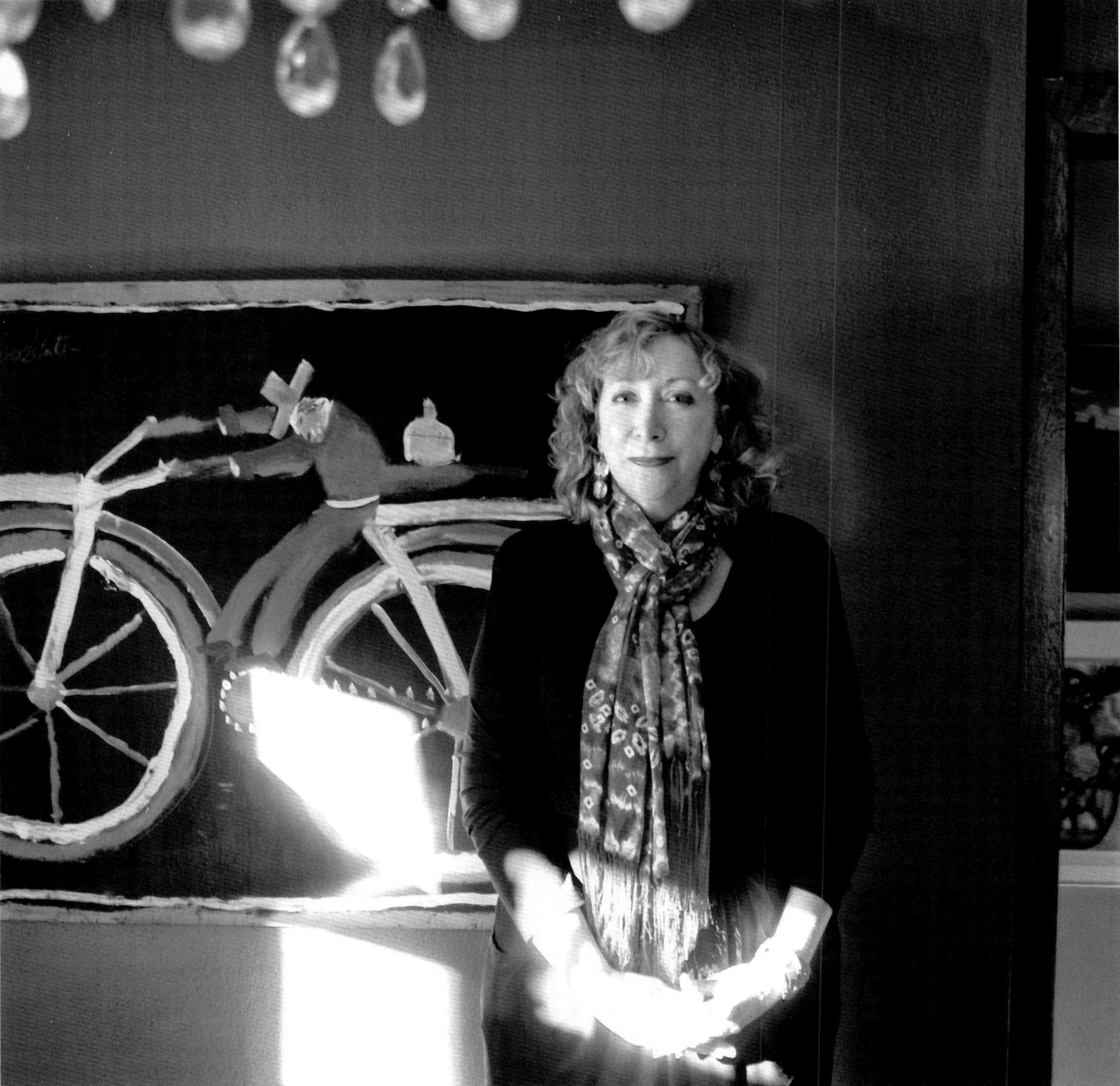

Dee Andrian

I came from a coal-mining town in Pennsylvania. We had no church, no post office, no doctor or dentist, no drug store. You name it and I'll bet we didn't have it. Except we did have two bars. I came from a big, fun family and we adored my mother. I wanted to be a model, but according to the agency, I needed to lose weight. I did lose weight, but my parents thought I looked like I had a disease. They set out to fatten me back up. I entered a local beauty pageant and won. From that experience I got on some television shows. That led to my co-anchoring a local news show.

One day a man I hardly knew told me I needed to go to New York. He said I was wasting my life where I was and that there were bigger things in store for me. He gave me an envelope with $300 with no strings attached. The next day I returned the money, as my parents were horrified. He told me that if I didn't take it, he was going to burn it in front of me. Well, I took it, and this time my parents gave me their blessing, thinking that burning money was an even greater sin.

I got a room in a lovely hotel for women. The world was a different place then. Men, who were mostly gentlemen, treated women like ladies. When you went on a date, it was for the fun of it or the romance of it. Nothing was expected at the end of the night, except maybe a kiss. I dated the handsomest men and was having the time of my life. I had a few passionate crushes, but nothing that turned into love. That is the reason I did not get married until I was forty.

Many of the network shows were in New York back then, so it was easier to find work and I did a lot of television. I was both a secretary and an actress. I met my husband at a charity event. He came up to me and asked for a date. I told him I had a list and would put him on it. He didn't think that was as funny as I did, and when I ran into him a year later, he asked if the list was getting any shorter. I teased him and said, "If you get tickets to *Applesauce*, you have yourself a date." The next day he called and had tickets. The play was amazing, but the dinner at Sardi's swept me off my feet. I had never met anyone who commanded my attention so fully.

I just wanted to hear him talk. We started a real courtship: roses, poems, love letters. This was the stuff dreams were made of. We married the year we met.

Soon I was pregnant, and we were ecstatic! The baby boy was born easily but had hyaline membrane disease and lived only eighteen hours. We had a chance to hold him and love him for less than a day. Neither of us ever recovered from that. Unlike many couples who lose children, it brought us even closer. We would talk about what he would have been, could have been, and agreed that he would have been extraordinary. Maybe he could have even been the President of the United States. We never forgot him.

As the years went on, I continued acting while Jim continued to amaze me with his wit and amazing mind. He did not need a dictionary—he was one. He was a golfer and a damn good one, too. He taught me to play, and the day I beat him, you would have thought he would be upset with me, but he was so proud. We were always big sports fans. For years, we rooted for the Giants, and then right after Jim died, they won.

That is one of the hardest things for me—I want to tell him everything. Of course I do, and so far he hasn't answered me back. At my age, that might be a good thing. We knew he was going to die and talked about it and made plans. He was going to be buried at Arlington, but stipulated that unless I could be buried beside him he would not do it.

Months later, after Jim had passed and he was buried at Arlington, I received a letter informing me that they were sorry, but I could not be buried next to my husband. I would be put on top of him instead. I looked up at the sky and laughed out loud. "You have outdone yourself this time, baby."

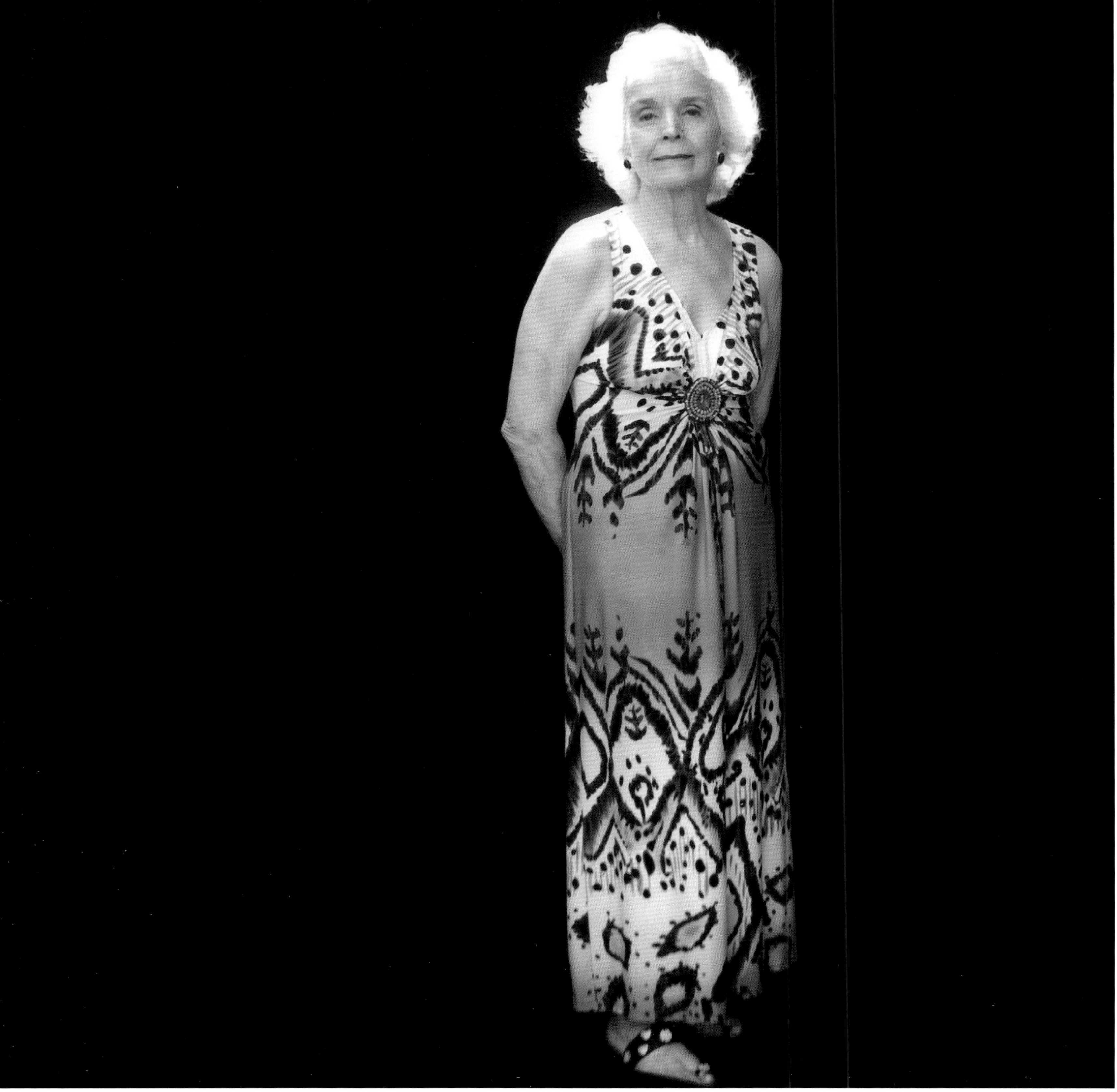

Teri Hairston

When I was three years old, my father altered my life. Whomever I might have been was lost forever. I loved my father back then. He would often tell me I was his favorite. He was a well-respected politician in the African-American community. He was elected president of the local branch of the NAACP, led marches on city hall, and organized and walked on picket lines. He was honored with awards, plaques, and certificates ranging from esteemed humanitarian to commendations as prestigious as the Nelson Mandela Award for Peace. Strangers approached him with outstretched hands to shake his. He was a big man, as big as a tree. He married my mother when she was fifteen and pregnant.

My mother worked all the time. When she wasn't working, she was drinking or having a nervous breakdown. When she had a breakdown, she would be gone for long periods. It was during one of these absences that my father molested me for the first time. I was warned not to tell anyone and took that warning seriously. After my mother returned, she took medicine and moved very slowly. She was withdrawn on the outside, and everyone noticed. My retreat was entirely hidden away. He did many inappropriate things in front of the family and masked them as affection.

Eventually my mother took me to the doctor because I could hardly walk. He told her that I was letting little boys do bad things to me. No one asked me what the truth was, and I knew the doctor was blaming me. I also knew he was not my friend, and if the truth came out, only worse things would follow. I was a tiny, little child with the mind of an adult.

I remember being thirteen and looking at my face in the mirror and realizing how much I looked like him. In my eyes I had the face of a monster. I had no desire to live because I had no control over what was happening to my body. I took pills, deciding to exit this life. Instead, I just became violently sick and wanted to die, instead of actually pulling it off. I never tried that again.

By sixteen, I was out of the house most of the time. I was boy crazy, and looking back, dressed for trouble. I looked and acted older than my years and had a knock-down fantastic figure with no self-esteem—a fatal combination. I now know that I had the word "victim" carved on my forehead. Abusers know their prey. I'm not just pointing my finger at the men either; women can be abusers, too.

During that time in my life, I married the handsomest man I'd ever seen. It was great in the beginning, until I didn't want to do what he demanded of me. The verbal abuse started and eventually became physical. I shielded my children as best as I could. One night, my three-year-old daughter came into my room and asked me if I was okay. I told her I was sad, that some people didn't like something I had done. Her response was unforgettable. "Mommy, don't worry about what anyone says. Just worry about who you are." In that moment, I knew she was smart. I had to show her courage and dignity. Soon after, I left my husband.

Against all odds, I became a police officer. In fact, I was the only woman to graduate in a class with eighty men. I was told from the start they would give me a chance but didn't expect me to make it. I was out to get those bad guys. You bet I wanted to get even, and I didn't want to live in a community riddled with gunshots, drug dealers, and rodents. I could outrun most of the men and was fearless. I did that until my children were teenagers and became afraid for me. One day I woke up and knew it was time to move on.

I am now in college, finishing my English degree. I am actively involved in gay rights and have a son and daughter who make me proud every day.

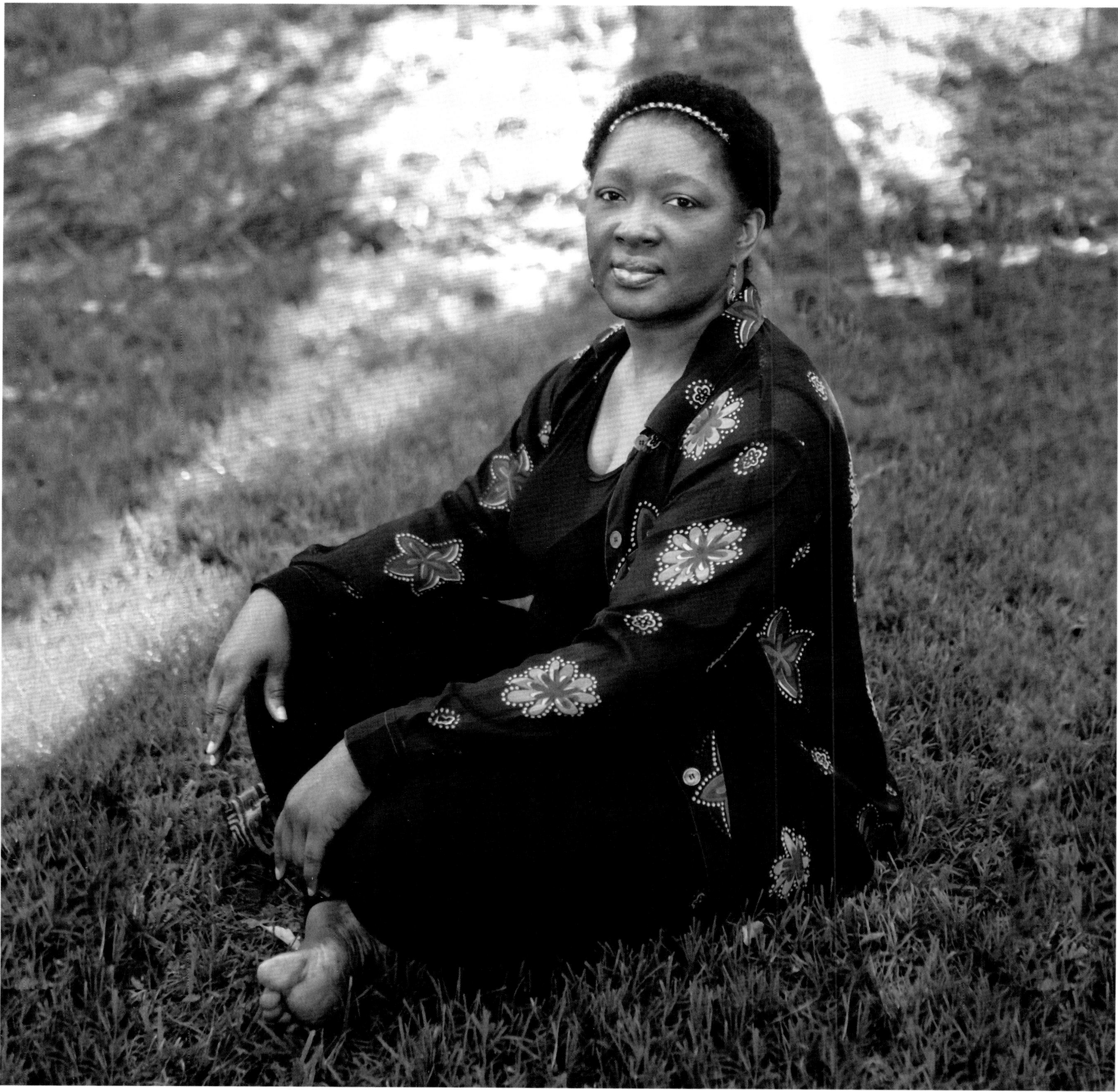

Micheline Chu

My parents came from a poor fishing village in China, where it was unusual for those born in the village to ever leave. My dad entered a contest and won a technical scholarship to a college in Germany. He was the only one in his family to get an education.

After college, he was offered a job in the United States. My parents wanted to be American and rarely spoke Chinese at home. They did not want their children to identify with any nationality except American. I knew they had succeeded when I traveled to Hong Kong, imagining that I was speaking perfect Chinese. Meanwhile, the Chinese people I talked to only responded in English.

I would have loved it if I had fallen in love and gotten married. I always wanted four children. I certainly dated and did the Match.com thing, but that magical feeling just never happened to me. I have always loved children so my career as an infertility doctor was perfect. I have had the joy of telling many couples who had given up on having children, that they were about to become parents. I have also seen it not work out for others, which is hard.

By the time I turned thirty-five, I understood my biological deadline better than anyone. I hinted to my parents that I was thinking of pregnancy without a husband. They did not like the idea of my being a single parent because they thought it would be unfair to the child. I vacillated, thinking that I might still meet someone.

Freezing my eggs was an option, and technology has come a long way in making that viable. It was not an easy decision for me to make without the approval of my family. Soon I decided to get pregnant on my own. If I had regrets, I would deal with them later.

I picked an anonymous donor. This means I had access to all the important criteria like education, family background, and health. There are many ways to have a baby and this is the one I chose. I felt it was not only the right thing for me but perfect for my job. Being able to talk about an experience that I had gone through myself makes the women I treat feel less terrified. It can often take twenty eggs for one to fertilize, if at all. I advise women to do it in their late thirties rather than follow the majority who leave it until their early to-mid-forties.

Once I was actually pregnant, I called my sister and begged her to tell my parents. It was Christmas, and I was afraid of ruining the holiday for all of us. I dreaded hurting them. In the morning, my sister told my parents the news. I did not expect to hear back for hours, but that's not what happened. In minutes, my mother was on the phone crying so hard, I could hardly understand a thing she was saying. I think most of it was in Chinese. I could understand "so happy," and then my father got on the phone, also crying. He told me that they would help me raise the baby.

The following spring I gave birth to my daughter. I can't imagine life without her. I look at that beautiful little face and thank God for all the guys who never called for a date.

I am not a risk-taker. I am not a procrastinator, either. Making quick decisions is a skill that many people lack and making thoughtful decisions and not following through is another problem. I see women taking chances they would not have dreamed of taking ten years ago. I get to help them. It's a wonderful world for women today.

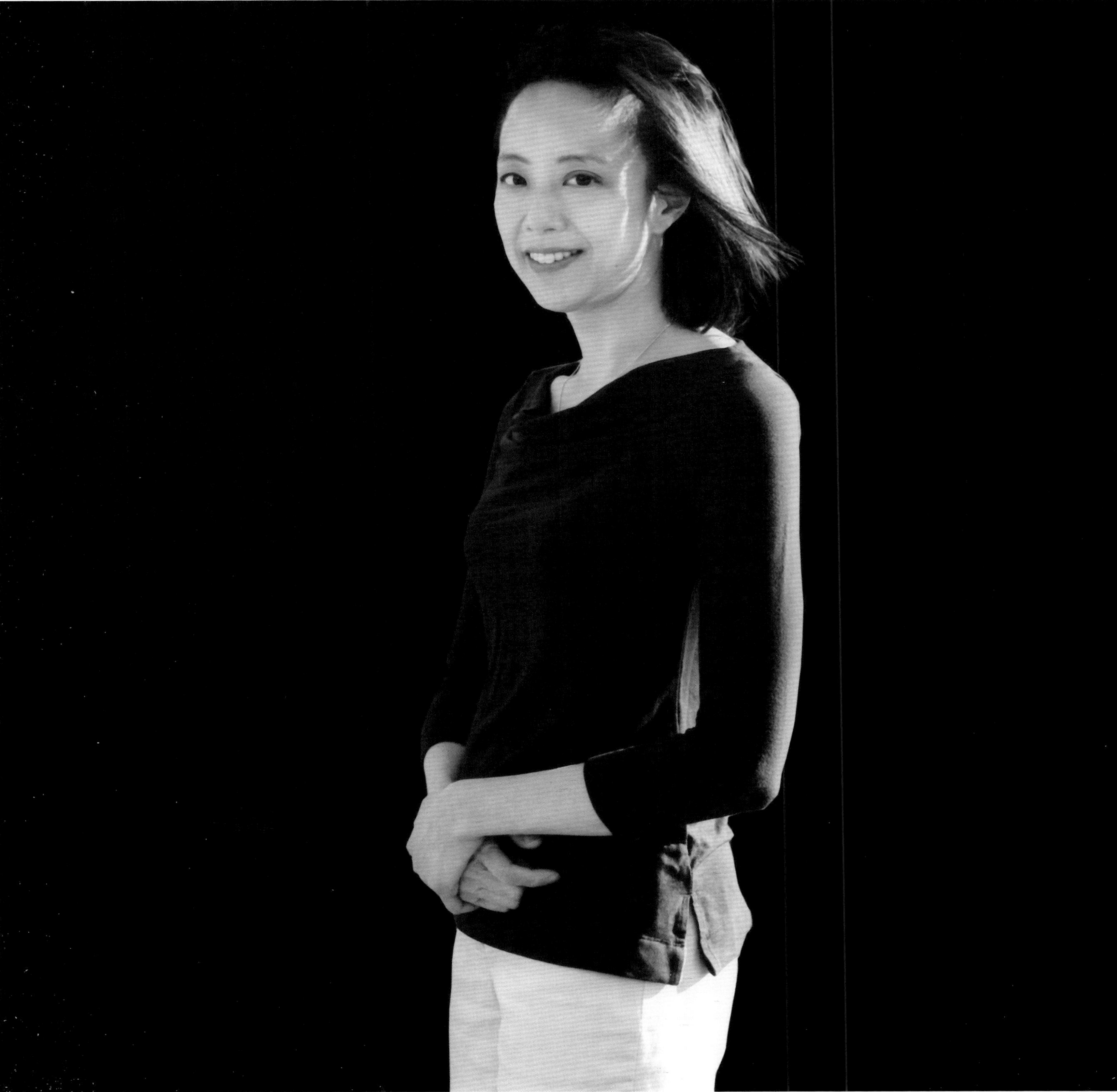

Daisy Rodriguez

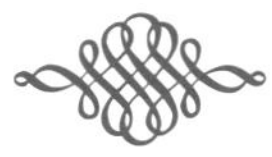

I was born to a woman who was mentally ill. She was not married to my father or to my sister's father. She would put electrical tape all over the walls to keep our neighbors from hearing our conversations and believed that people were trying to poison her. If it were not for my grandmother caring for us, I don't know if we would have survived. Very often, good people showed up unannounced. For instance, a friend's mother would show up with baked goods or a neighbor would knock on the door and tell us she had extra dinner and hoped we would like some. I do remember my mother would send me to the grocery store to get a potato for dinner. That one potato was supposed to feed my sister and me. More often than anyone knew, we went to bed starving.

Eventually, my mother married a distant cousin who had loved her from the time she was a teenager before she had developed problems. He remembered that young girl and took care of her, she was the love of his life. He got her on medication, and although things were not perfect, they were normal for us. He was a wonderful husband and to me the role model of what a man should be. We were not treated as or called step-anything—we were his own. Today, I look back at my mother and feel nothing but sorrow, knowing that it wasn't her choice to be sick.

After college, I married a Russian man. We had cultural differences from the beginning. Having my own family was everything for me. I wanted to be the mother I didn't have. We were constantly trying to make something fit that just didn't. Each of us was giving up a piece of ourselves to stay together. You can change people, but if change is not of their own free will, it will backfire at some point. The irony of this situation is that my mother-in-law is one of the greatest loves of my life and nothing will ever change that. For me, the truth should be up front. After we divorced, there were no mean or nasty scenes. We had once loved each other and now wished one another the best. We are the parents of three wonderful children and have four grandchildren. I have worked on finding the good inside the bad. We both learned to disagree, but with kindness.

Today, I do the same thing I have done for years, advocate for children. I am the outreach coordinator for the Second Harvest Food Bank of North Carolina and the director of childhood hunger programs. I received my degree in childhood development before I married and have worked in the field for years. I speak for the children who don't have voices. Sometimes I believe that what I went through as a child was an internship for this work.

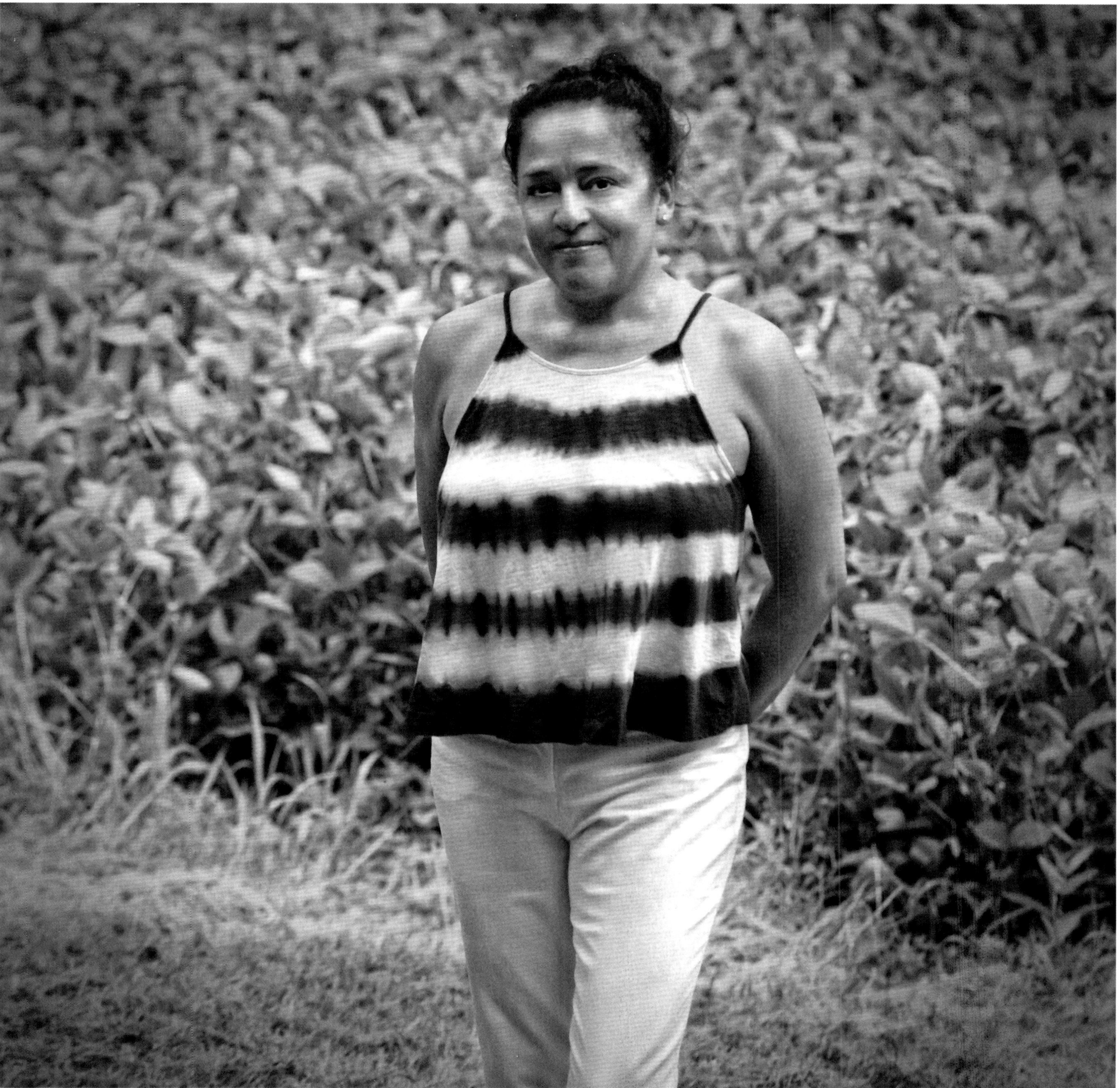

Deloris Davis

My mother was fifteen when I was born. My grandmother was raising me when a relative came to visit and found me filthy and starving. She offered to take me and met with no opposition. I don't remember that time, but I can tell you that my real mother—the woman who took me—gave me the best home any child can imagine. I was adored. My bedroom was fit for a princess, and the house was beautiful. It was like living in two houses, the way the curtains and carpets were switched out in the summer, for lighter and airier ones. Fresh flowers arrived weekly, and music was a part of family life. If I had a fantasy wish box, I could not have asked for more.

I married and had a son, but that marriage did not work out. He loved other women as much as my family loved me. I got married again after dating for eleven years. As soon as the ring was on my finger, he changed, and it wasn't for the better. I was working two jobs, while he didn't have even one. It was about this time that I decided to go to beauty school and end my marriage.

After graduating, I saw that Belk Department Store was hiring beauticians, so I went for the interview. They liked me but were looking for someone who already had a following. I was brand-spanking new at this and had no one following me. I asked them if I could set up a chair in the entrance and offer free haircuts to everyone until I developed my own clientele. To my surprise, they agreed. Before I knew it, I was working in the store and got not one station, but two, plus an assistant. Eventually I opened three of my own salons. I love making people feel beautiful.

I ended up with severe back pain and went to several doctors for physical therapy to treat it. I decided to get an epidural because the pain was getting worse. Something went wrong during that procedure, and I have not walked since. I have been to neurologists at Duke University and to the Mayo Clinic. So far, no one has given me an answer.

The good thing that came out of this for me was that I don't go to church anymore. I was unable to move for so long that I started reading the Bible by myself and learned that I was interpreting it differently than the interpretations of the pastor. I also stopped giving so much money to the church. After going for years, they never once called to see how I was doing. I have my own car now, all set up for my wheelchair. I am out and about and not letting this ruin my life. I would love to be married to a good man, but not one who is pushing my wheelchair. My entire life, I always had the feeling that I would marry an older, wiser man who was kind and charming. Now that I am seventy-four, that dream is less appealing.

Cathy Howe

How I turned out to be normal considering my upbringing is amazing. Both of my parents were orphans with no parenting skills. They rarely talked to each other and had nothing in common. I remember talking to a therapist once and she asked me what my expectations in life were. I couldn't answer, so she asked me what I did for fun. I was stricken because there was no fun in my life. But I had no intention of being boring, dull, fat or married.

When I met my husband, I thought he was perfect for me and that all my misgivings about marriage were untrue. The thought that I might not be good at marriage did enter my mind, but I would not allow it to stop me. I wanted to be what I considered normal. We married and moved into a new house. I should have been out of my mind with joy, instead I was of out of my mind with misery. I kept pushing my feelings back and hating myself for having them. Eventually, it was like a long, slow, never-ending death scene that everyone just wanted to see end. By the time it finally came to a breaking point, we had a daughter together. Because I loved his mother, we remained friends.

After the divorce, I found myself looking for another man. I had low self-confidence and found myself lowering my standards, hoping to find someone who would want to be with me. The lower they went, the more inappropriate the people were who entered my life. I was in a bad place and knew my big challenge was to get my self-respect back.

I decided that if I were destined to be a single person, I was going to be the happiest one I knew. I felt that copying the behavior I had seen in my life so far was not the way I wanted to go. I also acknowledged that unless I was willing to change, I would keep repeating the same mistakes. I knew exactly what to do and say when things were going bad but had no idea how to enjoy the good times.

I'm a reader and have read many books that have helped me grow and change. I have learned to stop fighting everything and accept life as it is. I have completely fallen in love with yoga and am proud to say that I am now teaching classes, along with my career of teaching women in third-world countries technical skills.

For my fiftieth birthday present, I went to London alone. The wonderful thing about traveling alone is that you can do whatever you want whenever you want to. I ended up meeting the loveliest people. I have lost the fear of doing things by myself and have taught myself not to allow the lack of a companion to stop me from doing anything. My greatest fear is living life on the sofa.

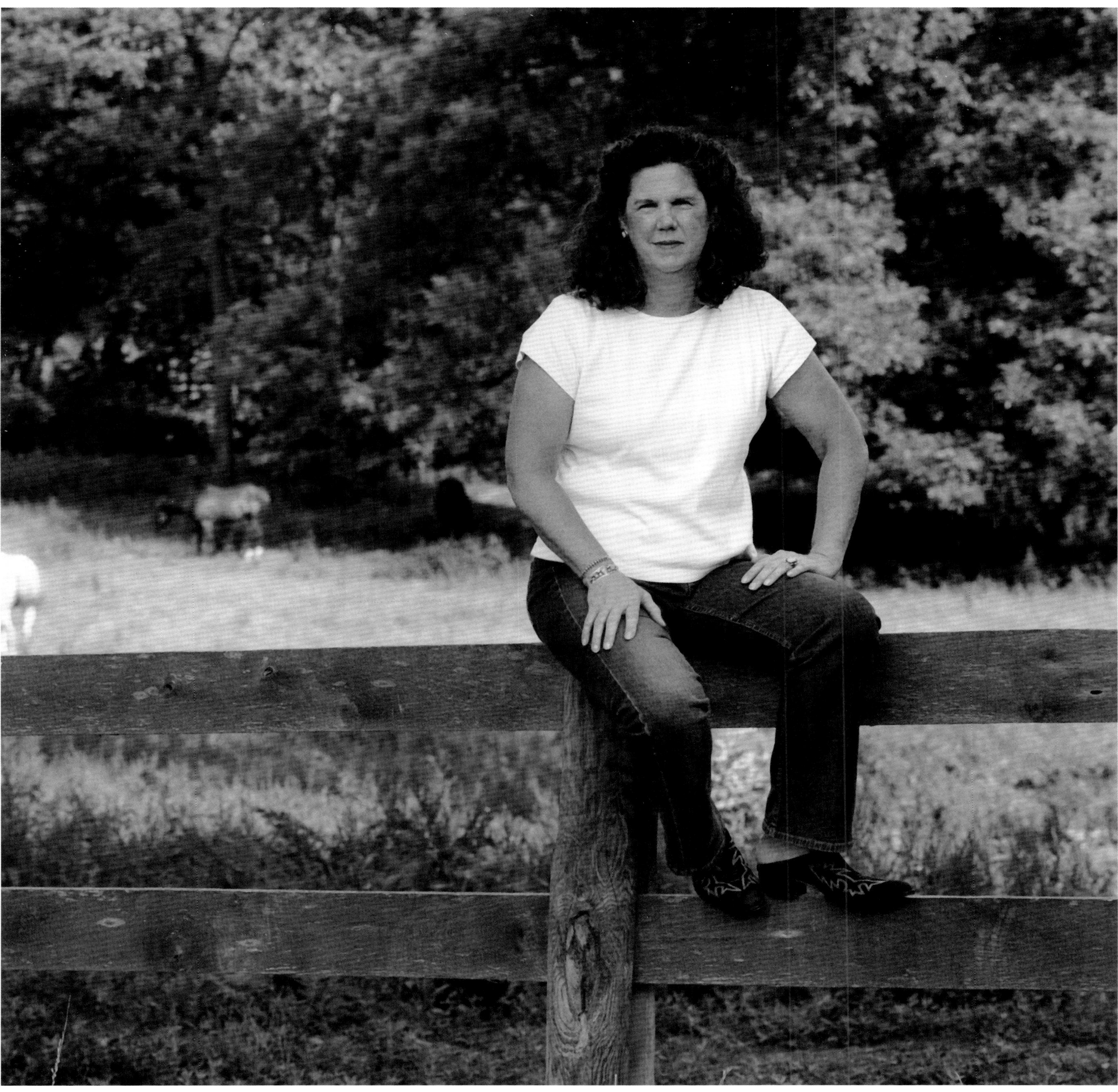

Tamara Michael

I had an aunt who never married. Her name was Aunt Bess. In a world of black-and-white photos, she was in Technicolor. The word "spinster" was used to describe unmarried women, but no one thought of her in those terms. She was gorgeous and a model who had an English degree. She was always preparing for a holiday and especially loved Paris. She had a cadre of fascinating friends: authors, designers, writers. I don't think she was ever bored. As a young girl, I adored her.

I never wanted to get married. I wanted to be like her—larger than life. However, I fell in love and like many plans, my single life was put on hold. I was married for eleven years before I found out that one of my closest friends was closer to my husband than to me. I had one son when my marriage ended.

After that, my life exploded—in a good way. I was a clerk at the post office part-time, working hard, when affirmative action kicked into place and I was offered the opportunity to become postmaster. My philosophy is that we all have defining moments that are golden—something like the Wheel of Fortune, and then it stops in front of you. You better know it's there and grab it. I had that job for many years, and as a saver, I was able to plan for an early retirement. Aunt Bess left me an inheritance and I wanted to take a risk, yet stay relatively safe. I did a lot of research and decided to buy some waterfront property. That could have been the stupidest thing I had ever done, but it wasn't. It was the smartest.

After retirement, I found myself becoming depressed. I remember being in New York and seeing an ad from a travel agency offering a trek in the Himalayan Mountains. I signed up to go alone, not knowing what it would be like. It turned out to be the beginning of an entirely new life for me. I met many people my own age, but I had the most fun with two brothers who were married and loved exotic travel. At the end of the trip we vowed to do it again but deep inside I felt like it was most likely a party promise, and dismissed it. A few months later, I received a call from one of the men's wives, inviting me to travel to China with them. Since then I have traveled to Nepal, Vietnam, Egypt, Saudi Arabia, and Iran with those two brothers. We are like family now, and I am good friends with their wives as well.

I don't have a lot of clothes, a car, or the latest in many things. I made choices along the way about what was most important to me. You can't have everything. Some things you have to give up to get what is more important. I am single and won't give up my freedom. I could have been married many times, but it's all about priorities.

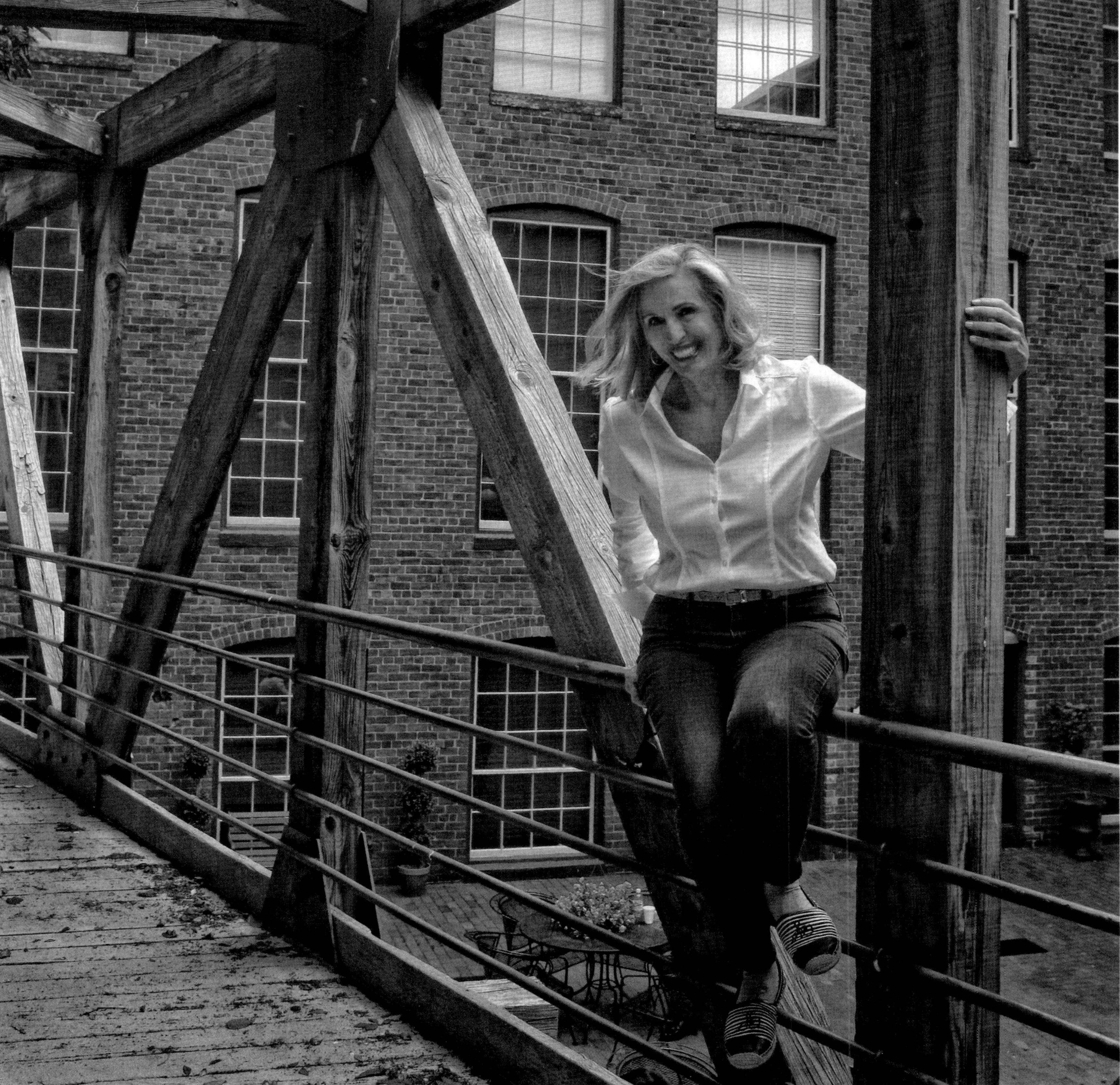

Earline King

I was an only child from a religious family. When I was a young girl, we lived on a block with many children. One of the games we played was called Statue. We would run around the lawn and the person who was "it" would choose the best statue, by facial expression and posture. I look back and find it such a foreshadowing that I ended up a sculptor, as I did not particularly enjoy that game.

I met my husband as a young teenager in school where we both took art classes together. In those days art was valued differently, and many people went on to have careers from the education they were provided. We got married in secret at sixteen. We were afraid to go against our strict upbringing, so sneaking away seemed the best option. Of course, our parents eventually found out. Thankfully, they accepted our marriage graciously.

I ended up winning a college scholarship, while singing in a talent contest. My husband started out as a commercial artist, drawing storefronts and such, but eventually became one of the best portrait artists in the world. He even received a commission to paint Queen Elizabeth II!

We had a busy and fun marriage, but we did not have any children. He was multi-talented and had a ventriloquist act while I sang in nightclubs in New York and Washington D.C. I loved him tremendously and was disappointed when I realized there were other women in his life. Like many women of my generation, to keep peace and save face, I turned the other cheek to his on-and-off affairs.

One night a friend urged me to accompany her to a sculpting class. I said no, but she would not give up. And so, I did her a favor and that changed my life. Before the end of the class, I was in love with what my hands were creating. I became obsessed and spent day and night at the studio, perfecting my art. Eventually, I had a hard time keeping up with all the commissions

We had been married for fifty years, and then everything fell apart. My husband was working with an Italian model who was twenty-two years old when he stopped coming home. The worst night of my life was the night I put everything he owned on the back porch and told him to come and get it. Not only did he not desire me, but he couldn't care less about my humiliation.

I know people don't want to be around bitter people, so I didn't talk much about it. I had never been alone before and was living from minute to minute.

Another night, a close friend of mine invited me to dinner. She had a charming business associate from out of town over, and he happened to be twenty-five years younger than me. The story is long, but the ending is short. We fell in love! It has been several years now since he started asking me to marry him. My answer is always the same: not today, but maybe tomorrow. I will love my ex-husband until the day I die, and I completely forgive him, but I have learned there is more room in my heart to love than I knew.

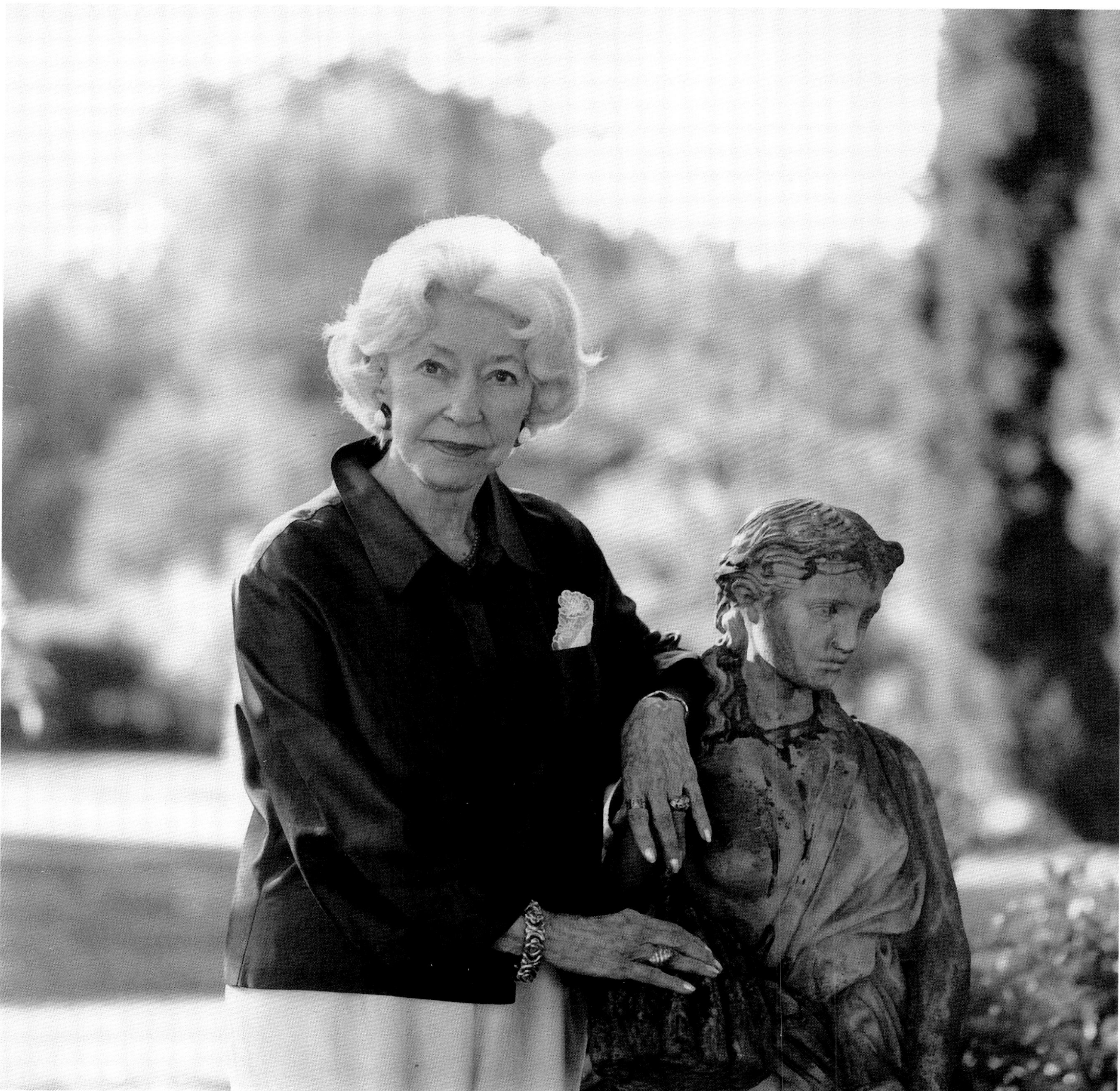

Jane Heaney

My mother was a perfectionist and did everything to a fault. She wanted to protect me and make sure I was safe. I didn't have the opportunity to learn from my mistakes, so I learned helplessness at an early age. I was born into an Irish Catholic family. If someone had asked my mother, grandmother, or aunts whether they would rather my sister or me be unmarried or run over by a truck, I know they would have had to pause to think about it.

In the beginning, I so wanted to please my family and make them proud. I got married as expected at 19, before anyone might steal my virginity. I walked down the aisle sobbing. Everyone thought it was from getting such a catch. He was handsome, with an impressive resume, yet all I could think of was that I was making a mistake. I had wanted to call off the wedding, but the embarrassment and potential financial loss for my father kept me from doing it. I felt as if I was the last virgin of the 1970s.

As time moved on, I was unhappy. My family said, "You've made your bed and now you have to lie in it." I decided in spite of disappointing them, I needed to get a divorce. I had been way too young to make a lifetime commitment. In their defense, I must say they felt that by my being married, I was going to be taken care of. I think a good age for marriage should be at least thirty. I have no regrets because I have my beautiful daughters. If I could give them one gift, it would be fearlessness and the knowledge that no matter how terrible things may seem, there is always a way out of a bad situation.

For many years, I was an office manager. It was a fun job and kept me busy. I did not date often because I was focused on my daughters. I would not introduce them to the men I was dating, unless I felt serious about them, which didn't happen often. The few times I did meet someone, they were professional business men. What would start out lovely, would end with them wanting me to be a little different than I was. I didn't want to be a size six or have a salad, when what I really wanted was a hamburger.

There was a man who was nothing like anyone I had ever dated. I saw him nearly every day. We had great chemistry and laughed a lot at the same things. I never thought of him to date, he was just a great friend. He happened to be the happy-go-lucky mailman from the office I worked in. He would come to deliver the mail and end up staying longer and longer. We both had relationship problems and were enormously comfortable sharing our deepest feelings. When I was being a little overly sensitive about something, he would call me on it. I listened to his advice. He comes from a family of eleven children and is the kindest person I've ever met. I fell for him long before we had our first date.

Now, we have been together for several years but will not marry. I believe there is a time for everything under the sun. I don't need the formality to be happy. My daughter, who got engaged at thirty-one, is getting married soon. I am so joyous about that. Her fiancé has a quiet intelligence, wit and quirky sense of humor that has made her a better version of herself. This time, when I walk down the aisle, as mother of the bride, I will be crying with happiness.

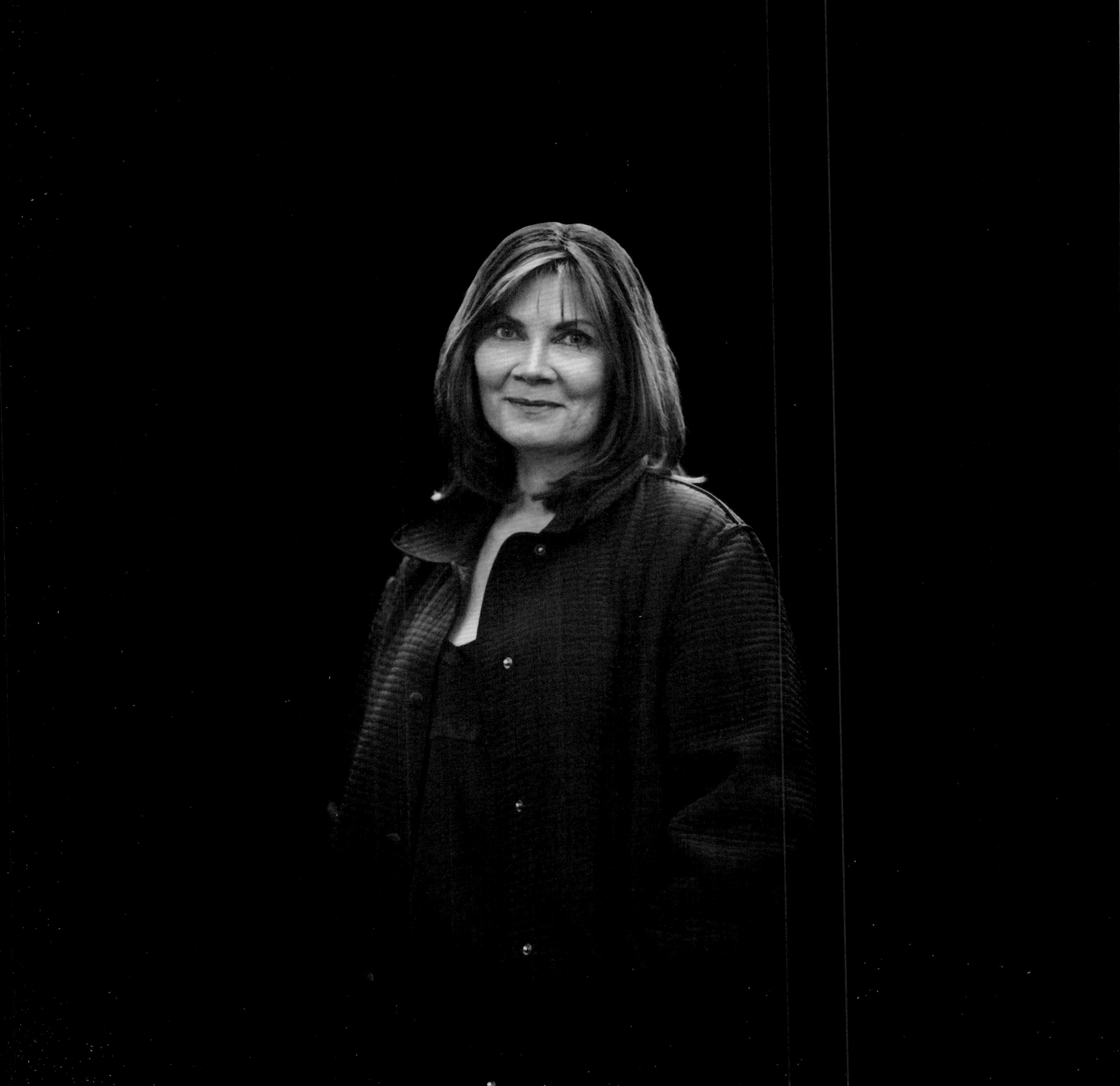

Marge Crunkleton

I was an airline stewardess when I met my husband. He was on his way home from the air force and had extra time between flights. He knocked on my door looking for an old girlfriend who lived in my building. I was wearing a tattered, old, quilted robe with no buttons, which was closed with a safety pin. Not the outfit I would have picked, if I knew I was about to meet my future husband. It goes to show no matter what you're wearing, you can't kill chemistry. We had fun talking while I tried to find his old flame with no luck. He promised to come back in a couple of weeks, this time to see me.

We had a long-distance courtship, seeing each other every week because I was able to schedule my trips to his home in the South. After five months of dating, we married. He was so handsome and also quiet. He excelled in all athletics and eventually went from an upbringing in poverty to a hero level in sports. I, on the other hand, came from a big Armenian family who expected me to marry one of my kind. It was *A Big Fat Greek Wedding* family drama, but eventually they came around.

After our marriage, I got pregnant, started college and had a baby all in our first year. We had a three-room house with no plumbing. At first, we had no heat and it was cold. I would go to bed first, followed by Ted. He would push me over and take my warm spot. I would push him back and in the end, we would end up laughing or making love.

In every marriage, eventually you hit that for better or worse wall. If it's getting worse, both people need to figure out what is really going on and fix it. Burying heads in the sand is the reason many marriages fail. I also believe compassion is right up there with commitment. You need to recognize the differences between the two of you and focus on the positive while working on the negative. We were total opposites, but I would not want anyone like me. He was sports obsessed: watching it, playing it, teaching it or talking about it. I am a nonstop, want-to-be, sometimes am, obsessed artist. I am creating in my sleep. That said, we were able to be cheerleaders for one another.

We had four children and I had a career for many years as a draftsman. I loved the job and didn't think of myself as a feminist, as the movement hadn't even started back then. I was finding my way in a man's world successfully.

While drafting, I also worked on many other things. I designed a line of baby dolls (ten in all) with learning lessons for behavior modification that was sold nationally. I created old lady and old men dolls and dressed them to match their unique personalities. I make life-size dolls, dolls you can hold in your hand, marionettes, Santa dolls, and fantasy dolls of all kinds. I knit, crochet, embroider, and sew without patterns. What I do makes many people happy, and as I create, my brain is often dreaming of the next project. We went from that three-room house to a stunning house on a lake. Ted was a successful, passionate baseball coach and I eventually opened an ice cream shop that also sold the many toys and dolls I made. When the children came in, I pretended to be asleep and snoring. You couldn't imagine the laughter when they thought they woke me up. It was one of the most fun things I have done.

Ted passed away a few years ago after a long illness. We were married sixty years. I cry easily and often. I know we had a great marriage, even though we didn't go to the movies or take walks together. Without even realizing it, sometimes I will be in my studio and yell out to him to look at my newest creation. Then I remember.

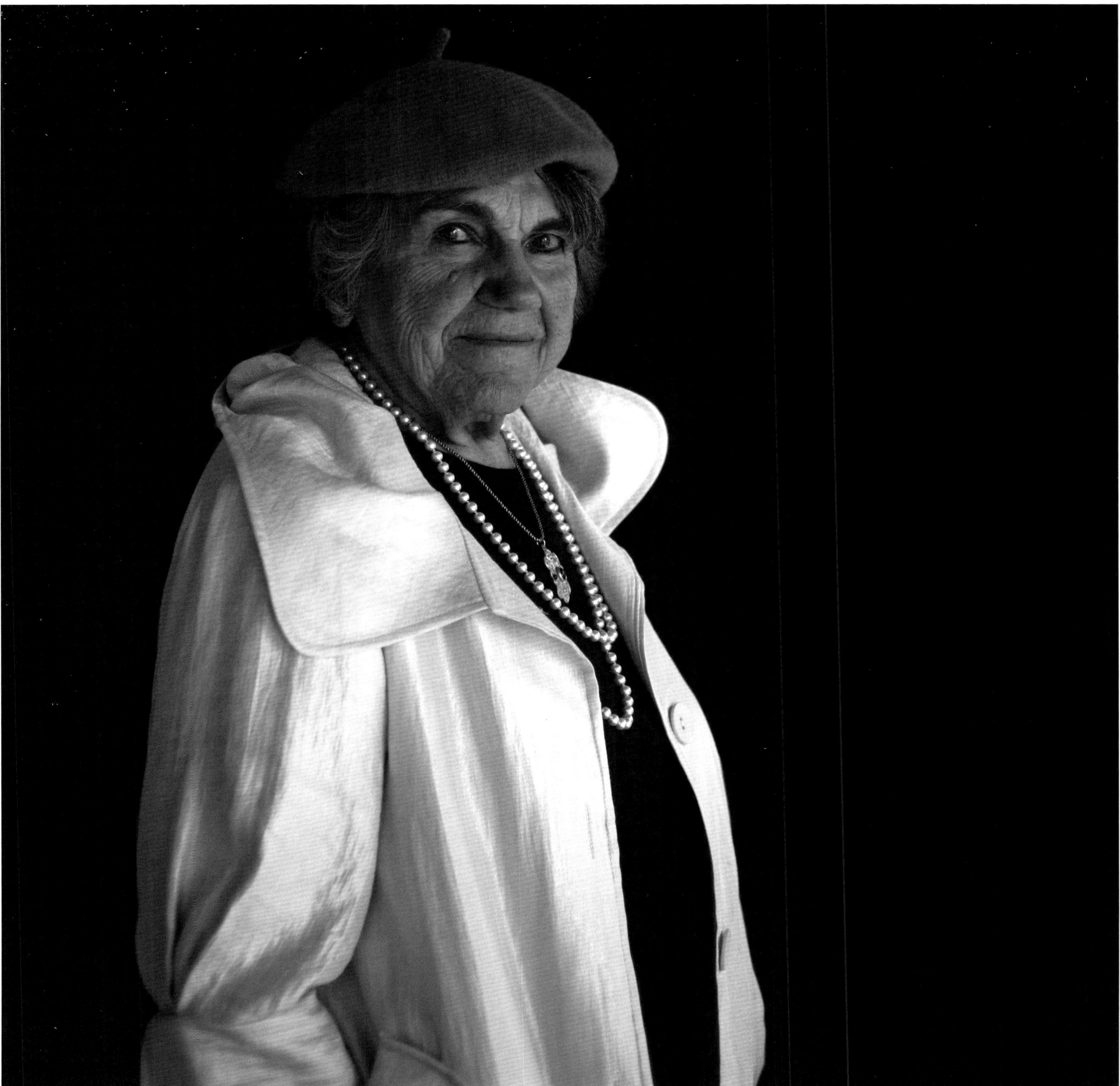

Amy Chenette

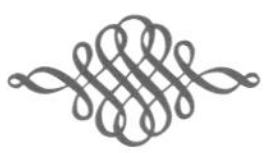

I grew up in a modest household with rules. The roar of my father's voice when angry and the guilt my mother doled out kept me on the straight and narrow. I had a paper route and babysat often. Those ethics around work and spending have been invaluable to me. I still shop at Goodwill and consignment shops.

I met my husband in the summer when we were both sharing rental homes with friends. When I first saw him across the room, the physical attraction was magnetic. We talked all night and began a whirlwind romance. He was so handsome, so kind, and to top it off, he was a wonderful listener. This was my Prince Charming.

Earlier in his life, the infidelity of his father had hurt both him and his family. He had terrible memories of that time and it never entered my mind he would emulate the behaviors he despised.

We got married. As his Wall Street career blossomed, we had four children. I often pinched myself to verify that my life was real. We had two stunning houses on the water, lots of friends, and were both involved with our church where he was a deacon. He told me he loved me all the time, and not once did it enter my mind that our marriage was in trouble.

One night out of the blue, while I was cooking dinner, I was told that I might receive an upsetting phone call. Before the statement was out of his mouth, the phone rang and a woman told me she'd been having an affair with my husband and had just found out that he was cheating on her.

In disbelief, I blamed the woman and myself for not seeing the signs, and yes, I blamed him. Even so, I quickly decided to stay and fight for my marriage. We had four children, and I didn't want them to suffer. He moved out and got therapy. I kept this time private, except for telling my two best friends. He moved back home, perhaps too quickly, and I started living a "Stepford Wife" existence.

Five years went by, and I believed we were finally healing. The children were always getting party invitations, which they would rip open with excitement. As I sorted through a stack of this already-opened mail, I found a blue envelope embossed with the name "Tiffany's." It was a thank-you note for purchasing the diamond necklace and explained that the bracelet was now available.

We had financial difficulties, so I knew it was not for me. I called him at his office and when confronted, he denied it, saying it was a mistake. The more he denied it, the angrier I became. Finally he said, "It was only a small diamond and didn't cost much," and hung up.

Shaking with emotion, I went to my computer and wrote a letter to all of our friends, family, and the congregation at church (more than 400 people). I told the entire story from five years earlier to the present day. I read it several times to make sure I was making sense and not embellishing. I kept pausing at the send button, knowing that if I hit it there would be no going back. In my head I kept hearing the words, it didn't cost much. I hit the send button.

That was several years ago. I have since started my own business helping people organize everything from their wardrobes to their attics and garages; I am great at de-cluttering extra space. The children are emotionally healthy and happy. I have had an outpouring of love and help from so many people. I have a new life, and it's still evolving. I learned that a lot can be taken away during a lifetime, you may lose your job, your house, your loved one, but one thing that can't be taken away is your values. So, my most important job is being the best mother I can be and living with honesty and integrity.

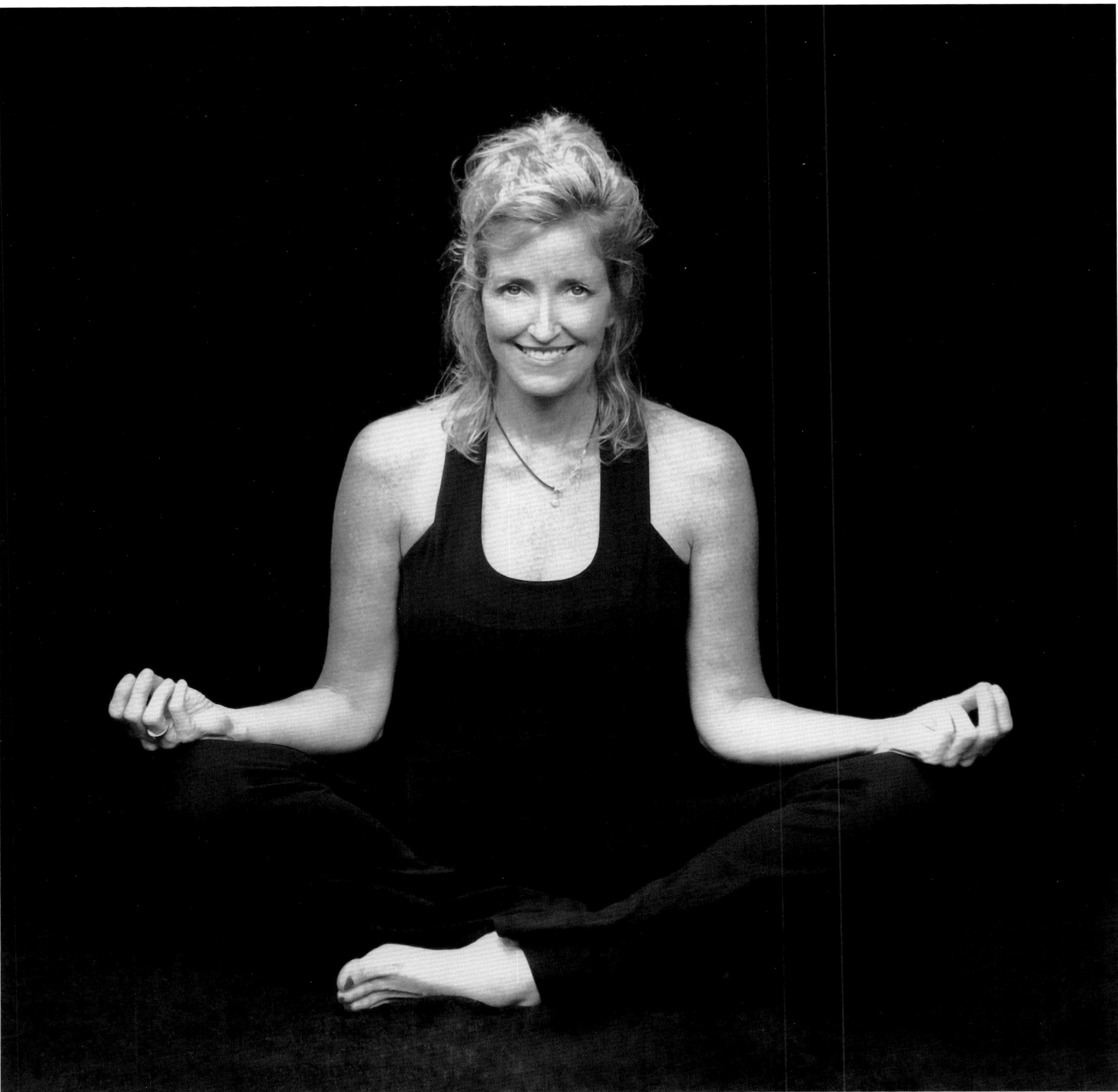

Mish Kara

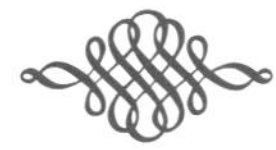

Both of my parents were Russian. They were very wealthy in Russia but not when they came to the United States. Leaving Russia, my father's mother put her jewelry in the hem of her coat. They always let us know that you had to work hard for what you got. They also let us know life was not always fair and therefore, we did not have unrealistic expectations. Their love of reading was passed onto all four children, perhaps because we were read to from an early age. The background music from my childhood was Russian classical, and I played the cello from third grade. I also played the piano early because I could read music without instruction. I started dancing lessons at seven and I knew, even at that young age, that the teachers spent more time correcting the good dancers.

When it came to going to college, I was not allowed to major in dance. How smart my parents were. They insisted I major in something that would allow me to be prepared to support myself or my family if I needed to. My parents did not spoil us with toys but took us to concerts, museums, the ballet and plays—anything to expand our minds.

My father was strict but always explained why he was saying what he said or doing what he did. He never yelled, he explained. To this day I rarely lose my temper, and I try to use reason. I lower my voice rather than raise it. From both my parents I learned the skill of non-confrontational conversation. The advice I often give to soon-to-be parents is, "Always listen to your children and you will know what they are thinking the rest of your life."

When I got divorced from my first husband, I learned if I did not argue with him, he couldn't fight with me. I was in a terrible situation. He was an alcoholic who lost his job and drove me to work everyday. I couldn't leave the house by myself or answer the phone. Eventually, I left in the middle of the night with my children, who were two and four years old. I had no idea how I would support myself but believed I could. Coming from a woman's college had given me a different confidence than many other women. I was offered a job in medical sales, before it was commonplace for women to have that career. I was told by many people I would never be successful and that was the fuel that catapulted me into the number one sales rep in the company. The second year, they did their best to make sure it didn't happen again and when it did, I was able to buy a house. Eventually, I traveled all over the world in that career. I respond in a good way to challenge.

I married my second husband, Jay, after years of being best friends. He was someone I could talk to about anything. He supported my dancing, even though he was not a dancer. He was my rock—someone I could lean on and be hugged by. He made me feel beautiful and I adored him. We were married twenty years when he passed. I have lost people before, but this has been the worst. It has left a big hole in my heart, but I am not trying to fill that hole. I take the memories out and savor them often. I have a busy life now bringing up my thirteen-year-old grandson. His mother is mentally ill and I am helping my son and his children get past this tragedy. I never expected to be a mother again at seventy-five, but it is a joy to see the positive changes taking place. Both of my children have turned out to be beautiful people who I talk to every day.

I both take and teach ballroom dancing lessons. I have enjoyed the process of competition in dance and made it through all the different levels and eventually won at the highest level. My love is in the teaching and seeing the joy it brings into people's lives: the waltz, fox trot, cha-cha, and tango are the most popular.

Recently, there have been reports that dancing is great for the brain. It forces multitasking, which is cognitively beneficial for everyone. I charge little for my instruction because it is a joy for me and I am a believer in paying it forward.

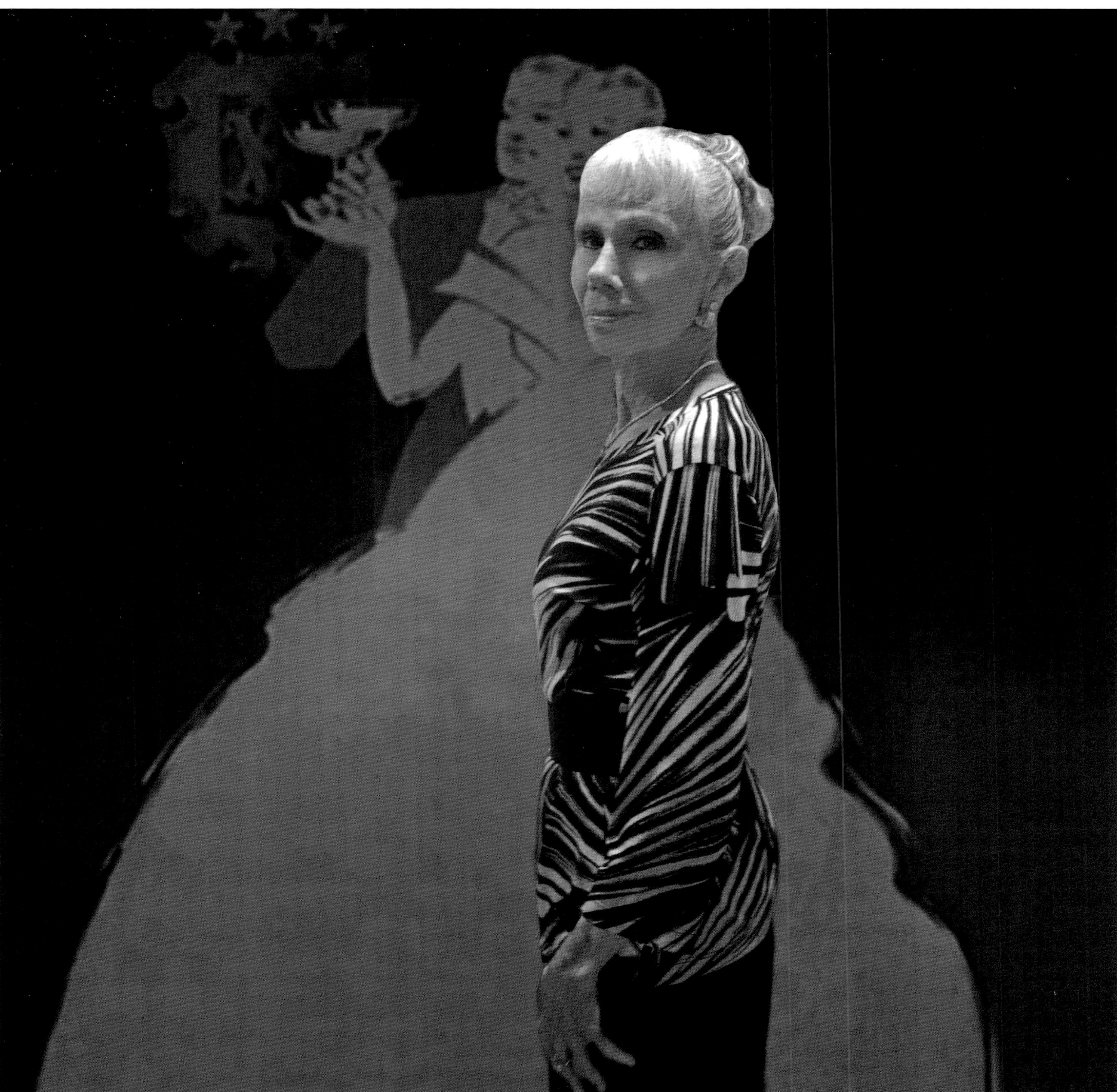

Jennifer Beuno

My maternal grandmother was the biggest influence in my life. She stood 4'10" and commanded a room without ever raising her voice. Her serious tone demanded respect and she had confidence about her that earned her respect. She was a young widow running a chicken farm with four children to take care of. She grew everything she needed to feed them. She was a redhead with brilliant green eyes. That's unusual for a full-blooded Italian woman. My mother, like my grandmother, held strong opinions. She said it "like it was," with no sugar coating. She had a kindness and fairness about her, that made her a wonderful mother.

I am a lot like my mother. I hope I've added a little more diplomacy into the mix. From the time I was ten years old, I knew I didn't want children. Please understand that I love children, I just did not want them for myself. When I was playing house with my little friends, they named their baby dolls and even in the pretend world, I did not name mine. It's surprising how many people give their opinion on how other people should live their lives. The decision to or not to have children does not make someone unkind or less of a woman.

I met my husband on a dating site. My attraction to him was immediate. He was adventurous, spontaneous and he brought excitement into my otherwise quiet life. I was often told by my friends that I was too picky and difficult to please. I took those comments to heart and decided to dive in head first. It was not long before he revealed his Jekyll and Hyde behaviors. He was spending money recklessly and being noncommunicative for days on end. He said that I was ruining his life. I lived in fear of even our simplest interaction. We tried therapy, but he refused to work through it. When glass started breaking, I knew I had to leave. I was heartbroken.

During this period, I was working in IT and unhappy in my job. Despite having a degree in architecture and interior design, I felt having money represented success and provided security. I thought being in IT was going to provide a great salary, even though my heart was not in it. I was miserable and no bonus could hide it. To relieve stress, I went back to my roots and started gardening again. In addition to my Italian grandmother, my paternal grandmother was a Hawaiian farmer who grew unusual tropical flowers and orchards of fruit. Farming was in my DNA. It was incredibly rewarding to see what sprang from the ground. I felt that I was giving birth to beauty every day. It was not long before people started asking me if I went to horticultural school. While keeping my job in IT, I went back to school and got an additional degree in horticulture. Soon after, I volunteered at an old historical estate helping tend their gardens. Then, I received a call from my sister telling me about an opening at the Botanical Gardens near where she lived. I went ahead and sent in my resume and I was thrilled to be hired! I was delighted to be in my element, playing in the dirt full time. I now can say that money is not as important as I thought it was. Now my work is play!

I have learned that everyone has challenges, including me. It's easy to see why people think that their problems are the worst. I try to be sensitive about how I interact with others, as I don't know anything about their heartbreak. As far has finding a new man, I would like that to happen. I could use somebody that treats me with kindness and respect. I'd like to see myself with a fixer-upper, but I mean a house—not a husband.

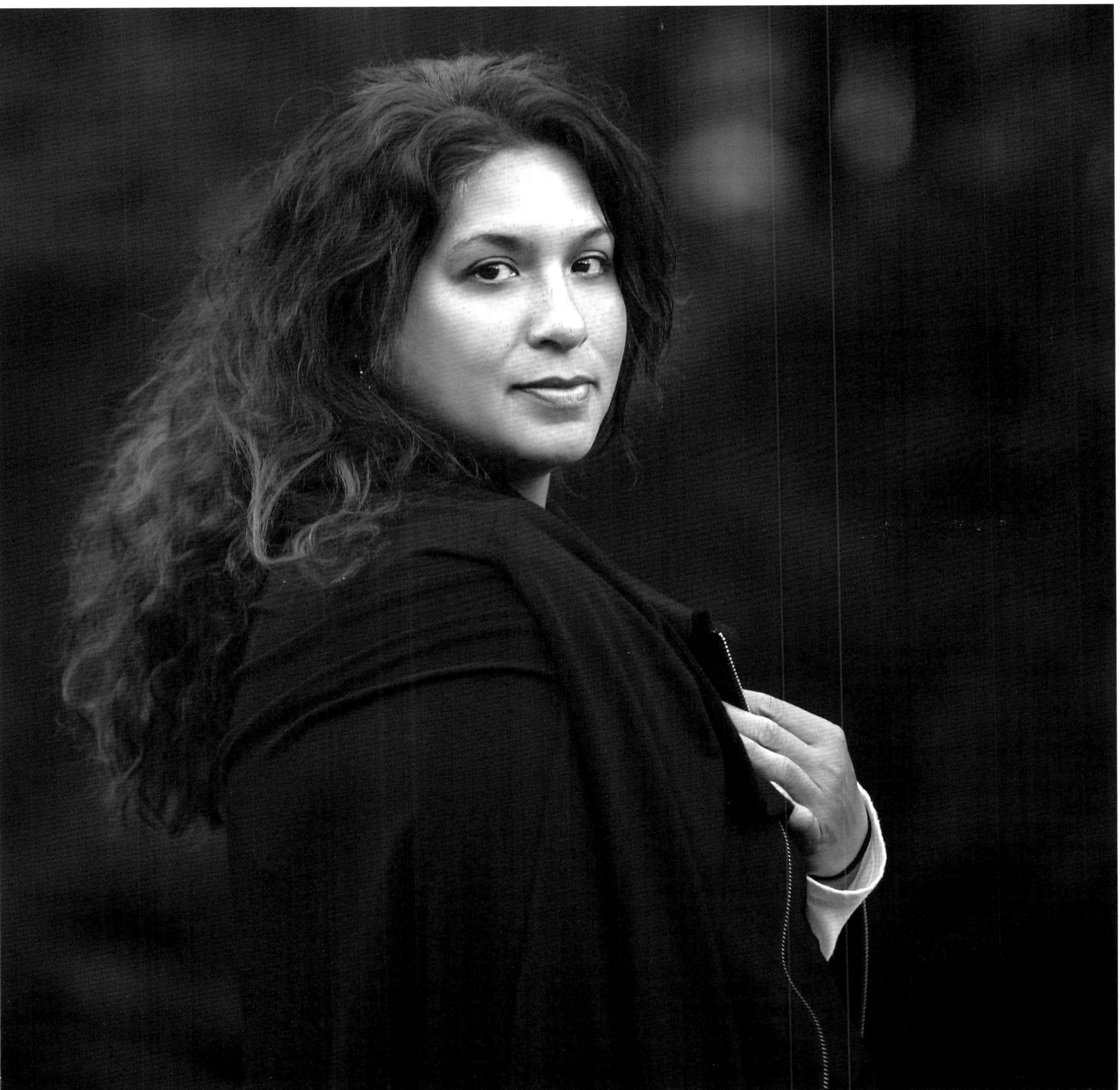

Madeleine Park

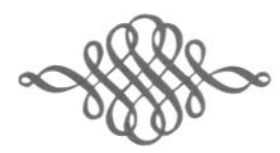

My mother and father were a perfect parenting combination. They were a blending of both love and lessons. We lived in Colorado back then and one of my favorite memories was being at a cookout. It was late in the evening, and although I was only five years old, I noticed my mother getting a second plate of food. Then I watched as she asked my father to escort her over the street, across the train tracks, to a homeless man she had spotted under a bridge.

Weeks later, I followed in her footsteps. My father took me to McDonald's and as I was handed my chicken nuggets, I noticed a homeless man outside. I asked my father if I could give him my food, and he said yes. That was the moment I felt the emotion of pride for the first time.

At a young age, I picked up a passion for playing basketball, which became my primary focus from age eight to eighteen. After high school, I continued playing in college and then semiprofessionally. That experience taught me incredible lessons about teamwork, winning and losing, perseverance and problem solving. Eventually, when I stopped playing, I was the director of coaching for an amateur basketball club. I was able to mentor girls from fourth grade through college.

In time, I started my own marketing and PR firm, helping small businesses to grow using digital marketing. I have learned that once you push yourself to take that first step, scared or not, growth will come organically. Since businesses can't do it alone, whether just starting out or an experienced professional, everyone needs good people behind them. Sometimes getting those people and keeping them is not easy. I do my best to hold onto those who are intelligent and passionate. With good people and persistence, you can build an empire.

My firm continues to do wonderfully. I volunteer with young female entrepreneurs to help them start businesses, and I have also started an organization called, "Together She Can," working with hygiene care for homeless people. This all started because I was de-cluttering my home and had a lot of perfectly good products that I wasn't using. I packaged them and gave them to homeless shelters. I decided to go on social media and ask people if they had any products they would like to give away. I was overwhelmed by the enthusiastic response I received. I gave out toiletry bags to both the shelters and people on the streets.

Today we have given out thousands of bags just in the Boston area, where I now live. We have also partnered with local companies to run educational programs to help people work toward the next stage of life. We partner with Sephora, Girl Scouts of America, Garnett Hill and Warby Parker. Our goal is to be in five major cities in the next five years. One hundred percent of the donations go directly toward our mission. togthershecan.org.

I used to be afraid that one day I would wake up and wish I hadn't dedicated so much of my life to work. Dating had always been tough for me. I'm independent, outgoing and always busy. I hated it when I was told I would meet someone if I slowed down. It was the exact opposite of what I wanted. I never focused on dating, I just let the chips fall where they may, as some would say. I always believed in love, but I was nervous that it didn't believe in me.

Just when I least expected, a few years ago, I started working with a man who became a dear friend. We had the same core values and as I shared my experiences with him, they were enhanced. Today, I finally have a teammate that I can run with. We support one another, we laugh, we love, and most importantly neither one of us would ever slow the other down.

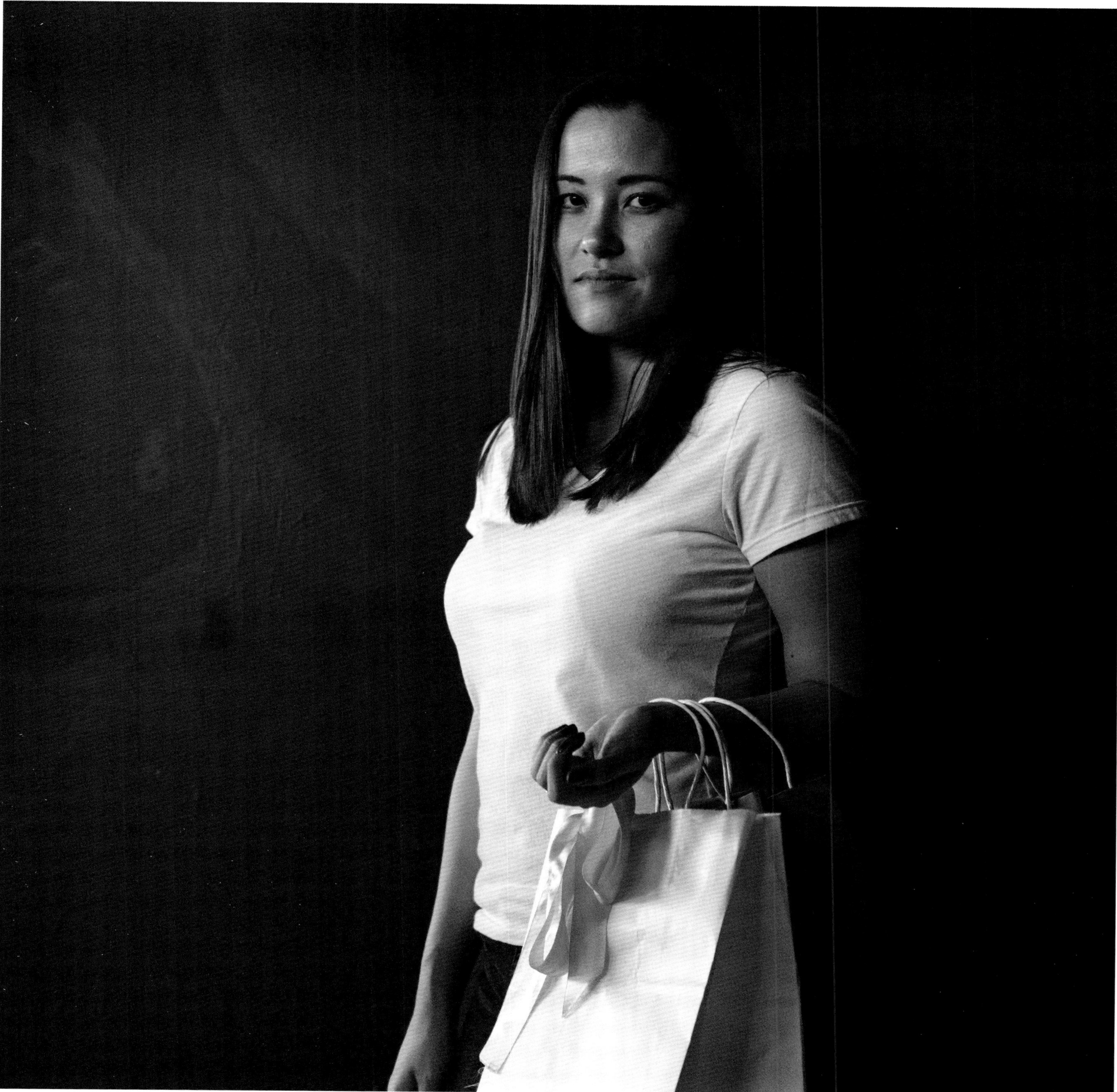

Jan Detter

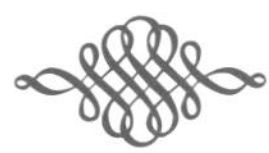

I was thirteen when I met my husband at the town fair. I remember thinking I would marry him and tried to remember everything about that moment. I was wearing a white shirt and brown-and-white shorts. I just knew.

My parents fought like cats and dogs. As the eldest child, I saw a lot of violence. My coping method was to read and when I did, all my problems became invisible and I escaped into a bigger world.

I had an immense curiosity and wanted to be an artist. I learned like a sponge and started by studying art history. I think artists see the world a certain way and through whatever medium they have chosen, they tell their vision.

I did marry the boy from the fair. We had a fantastic marriage. He was in the toy industry and a fun guy (almost as much as the toys themselves). He was the kid who never grew up, in the best sense. We wanted a baby, but I did not get pregnant for twenty years. No one could imagine the happiness we felt when I finally did!

Baby Zoe arrived and now, we were no longer a couple but a family. It was a wonderful time. When she was twelve, Dan was diagnosed with melanoma. It felt as if our lives had been ambushed. We were usually prepared for good news but never for bad. I can admit now that I had a hard time accepting the diagnosis. It's the kind of on-the-job training no one wants to have. He was skin and bones in a matter of months.

When he passed, I went into hypervigilant mode. I needed to get back to work and to move into a different house closer to town. My mind was racing around the to-do list. To stay somewhat sane, I started working on a cast I did of my body while pregnant years before. I had always hoped to make it into an interesting piece of art. I needed to keep moving but had no desire to feel anything. I made no allowance for grief. After all, I was the one who was alive. I did not want to be the pathetic widow. I started shredding tons of paperwork but had a difficult time throwing anything away. Eventually, I buried many remnants of our years together in the backyard. Someday, I would grow a garden there.

I was teaching art to children. To my surprise, I was offered an internship at a well-known and well-respected college. I was getting some serious commissions as well. I won the Teacher of the Year award. Then I had an eight-page spread in an academic magazine, showcasing not only my art, but also my philosophy regarding art itself. I was living a dream I'd never allowed myself to imagine.

The dark cloud that was about to suffocate me offered no warning of its arrival. One ordinary morning, I woke up and didn't want to go to work. In fact, I had no desire to eat, talk, or even breathe. My daughter was in college now, and I had wonderful friends and a job I could never have imagined. Yet, here I was with no desire to see another day.

I decided to go on a retreat to the ocean for a time of solitude. I was able to confront myself there and realized I had buried all the grief, just as I had Dan's possessions. I felt as though a big black ball was rolling off my back. I realized the person I had shared most of my life with, the person I had loved the most and couldn't wait to tell everything to, was gone. I not only missed him. I missed us.

Since that time, I've started reaching out and telling friends what I'm going through. It was time to bury the brave front, be honest, and confront my depression. I have joined a group of widows who share many of the same feelings. It's a long process toward feeling whole again, but I have taken the first steps.

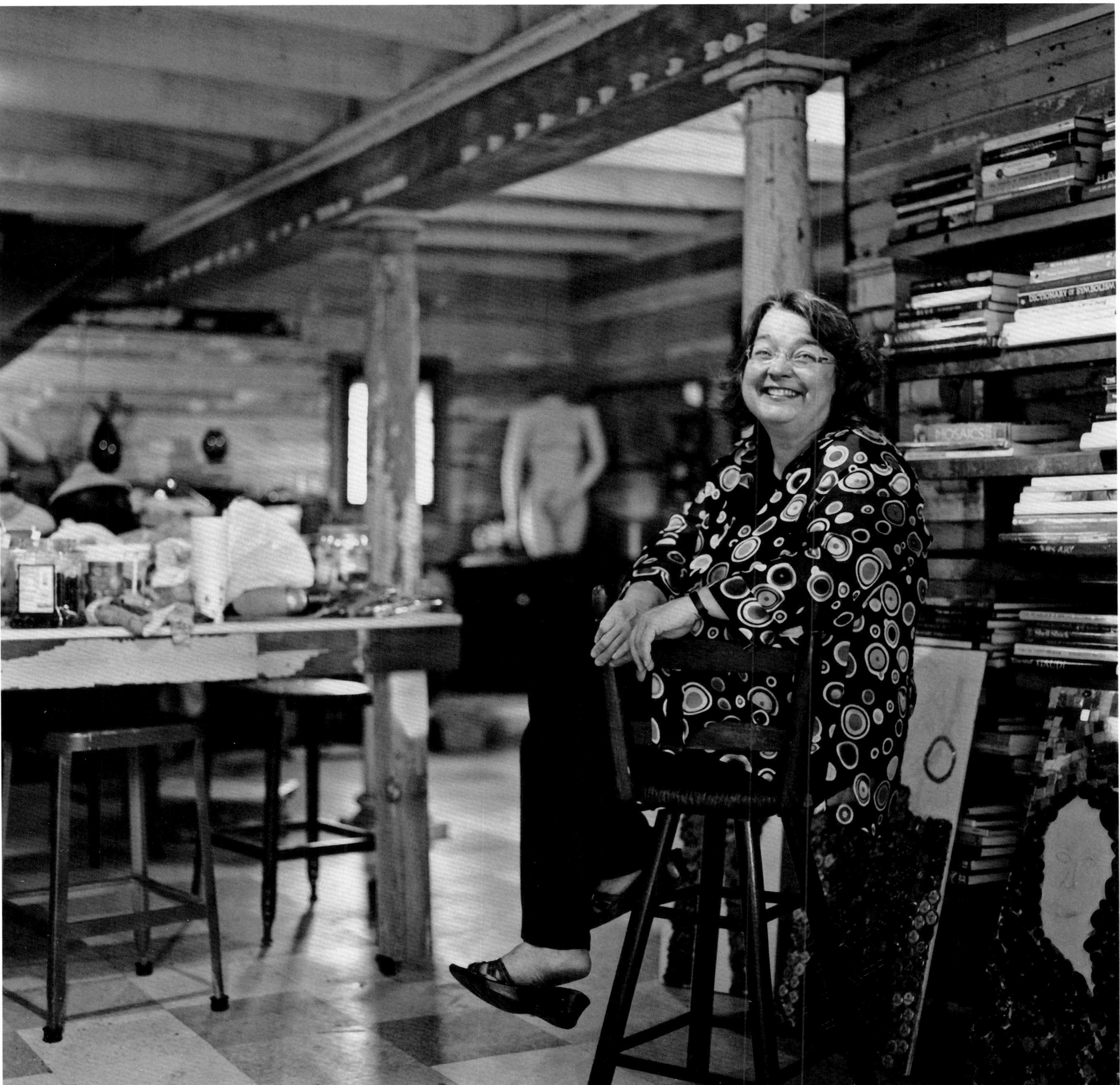
DICTIONARY OF SYMBOLISM
MOSAICS

Mary Ann Jones

I started college right after high school but was bored. I ended up in an uninteresting job, which led to a reckless social life. This, of course, led right into pregnancy. My devout Catholic family was horrified. My parents sent me to a home for unwed mothers, where I witnessed the emphasis on signing babies over for adoption. My true education started there. So, as a young woman in the 1950s, I gave birth to my first son and married his father—a man I hardly knew.

I had three more sons while holding down several part-time jobs. I had the companionship of old friends who shared a ski house. The men skied, but the women didn't have that luxury. Instead, we held a garage sale to earn enough money for ski lessons for the children and for ourselves. We stayed near the bottom of the slopes while the men tackled the mountains.

Eventually, many of our friends bought summer cottages, and the women were often on their own. Only my man objected to my leaving the nest. I felt increasingly trapped in a life not suited to the new-age '60s. He loved saying that I was a giver and he was a taker and we were the perfect match.

I started back on the path I had given up years before, my education. I signed up for evening courses at a state college. Religious expression and thought intrigued me. My academic interests illuminated the chasm that had developed in my marriage. He resented my wanting to learn and was negative in every way possible. After a summer of maze-like discussions with no end in sight, we separated.

He filed for divorce and didn't show up on the appointed day. I filed and did. The judge announced he couldn't possibly award me the family home because I might marry again. I responded by promising the court I would never marry again, causing laughter from everyone, except the judge. My husband's lawyer asked how my children were conceived. I wasn't sure if he wanted to bring out my eldest child's out-of-wedlock birth or cast doubt on paternity. My answer was sharp, "The usual way." More laughter.

Our friends were conflicted in their loyalties and once again, my mother was ashamed of me. Many women I considered close friends turned their backs as well. I not only ended my marriage but also lost my lifestyle. At the same time, I was meeting new women friends as I pursued an undergraduate degree in Western religion and psychology. My divorce became final the same month I graduated cum laude. Margaret Mead handed me my diploma. It was the year I turned forty.

I worked at Rosie's Place, a shelter for homeless women in Boston. This choice was probably prompted by the lingering fear that I would be homeless one day. Eventually, I took a job developing programs for urban non-profits. It was around this time that my boys began acting out on a regular basis. There were weekly calls from the vice principal, therapy, a change of schools, and an absent, but undermining father which just about crushed me.

Harvard Divinity School took me away from my own problems and allowed me to learn from women scholars all over the world. Maybe because I have no sister, nor a daughter, or much of a relationship with my mother, seeking and finding female wisdom has been a recurring theme in my life. Yet, female housemates are no easier than men. Those intense female friendships can be as difficult as marriage. As far as religious beliefs go, I believe that everyone needs to find his and her own answers to what God means to them, and that blind faith often replaces intellect.

As time moved on, I was invited on a trip to the island of Jamaica. It exposed me to art, literature, customs and rituals of healing, I would never have believed. I started doing writing workshops, which I have done for years now. My three brothers and sons provide me with enough male energy and I cherish them all.

I did keep my promise to the judge and did not re-marry. I am still writing and teaching and recently have been given one of my greatest gifts, a granddaughter.

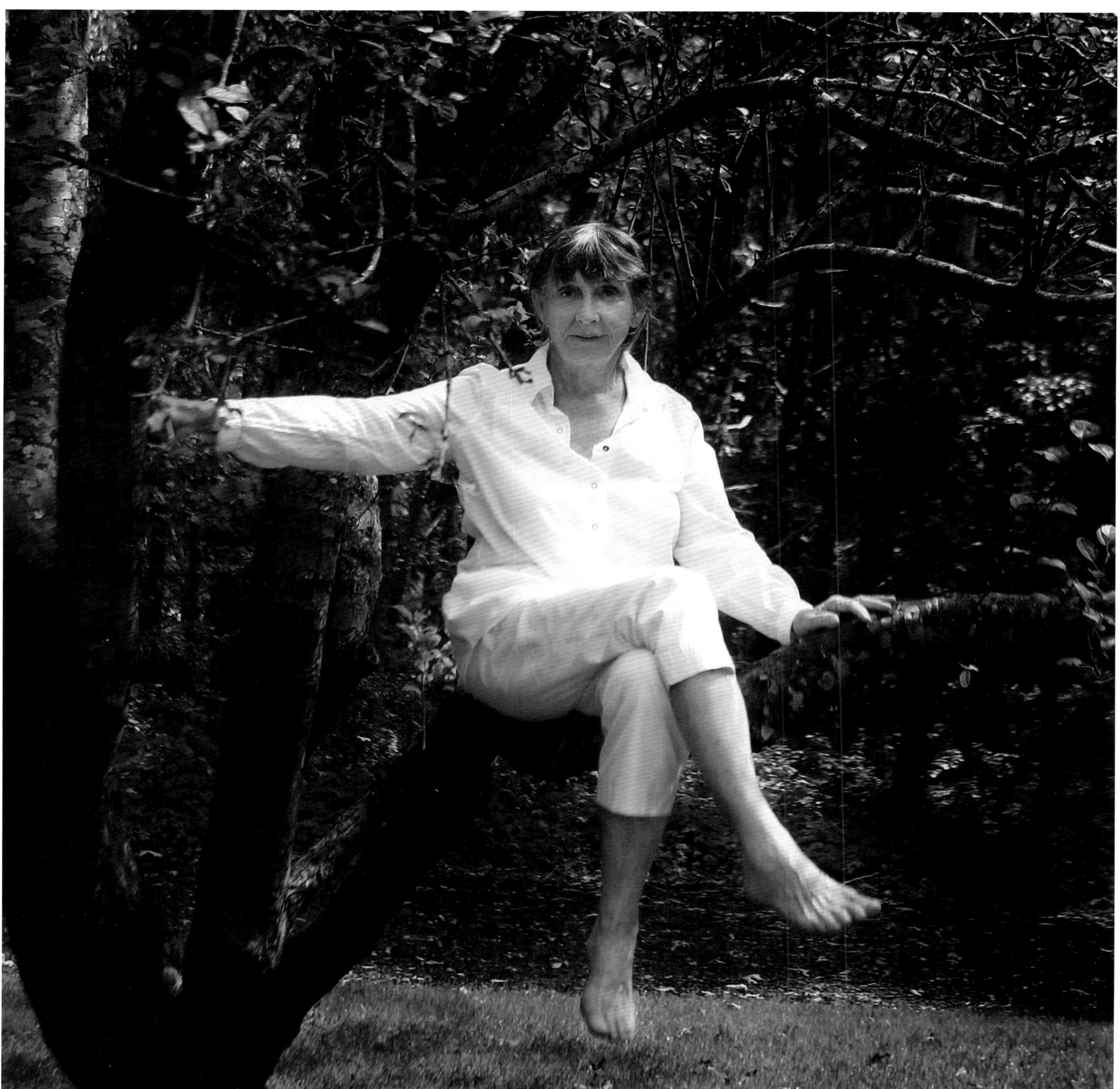

Brenda Kulp

I grew up on a hundred-acre farm. My mother had a sixth-grade education and my father was a fourth-generation farmer. In those hundred acres, my world was small. I did the typical things you do on a farm: got up at five in the morning to start household chores, helped grow the food we ate, sewed my own clothes, and quilted. I was taught early on that there was no free ride. My parents instilled in me a determined work ethic that has propelled me throughout my life.

I was tenacious about my goals and saved enough money to put myself through nursing school. After years of hard work, I became the Director of Nursing in our community Health Department. While working on my graduate degree, I met my husband. He was a doctor and without a doubt became the most influential person in my life, in both positive and negative ways. Initially, I believed I did not want to have children. I think I had some religious-based fears about bringing a child into a chaotic world, but eventually he convinced me to have a baby. Before long, I gave birth to my daughter.

After a few years of being in a happy marriage, I realized my husband had changed. He went from kind and loving to verbally abusive. It took me awhile to find out he was using drugs. More than once, he claimed he was going to bring me down. While I made a plan to leave the relationship, I used every psychological skill I had to keep the peace. I wanted to get safely away without any drama. I was in counseling with a brilliant therapist, when I made the decision to wait until my daughter was five and could understand why I was leaving her father.

My father always spoke about the "light at the end of the tunnel." I believe what he meant was the light represented the comfort that would come once hard times were resolved and as a metaphorical guide through the darkness, like a lighthouse. Throughout my life, I have used that image to calm me and keep me grounded. My husband did get into treatment, and I hoped and prayed he would be back to normal after rehabilitation, but sadly that didn't happen.

I worked a long time before I got married, so going back to what I loved was easy after the divorce. I have been a registered nurse for forty-three years. I've got a master's degree and serve on advisory boards. I also became the sole custody parent to my daughter. We weathered some difficult times with her father, but I made sure we had wonderful times, too. She is without a doubt, my best friend. My daughter's father passed away last year. I am happy they were able to have a relationship together despite his illness.

I am a busy person between my career and daughter. It would be a tall order for a new man to fit into my life. My mother loved gardening and before we sold the farm, my father and I dug up her iris bulbs that she had so lovingly planted many years ago. Over three hundred flowers are now in my backyard. A beautiful field of pastel greets me every spring and is a testament to how much I love my family and all they have taught me.

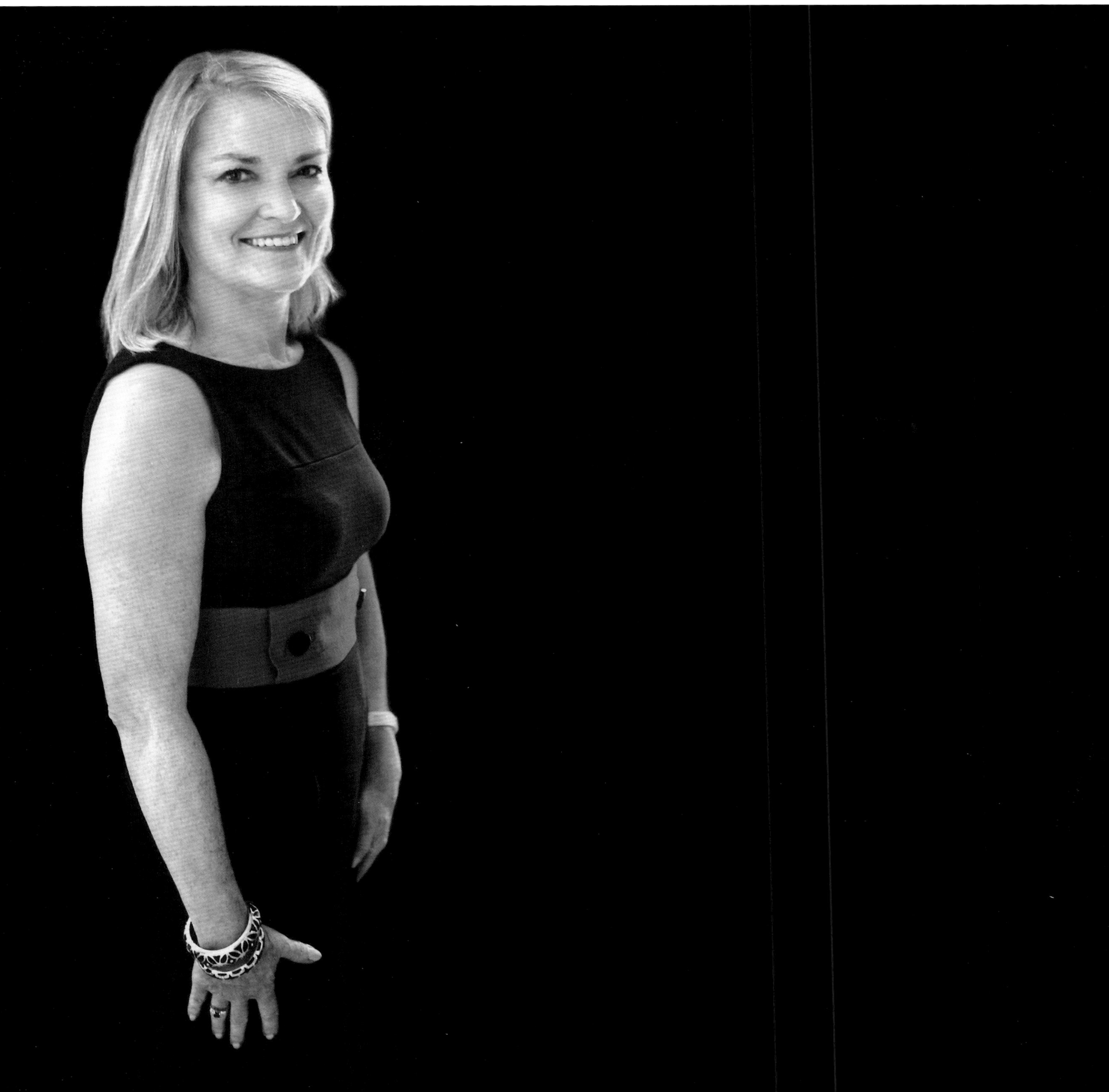

Xinxin Xiao

I relate to the American novel *Jane Eyre*. Like Jane, I had a miserable childhood in China. My father was never home because of constant business travel, and my mother was unhappy. Girls did not hold the same value as boys. If my brother said I did something wrong, he was believed and I got punished. I put up with constant verbal abuse from a woman who received the most joy from complaining.

I was consistently at the top of my class. I wanted to go to college but was not allowed to because a girl's real mission was to find a husband and have a family—hopefully sons. If I went to technical school, I would be guaranteed a job until I found that husband. It was a boarding school with no hot water, electricity, or heat. I shared a bathroom with 128 other girls. There were no doors or privacy anywhere.

I stayed for three years and earned the right to become a teacher. When I returned home, I begged to take a test similar to the SAT but had no English, math, or chemistry and needed to pass tests in all three. I borrowed books and studied from early morning until late at night. My mother was not happy about it, but she didn't stop me this time. I passed the test and began studying to become an architect. I had my degree in three years.

At thirteen, I had seen a city I wanted to live in—an old, historical city that fascinated me. I took all my belongings and savings and started interviewing. Finding a real job was not as easy as I had hoped. During this process I was making lots of foreign friends, and one of them asked me to be a tour guide for his company. He liked me, and the fact that I spoke English helped a lot. I went back and forth to different places, especially Beijing. On one of my in-between days, I met a handsome man who started calling me every day. He was romantic and kind. He lived in the United States but was back and forth every few months. After a year, he proposed and I accepted. We got married and moved to South Carolina.

After the honeymoon, he stopped being kind to me. I could not imagine what I had done wrong. He kept saying he didn't feel well or was tired or was not in the mood. I wanted to have a family and did everything I could think of to make myself attractive. The truth was that he was addicted to video games and wanted his laptop on his lap instead of me. After four years, I moved out.

I will not go back to China. I love this country—the heating in winter, the air conditioning in summer, the ability to see or not see whomever you choose, the freedom to conform or not to conform—it's all amazing. I am now working for Welcome Neighbors. I go from door-to-door welcoming new people. I have made many friends. I get to help people adjust to their life situations a world away from where I was born. I hike and dance and have no trouble walking through a new door to see where it might lead. Some doors you walk through and learn to head in a different direction next time.

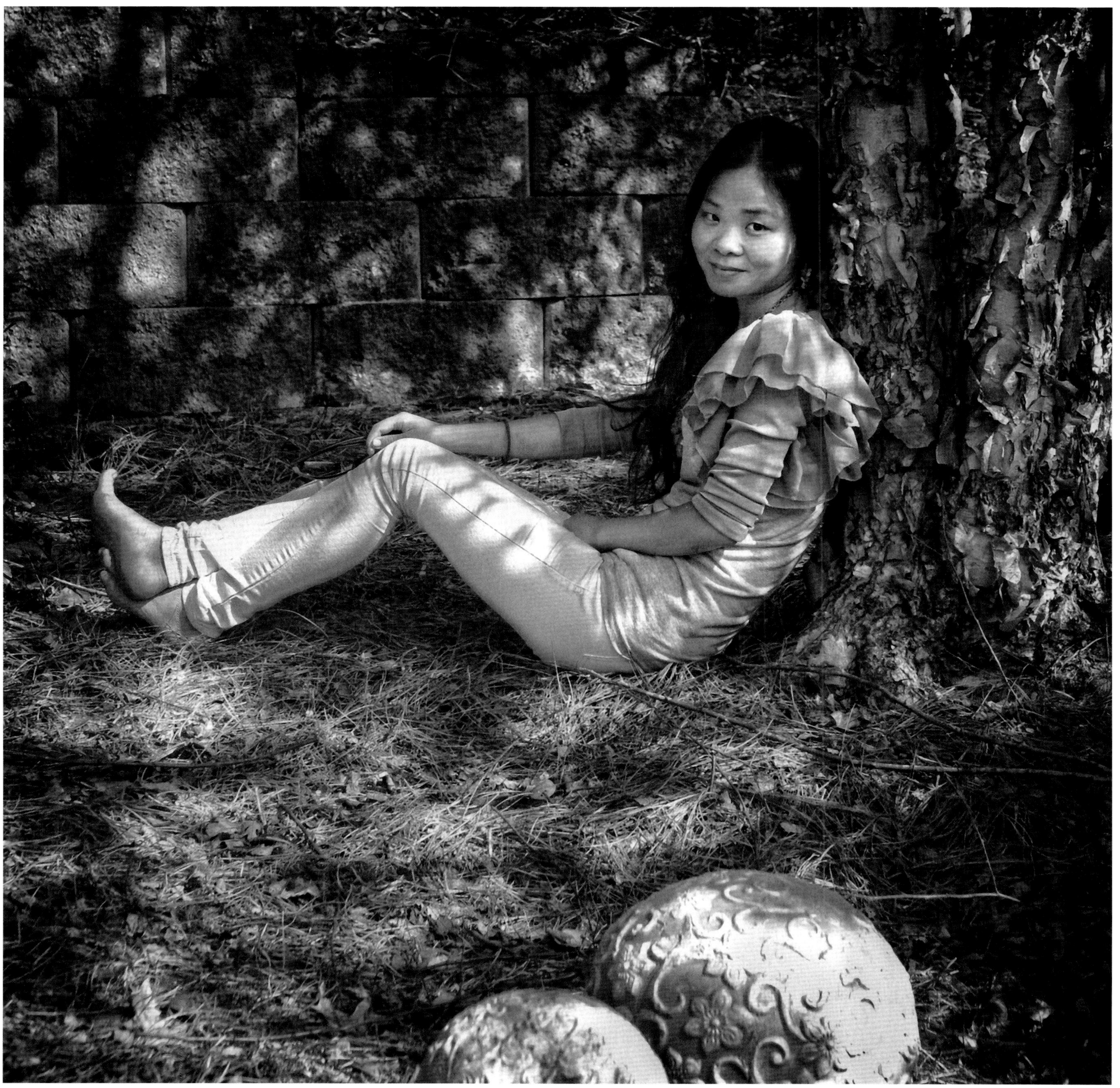

Jane Kelly

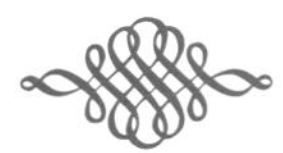

I came from a divorced family, which is not unusual today, but it was back then. There were no self-help books and fewer marriage counselors. I have often wondered how my parents and extended family knew how to make sure my brother and I didn't come out of it with the emotional baggage often associated with broken homes. I never heard my parents speak a bad word about each other. Both sets of grandparents said every good thing they possibly could about their former in-law.

I had a lovely marriage. We had two children and did not have more for several years. It wasn't planned that way, it just happened. My husband was the editor of the local city newspaper, we had an active social life, and we were both involved in politics and cultural activities.

Just when my years as a young mother were dwindling, I had two more children, one right after the other. Lives for women were changing, and I decided to go back to work. For many years, I was in the publishing business both on the editorial side and in design. When you are working and not aware of time passing, you are no doubt doing the right thing. At least that was what I thought. I felt that way for years.

As time went by my husband became ill, and I had time to prepare myself for living alone. The blessings of having older children were apparent to me from the beginning because they were not only able to help me survive emotionally but also helped raise their younger siblings.

I have dated very little in the years since my husband passed. I often thought that some friend would invite me to dinner and sit me next to the perfect man. That never happened. I did go on some blind dates, and by the end of the evening I often wished I was blind.

I am a serious reader and some of the greatest characters I've met have been in books. I look back on my life with astonishment because I never felt I was changing. I don't remember having any major epiphanies. My life lessons were learned subconsciously, without my being aware that I was learning at all.

Today, I have many women friends, but more importantly, I have closer relationships with all of my children. I don't take being invited for vacations or spending the summer with my grandchildren for granted. If you were to ask me what I did to have that dynamic, I would guess that minding my own business is at the top of the list. I only give advice if I am asked, and even then, I am careful not to overstep my boundaries.

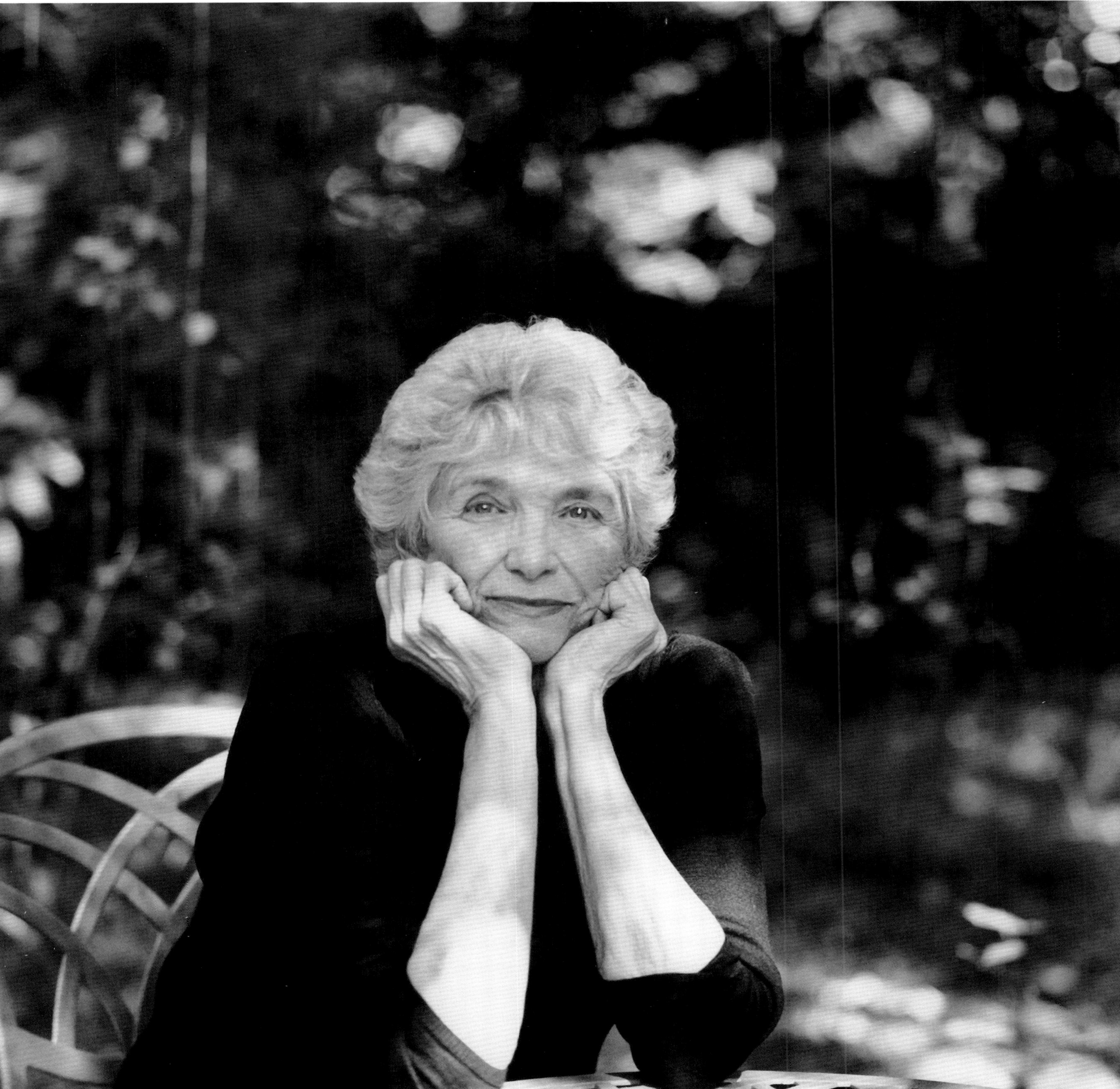

Helen Naples

My childhood was filled with transition and chaos. We were always starting over because of my father's job. I had no sense of stability or security. I guess I would say that I had a free-floating anxiety about what would happen next. On a positive side, I learned how to survive in an atmosphere of change. I would have gotten an "A" on how to be the new girl.

After being married for twenty years, my husband, whom I adored, left me. If I were writing a song about it, it would have to be a bad country song. It was like my husband left me for a skinny waitress and a bottle of beer. He fell for someone half his age.

Denial was a lifesaving skill that I had developed early in my life. I clung to my marriage as if I were a drowning woman with a single piece of driftwood. I knew something was terribly wrong but thought that if I lost weight or cooked better meals, everything would be fine. But the more I tried, the worse it got. In desperation, I hired a private detective, thinking he would tell me that I was just being paranoid.

I have a hard time believing that a divorce can be a happy one. If there is no love, there is no pain. I wanted to go off a cliff, but I had children to care for. I was able to fall back on the hard lessons of childhood. I did not say a word to my husband. I became an Academy Award-winning actress for weeks, while I gathered evidence and figured out what to do legally, financially, and as best as I could, emotionally. A year before, I would have laid my life on the line over the belief that I would never face infidelity. I learned that you don't know what you'll do in a situation until you face it. I also learned never to project myself onto anyone else in terms of life lessons.

I was not a perfect person. Somehow, early in life, I got the message that I needed to be. It played out in my life with my controlling what I ate. I did not understand that my obsession was controlling me. I had been on a diet for years. While thinking I was in control on the outside, I lost myself on the inside. I loved being pregnant because it actually saved me from starvation.

I went to a Christian church for the sake of my daughters. I wanted them to have some spiritual grounding. I sat there, week after week, bored to tears, but feeling good about being a good mom. Over time, I began listening with one ear. Eventually, without even knowing it, I started to change. I felt loved, valued, and forgiven. I also found out that the only control I have is to accept a lack of control. It was never in my hands anyway. Talk about freeing!

Today, I practice self-care rather than self-flagellation. I started exercise as a form of self-punishment and a way to get even with myself for having faults. I was reckless and self-destructive. In hindsight, I was a self-inflicted victim. I wanted to feel good in the moment and was unable to project how that was affecting my future.

A few years ago, I opened a gym exclusively for women. We offer everything from Zumba to yoga, and I teach several classes a week. I get to be a cheerleader every day, and I often feel like Peter Pan when he sings, "I'm flying."

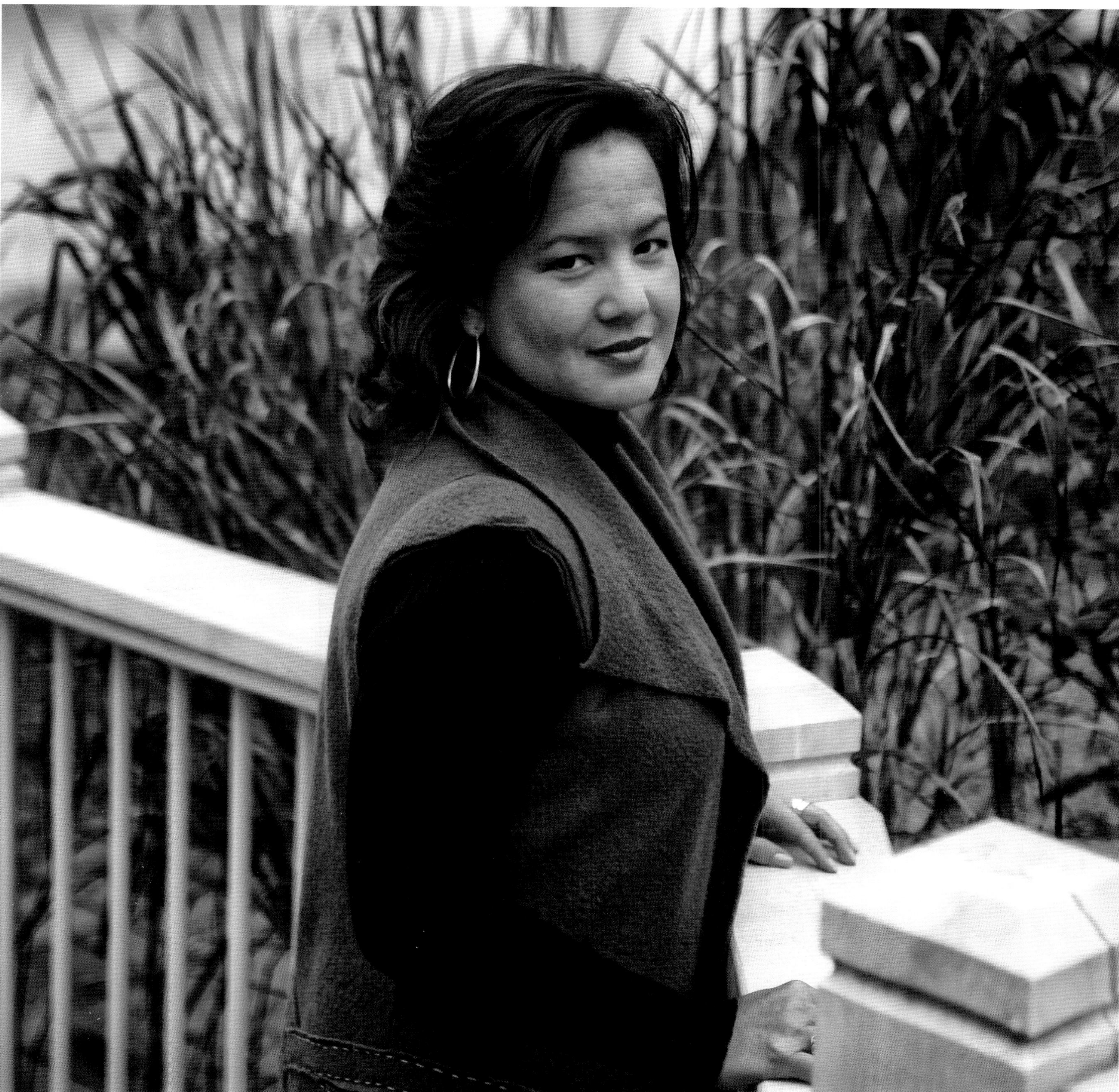

Paula Solano

I grew up in Costa Rica in a family in which fighting and jealousy were part of life. That dynamic was invited to dinner far too often. I believe parents have a responsibility to protect children from the harsh realities of life at least at an early age. They say the first seven years of life form your blueprint, when your values and self-esteem are either created or not created. As a small child, I saw and heard far too much for my age. They probably thought I didn't understand, but I did, and their problems became my insecurity.

I knew I was different from the other children in kindergarten. I didn't have crushes on the little boys like most of my friends did. I loved the woman who was my teacher. I couldn't wait to get to school every day—not just to learn but to see her. She was kind, and I adored her. Time went on and I dated boys like all my friends did, but I was never emotionally or physically involved in any way. I fell in love when I was nineteen, and it was with a girl. Her name was Katya and today we are no longer a couple, but she is my family and best friend.

Eventually I entered medical school because I really wanted to help people, but I wasn't good enough at chemistry, so I tried dental school. I did that for two years before deciding to live in the United States. When I got here, I found out that many of the courses I had taken were useless in this country, so that ended my dental dream. I didn't have it in me to go do it all over again.

I did want to help people, but I was also quite materialistic back then. My higher self had more to do with my height than my spirituality. I am Catholic by birth, but today I love to learn about anything metaphysical. Give me a Wayne Dyer or Marianne Williamson book, and I am lost for days in contemplation.

I have my own herb shop now and give cooking classes. This is a part of my life that I never foresaw. I have a long-term love, though we probably won't get married. We don't think signing a piece of paper really means anything. There is a part of me that likes the idea of marriage, but I'm not a believer in the reality. There are all kinds of rules of society that I think are ridiculous. How do you promise you will love someone forever when you don't know what the future holds? That said, the way life is, I know it's possible that I could change my mind.

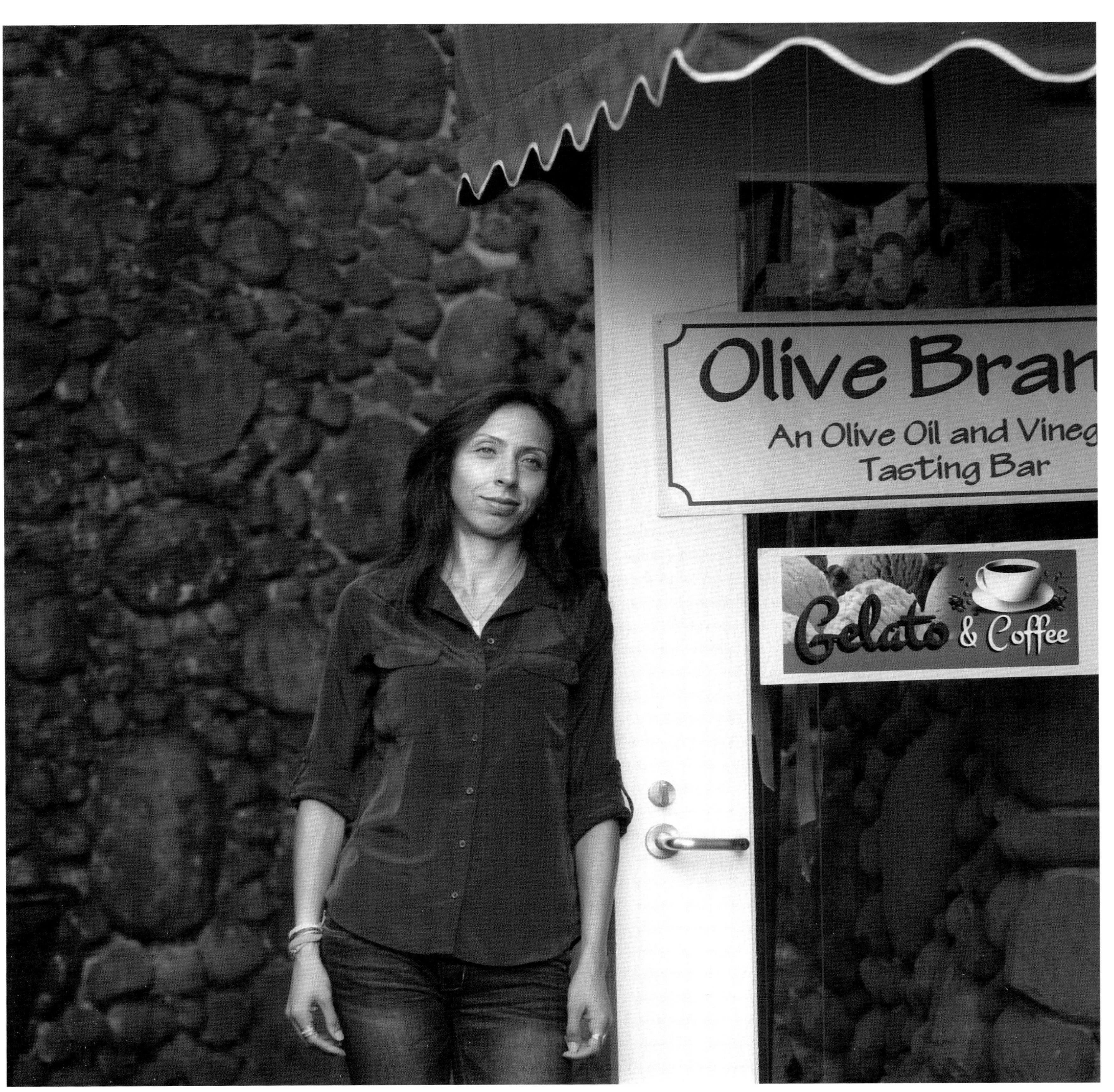
Olive Bran
An Olive Oil and Vineg
Tasting Bar
Gelato & Coffee

Susanna Gates

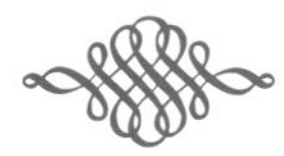

When I look back at my life, I see myself as an egomaniac with an inferiority complex.

I came from a strong, encouraging, and supportive family. In spite of that, I never felt I fit in anywhere. I got along just enough without forming bonds. The word "introvert" describes me accurately, I've often thought that I got my energy by being alone.

I fell in love with a man who had three children. He divorced, and then we married. It was a toxic relationship from the beginning. We simply brought out the worst in each other. I became pregnant with twins, and that was an exciting time. How wonderful it was that we were having a boy and a girl at the same time. All the craziness was on hold, as we waited for them to be born.

I gave birth to Katie and Stephen and found out immediately that Stephen had a heart problem. He did not go home from the hospital for several weeks, and we were told he would have surgery as soon as he was strong enough. After several months he had the surgery and did not survive. I will never understand nor appreciate what happened. I do know I have to accept it. Kate is a constant reminder of how lucky I am to not have lost her as well.

After that, our marriage fell apart. We were grieving differently and were unable to comfort one another. I wanted it to not have happened, while he wanted retribution against the doctors. The doctors gave me prescriptions for the grief. Eventually, after the divorce, I started waking up and having a drink. People would say I was strong, but the truth was I was numb.

After being diagnosed with Type I diabetes, I recognized I needed help and went into a rehabilitation facility. This led me into recovery. Honestly, I think my sponsor saved my life. My problems were inside, but help was on the outside. I recognized that the advice my mother had given me for years was true—she always said life was a journey, and I needed to do things in small steps. She also said I should not jump ahead, but accept life as it appeared. That was not my MO. I liked to get to the end quickly, so I could start over again.

Drinking was my social life, and drugs took away the pain. Like many others, the hardest thing I ever did was fight for my sobriety. I love the saying that one is too many and one thousand is not enough.

I bought a little house for Katie and me. I'm changing all the time. I had a few close friends before recovery, but nothing like the intimacy I now have in my life. I do hope I will marry again, and this time it will have sanity and balance. No more living in the extremes.

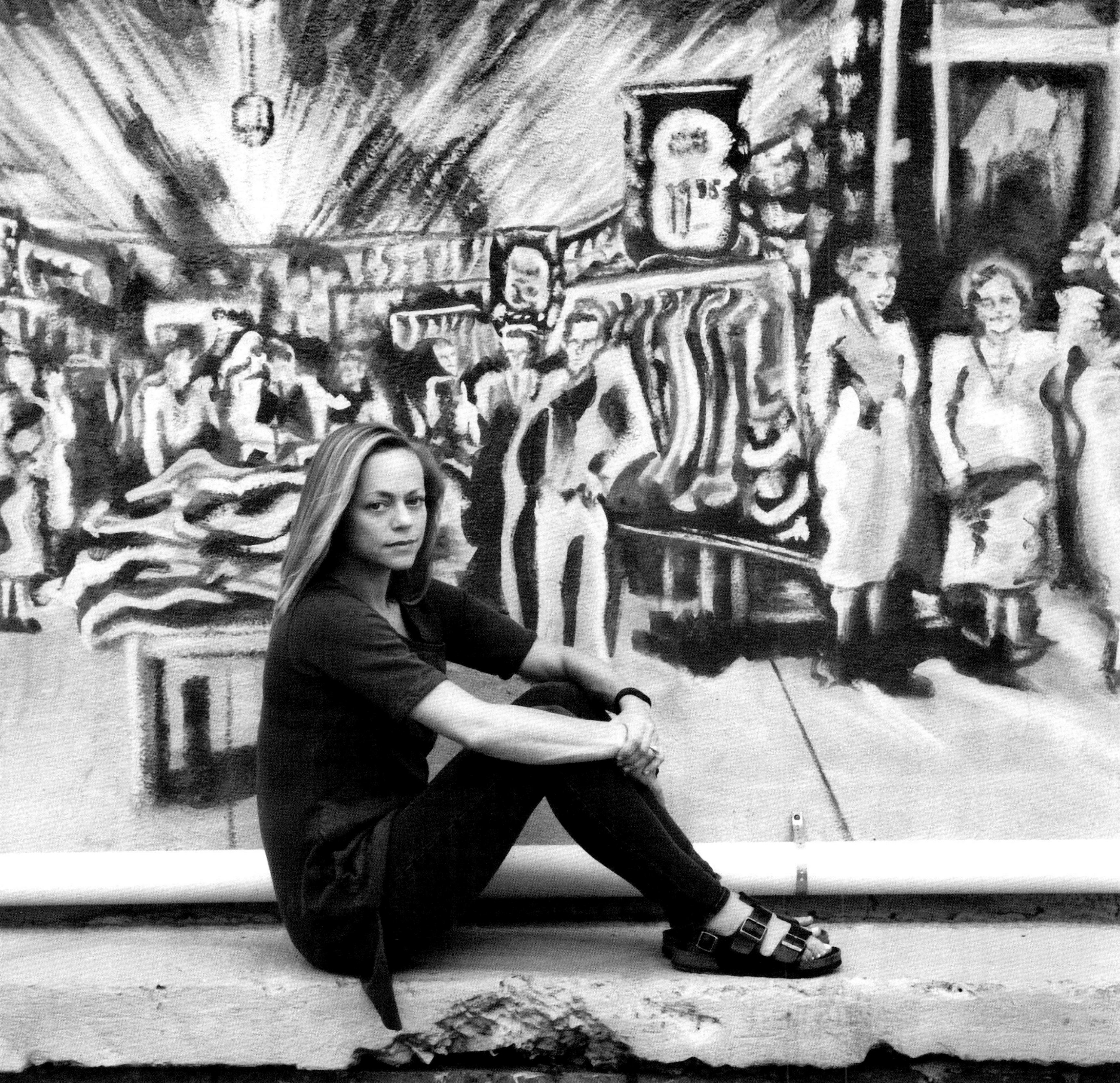

Joni Aldrich

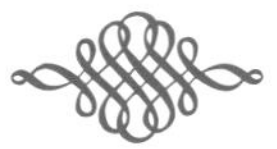

I grew up in a poor area, but my mother instilled in me the importance of good diction and grammar. There was no slang used in our house. We were the downstairs folks with the manners of gentry.

I encountered illness early in life. My father was a Marine and an amputee who fought in World War II. He had been stationed at Hiroshima and suffered many complications from that time. Back then, doctors encouraged people to smoke to settle nerves. Without encouragement, he drank and was a nasty drunk. The weekends were unbearable. We would pack up and leave rather than face the insanity. From that, I learned to take action when something was wrong.

I believe we all have a series of lives. We have our childhood life, followed by our teenage life, and then the early twenties life. I think all those times are like the foundation of a house. The lessons presented and how we respond to those lessons form the person we become.

When I was in college, I met my husband, Gordon, in a bar. He was a big, burly teddy bear of a man with a bigger personality than his smile, which was no easy feat. We both fell in love hard and fast. We did not have children, so we were able to focus exclusively on one another. He was in sales and traveled often during the week. We could not wait to see one another on the weekends. We loved our big house and eventually bought a motorhome and hit the road on weekends.

After twenty years, my husband was diagnosed with terminal brain cancer. He was determined to beat the catastrophic disease. Here he was in the prime of his life, feeling completely normal and told he was going to die. We'd had nothing but happiness for twenty years, and that made the thought of losing him even more devastating. I would often wish it were me instead, rather than watch him suffer.

For two years we were on a roller coaster. Sometimes things looked optimistic, then not. His personality changed dramatically, and so did my feelings. People under extreme stress do reckless things. My doctor put me on anti-depressants, but I couldn't tolerate the side effects. I dragged myself to the gym and got the correct chemicals going through my body.

While I was fighting for Gordon to live, the magnitude of how my life would change did not enter my mind. I didn't know how to be single. After he passed, I learned that you can't change reality. I wanted nothing more than to get away from illness. I would talk to Gordon and ask him to help me. I talked to God, but I didn't have anything nice to say to Him. The word "why" was the most common word in my conversations with God.

One summer day, I was walking along the beach thinking about all that had happened, when I realized I was writing a book. But I wasn't a writer. I remember running back to the room and frantically scribbling my thoughts down before they disappeared. This was the introduction to my first book.

That was several years ago. I have written six books, appeared on a radio show five days a week, and focused on everything imaginable about cancer. I have interviewed many people involved in miracle cases we know so little about. Cancer is still pervasive, but the survival rate is skyrocketing.

I never imagined I'd be on this path, which I believe has been divinely directed. I get up every morning, knowing that I am going to make a difference in someone's life.

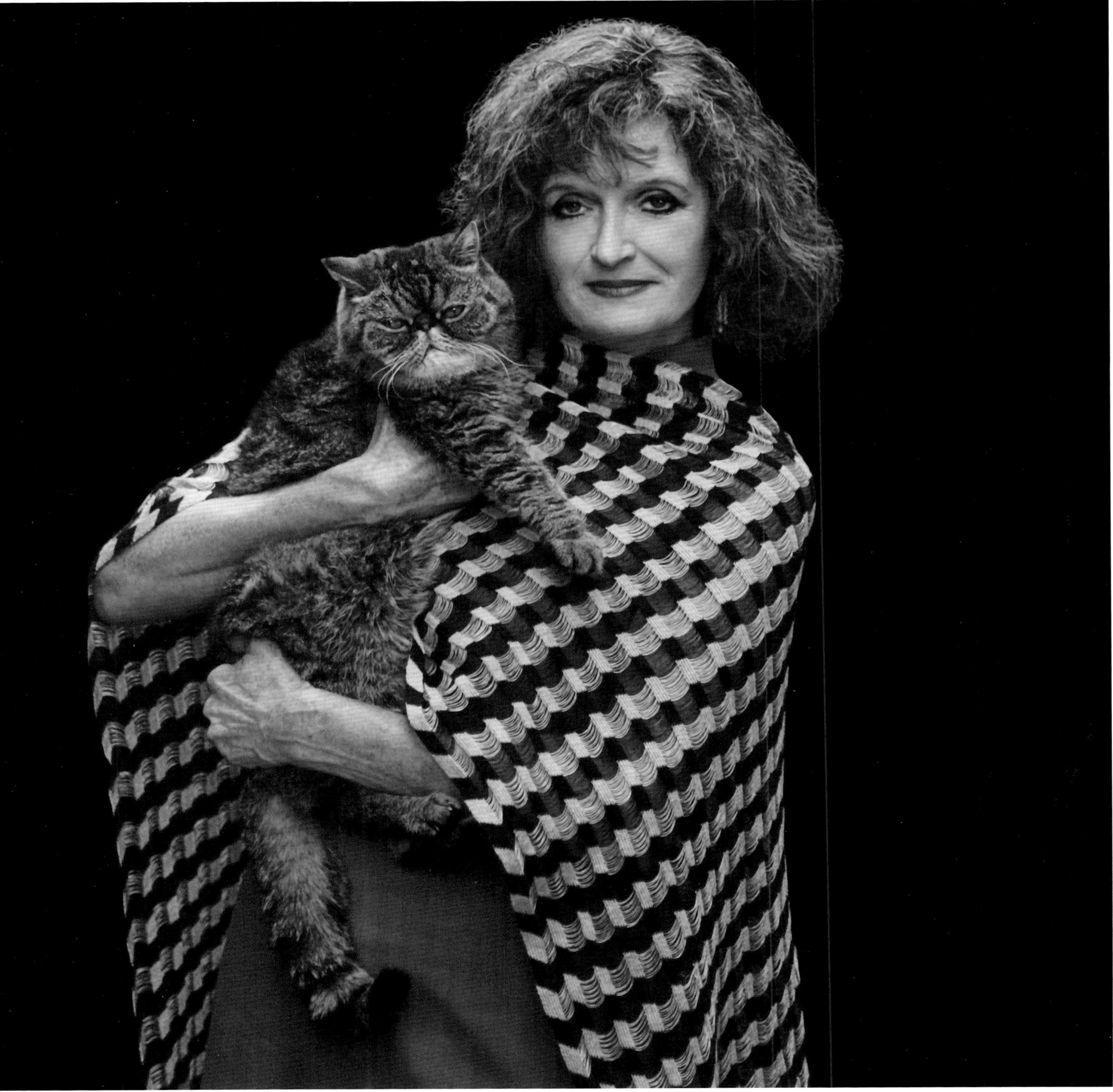

Mary Jo Dorman

My parents were midwesterners. My dad was a lawyer and my mother, a housewife. They were affluent, but I did not know that. We didn't own a house, belong to a country club or drive a fancy car. If I had to use a word to describe my life back then, I would say "wholesome." Our one indulgence was to spend a month every summer in Provincetown on Cape Cod. The seaside town was very idyllic and lively.

I went to college and got a degree in psychology. Instead of becoming a practicing psychologist, I became a flight attendant for American Airlines. It was not long before I fell in love with a man whom I married and had a son with. It seemed like a great marriage until the night we had a big disagreement, and he knocked my teeth out. Having studied psychology, I knew enough not to be around for any further disagreements.

My next love was a long-distance relationship that appeared to be wonderful. He was the kind of man who volunteered to help the blind swim and ski. I thought it made him a good person. Again, I should have known better. Very often people cover up who they are with a false front. It took me ten years to see his dark side, but when I saw it, it was over.

As a young mother, I worked part-time as a manager in an aerobics studio that allowed me to still be able to care for my young son. I'd had that job for years, and eventually I was given the opportunity to manage an entire resort. I ran the resort successfully for ten years and loved every day. There was a lot of action and being busy was great for me.

Happily, I returned to the Provincetown of my youth. A friend had asked me to house sit, and I was more than glad to help. I did that for a while, till another friend asked me to help him out by driving his cab a few days a week. I was just going to cover a shift or two, but I ended up meeting the most interesting people, and found myself doing it full-time. I get all kinds: drunks, drag queens, executives, families and foreigners. I have so many great stories about my crazy rides, I feel like I could write a book! People tend to confide in me about their problems when I drive, and I sort of get to use my psychology degree after all.

When I am not driving the cab, I completely enjoy my own company. I have thrown myself birthday parties with candles, wine and even sent myself flowers. I even go to restaurants in fine clothes and eat alone. There is a world of difference between solitude and loneliness. I meet new people wherever I go and don't feel the need to have a partner to complete the picture of myself.

Now my son, his wife and my grandson live in California. My son says his wife "rules the roost" and I concur saying "as it should be!" I try to visit them as much as possible. I swim in the ocean every day and often I ride my bike. My goal is to be like my mother, who never stopped growing and keeping her mind open to new ideas. It was not surprising to see her at ninety-two standing on her head in a yoga class. Yes, I want to be just like that.

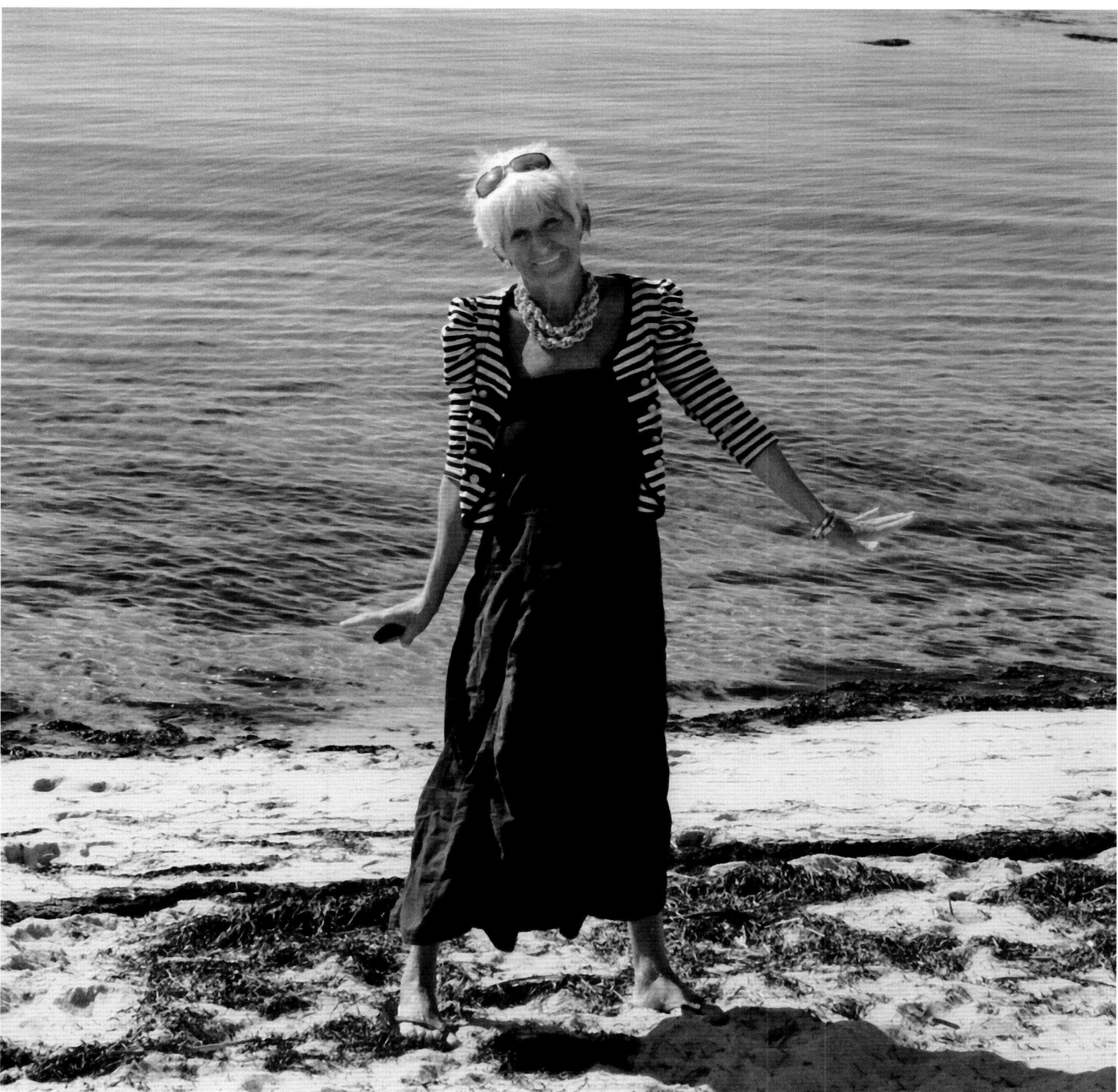

Michelle Eller

Life is not what I imagined. I had no idea I would have two children with different fathers. I grew up hearing I should not associate with certain kinds of people. Now, I am afraid they were talking about me.

I married my high school sweetheart. As I went to work, he played around—and I don't mean with the guitar. He was not a respectful man, and I felt used. Eventually our marriage fell apart. My second husband was all passion—adventurous and fun. I was not looking for the "bad boy," but that is what I got. In time, he became abusive and my self-esteem fell apart. We divorced. My third husband was on the rebound. He was adorable, but I had a hysterectomy at thirty-four and my hormones were all over the place. I was exhausted and he wanted his own biological child, which I could not give him. I did not feel like a woman, much less a decent human being. If I could have divorced myself, I would have.

Counseling helped me through this time in my life. I have been working on creating my own values and not listening to the critical voice in my head about my early choices. As I learn to accept the decisions I have made, I am also learning not to judge anyone else. My mistakes have given me a newfound compassion.

I am an aesthetician and care for skin in every way. I love my job. I touch people one at a time, and I know that what I do makes them feel wonderful. I especially love to treat young people with acne or rosacea and watch them go from sadness to glowing human beings.

I am now buying my own house. It's old and it creaks and the outside doesn't match the inside. There are fruit trees and hidden gardens waiting to be resurrected. I hope I die in this house, tending the gardens and taking care of my children and grandchildren. If I meet a new man who is a good person and who loves me, and I love him, I would consider marrying again. If that doesn't happen, I will get a cat.

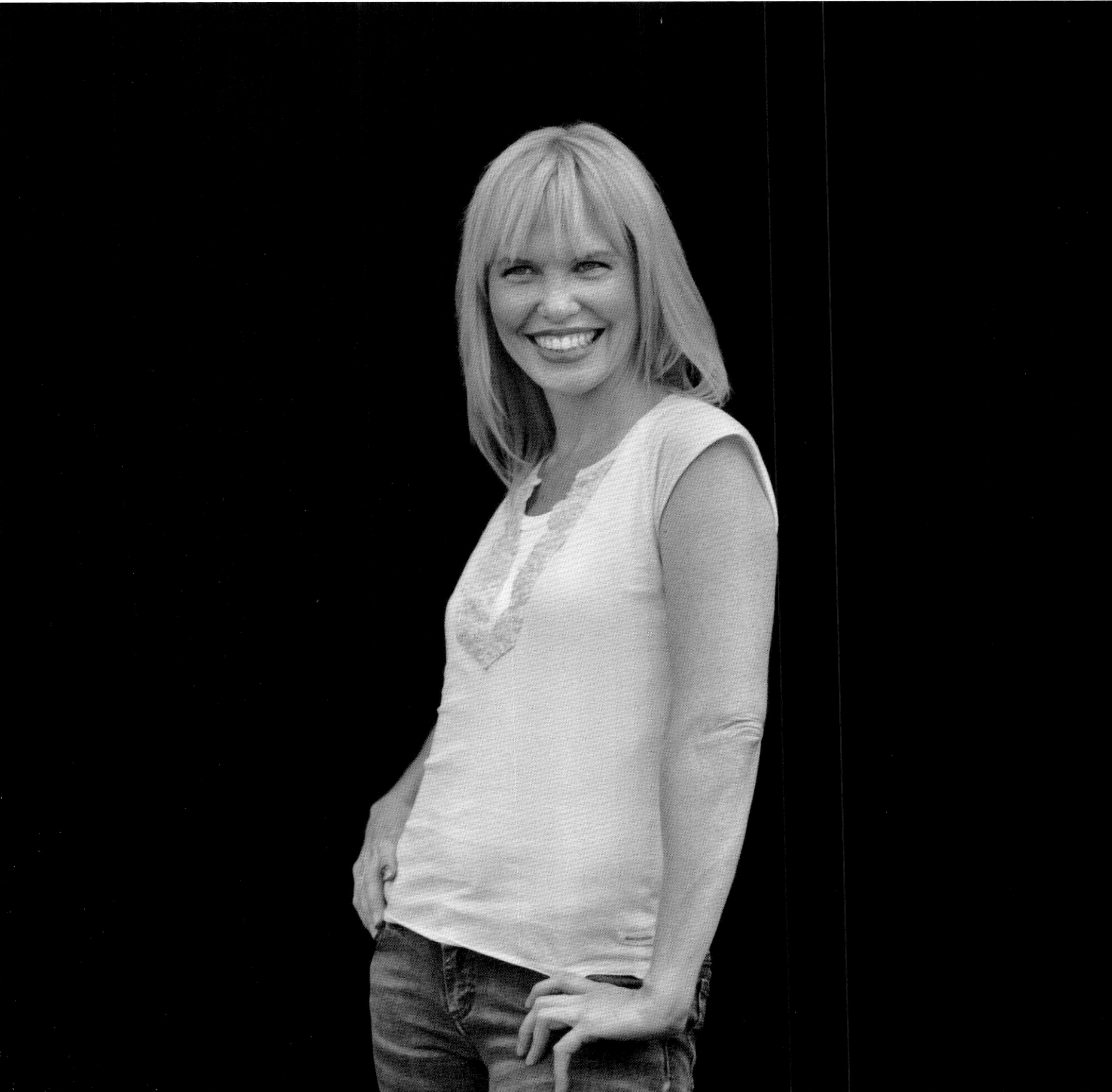

Michaele Cascone

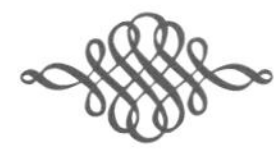

My grandmother was educated by nuns. They saw something special in her and encouraged her to become a teacher. When my great-grandfather died, she had to stop school, as it became her responsibility to support her mother and siblings. It broke her heart to leave school and she said it was the biggest regret of her life. She was my heroine. The story had a lasting effect on me and I wrote about it in an essay titled, "What Being A Teacher Means To Me." The essay won a scholarship to Hunter College in New York.

My first marriage was to my childhood sweetheart. I was pregnant before we were even married. While he was in the service in Vietnam, I was alone and lonely for a long time. I was envious of my friends who had their husbands with them. When I gave birth to my second child, he was not present at the hospital once again. I wanted the flowers, cards and adoring looks I saw the other women sharing with their spouses. I longed for him to come home, so we could live a normal life. Without asking me, he re-enlisted and I was devastated. I concluded that he could not possibly love me. While married to my first husband, I met another man whom I eventually married. My parents said my first marriage was a mistake. They pressured me to divorce and marry the new man, as they thought he would be a good father and husband. I was just twenty years old and had my doubts but agreed.

The second marriage started off well, and I became pregnant with my third child. It was not too long before he revealed his darker side. Once my daughter was born, the marriage had already reached a breaking point. I was ashamed, embarrassed and felt that there must have been something wrong with me. I felt guilty about the impact the divorce would have on all of my children. Hell, I still do. I tend to see good in people and ignore the bad. I wished I had listened to those internal warning bells and paid attention to the signs. It took me eight years to be able to afford a divorce, but at least it kept me from making another mistake.

Once you have been married and have children, there is no way to go back to being single. Despite a divorce, you remain "married" to your children. However, you may experience some freedom between your children's crises! A parent is on-all 24/7 with no breaks, holidays or days off. You then experience the whole bag of "goodies" and next up is grandparenthood. Single? Forgetaboutit.

Today, I am a science teacher at a public school. I love getting up every day knowing something I might say or do could change a life for the better. I am passionate about my students and get such joy when I see their eyes light up when they are learning something new.

Being a single mother was some of the best years of my life. I wish I had paid more attention and not been scattered in a hundred directions. I am proud of the fact I was the sole provider financially, physically, emotionally and socially to my kids. Amazingly, all three came out just fine. I am blessed with wonderful children and lovely grandchildren. Clearly, I did not mess up too much.

As far as meeting a new man, sure that sounds good—but there is a drastic shortage of saints in suits of armor riding white horses. I don't think anyone would stand a chance with me. I am not anybody's dream girl. The longer you are by yourself, the more you realize you can be lonelier with someone than without someone.

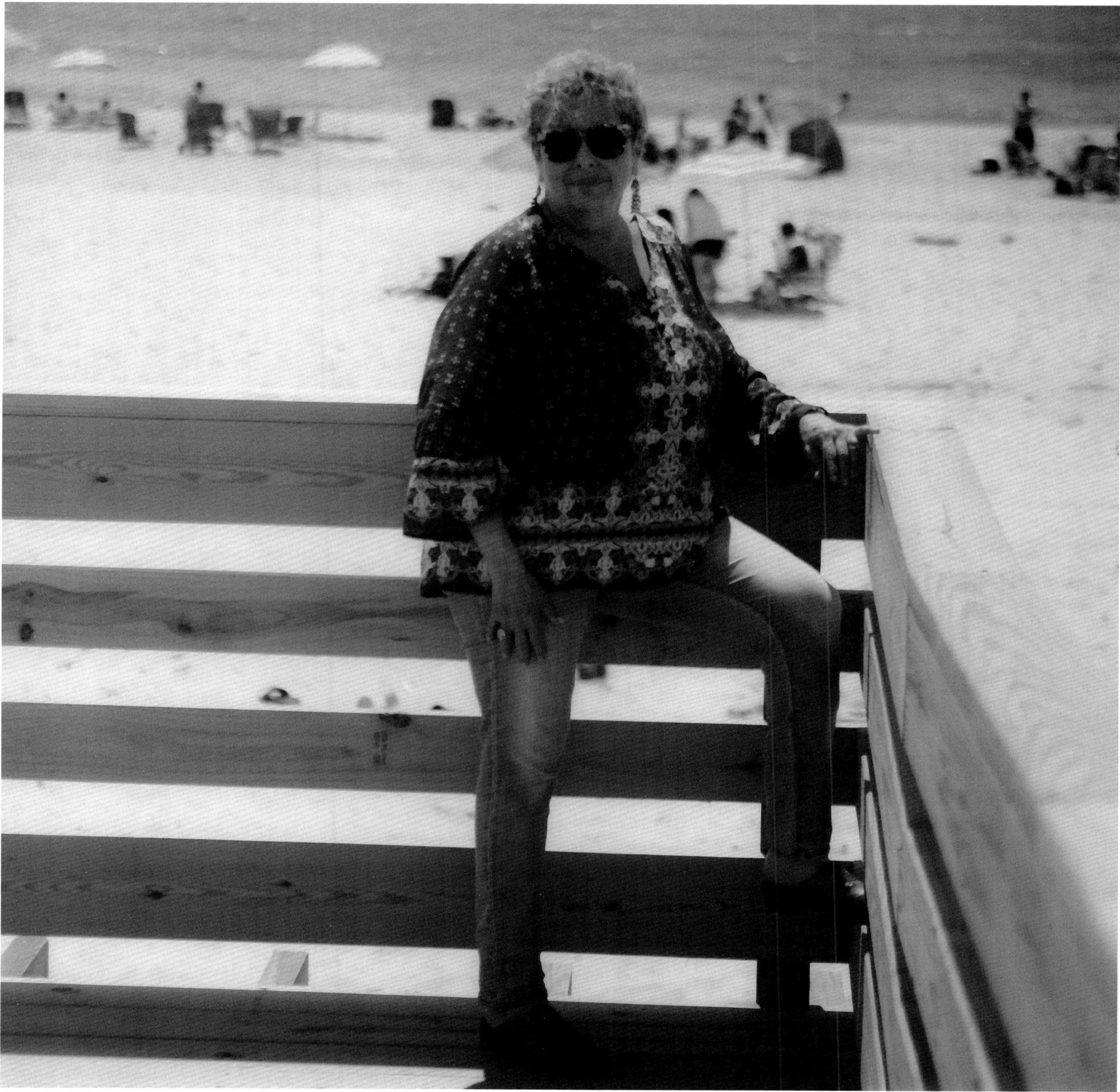

Kendall Ferguson

My father died when I was seven from melanoma on his back, in an area where no one could see. I come from a long line of solo women. My mother had three daughters and my grandmothers were both widows who raised their families alone. I had a front row view of the juggling that takes place to do that successfully.

I had a husband who I was totally compatible with, and we were madly in love! We even shared a birthday. At thirty-two years old, he had a massive heart attack due to an unknown defect. I remember every moment of that night, as if I were frozen in time. Within a five-minute time frame, my world fell apart. I had two kids, a three-year-old and a three-month-old. I was even interrogated by the police because they, too, did not know what happened. For two years, I would say I was in shock. I sold my house and moved back to my old neighborhood. I needed to be surrounded by friends and family.

My husband grew up in a faith-based home. After his death, his sister got me involved with a group of women who studied the Bible. They also have an active ministry of helping those in need. I don't belong to any particular religion. I look at "Jesus" as a moral way of life. For me it's a way of being that teaches us how to treat others. For several years now I have taught Bible to young children starting at two years old.

I have maintained part-time jobs while remaining a full-time mom. I bartended and waitressed a few nights a week. I have also worked weddings and events at "Grayland," a beautiful fairy-tale castle my grandfather helped design and build. During this time, while raising my own kids, I have been a "nanny" to three children who are now teenagers. At last, for the first time, I have a full-time job as an insurance claims investigator.

It won't be long till I will be an empty nester. I will then have the opportunity to make new and different choices for myself. My dream is to be on the show, *Survivor*. I have been working on that challenge for a long time. I've just completed an audition video that I will be submitting to the production company to get on the show. I know you would not believe it by looking at me, but there is nothing more I love than running in mud and swinging from trees.

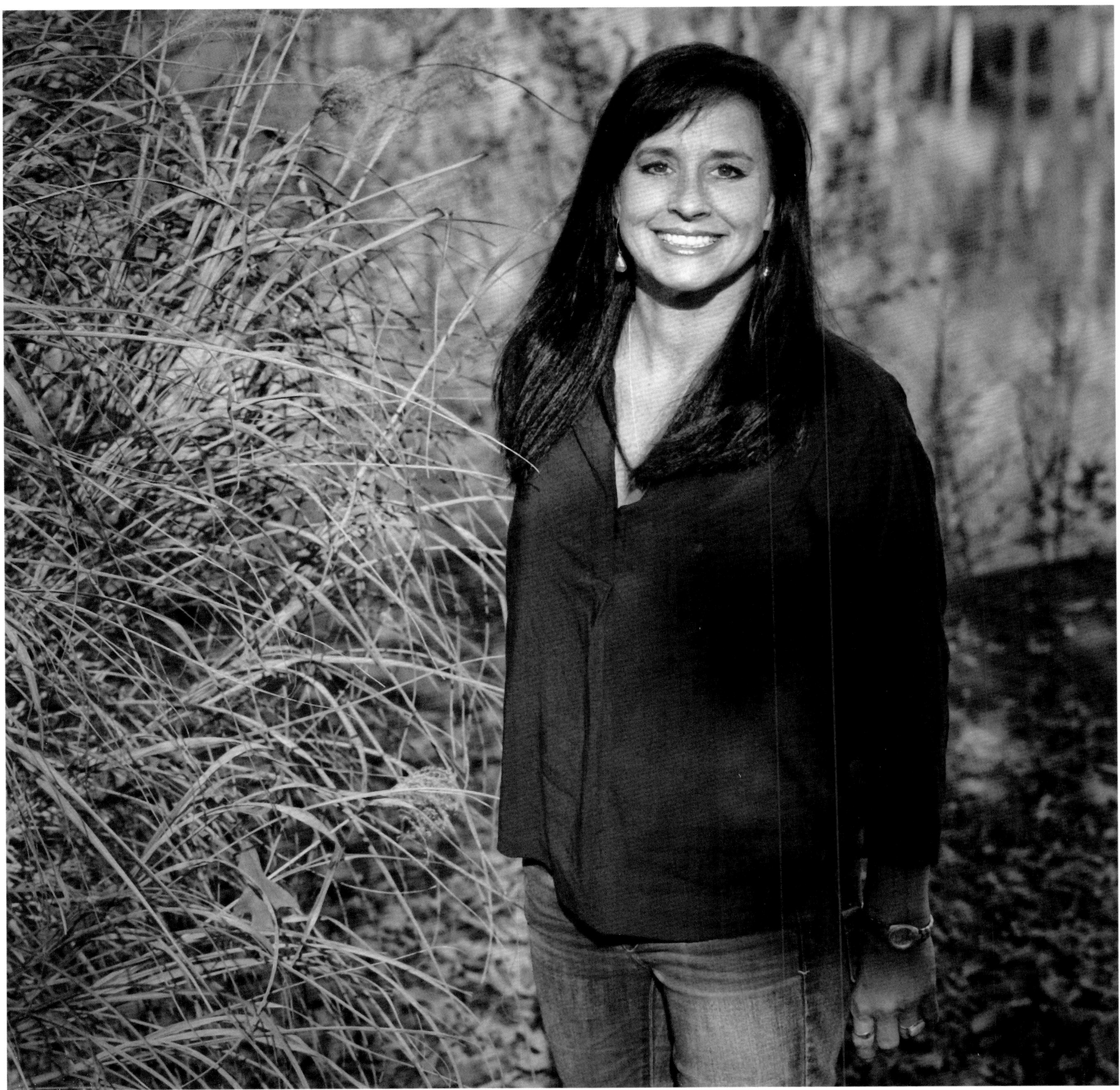

Vickie Toner

I was encouraged to be a free thinker from the very beginning. I went to kindergarten for one day and refused to go back. Instead, I insisted on taking tap and ballet lessons. I was never very good, but I danced my little heart out. I always had a very unique way of looking at things. In first grade, I participated in a creative contest sponsored by Carnegie Mellon College. I drew a memorable picture of a bulldog in an oriental jacket wearing ballet slippers. I won the contest and received free art lessons!

The biggest influence on my life has been my dad. He was honest, kind and supportive my entire life. He knew that I was strong-willed and spoke my mind. He endeavored to teach me to temper my disposition with tact and compassion. My parents were each other's best friends and really loved each other. I've always regretted never finding that kind of close relationship. Although, it has not stopped me from trying. I spent a lot of time making poor choices with men and having my heart broken. So much so that I felt the need to take a ten-year break in dating.

As I have grown older, I've come to the realization that I see things as they could be and not necessarily as they are. The term cockeyed optimist fits me perfectly. After lots of soul searching, I realize that for me, being true to myself is more important than being diplomatic. I am not willing to lose who I am in order to keep the peace.

I am passionate about what I do for a living. I graduated college with a degree in biology, but I had no idea of what I was going to do with it. One might say that film production found me. From my first day being a production assistant, I was hooked. Over the years, I have worked with TV shows, commercials and some aspects of movie making. I am a hard worker and take pride in the work I do. Because I endeavor to do a "above and beyond" job for my clients, I continue to get work in a youth-obsessed industry.

I am not a fan of dating websites. Most of the men I have met through there, I don't care for. I just don't want to start from scratch explaining my life choices to a stranger. The things that attract me to a man cannot be found in a photo. I am looking for that special spark that can only happen in person. I am open to dating again and would actually like to go on a blind date or two. I think it would work better to be introduced by people who know both of you.

I live in an old sun-drenched Victorian house with my pets. No one would ever accuse me of being a minimalist. One of my favorite things is finding funky antique shops that have unusual things with an element of surprise.

One of these days, when I am too old and gray to work, I hope to travel the world. I have always wanted that freedom. I have a saying affixed to my refrigerator that says, "The world is a book and those who don't travel read only a page." My next plan is to read the entire book!

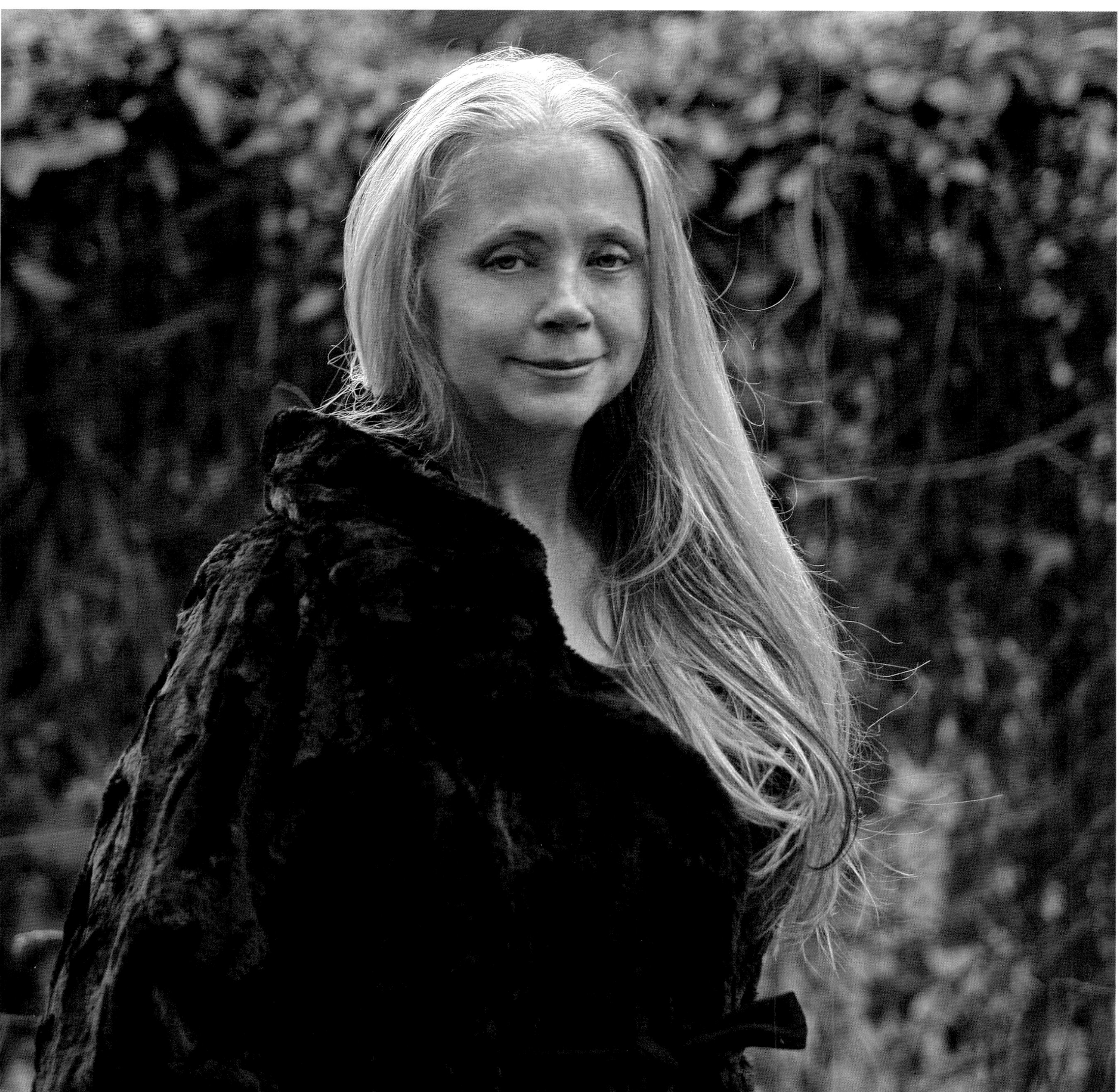

Christine Wilkie

From the time I can remember, my sister Susie has been my best friend. When I was five and crossing the street on a trip to the candy store, I walked out between two cars and was hit by a car. My head was nearly severed. My seven-year-old sister started running home with me in her arms. Someone saw us and called an ambulance which no doubt saved my life. For days, my family did not know if I would be a vegetable, die or suffer brain damage. The near-death experience has shaped my life. I know that people cross paths for a reason and every life has meaning. I also know that divine power is not revealed to us while we are in this world.

I grew up in the Midwest. My first job was shucking corn all day. Life was family, church, and school. We had no microwave, no color TV, no concerts, no air conditioning and Sunday was a day of rest with stores closed. Parks were open and we had family picnics. The men got the biggest pieces of meat and women were submissive. Out of this upbringing, I decided to take off for France.

I thought I spoke French decently until I arrived. The French have a way of telling it like it is. I lived with a family of ten and that experience gave me a feeling of accomplishment and sophistication. It also opened my eyes to different ways of life. I was proud of myself for doing what no one I knew had done. After a year I came home but didn't want to stay. I went to Montana and studied chemistry relating to animal behavior. I got a job with Wilderness Trails. I built bridges, cut down trees, fought forest fires, flew in helicopters and slept in tents.

When my education was complete, I moved to North Carolina to be near my sister. I met a charismatic man on a sailing trip. We dated for two years before we got married. We honeymooned in Africa followed by a two-week trip down the Nile. When we arrived home, he asked me to sign some papers he forgot to mention before our wedding. I was dumbfounded by the fifteen-page prenuptial agreement. How do you forget to mention that? An attorney advised me not to sign. My husband accepted my decision, but I felt deceived by him and he was annoyed with me. I felt distant from him after that and it was clear pretty quickly that there was no "We," only two "I's."

By all appearances I had a great life. We had money, belonged to a country club, lived in a gorgeous home, owned a beautiful boat and had an active social life. However, as time moved on, I felt more and more suffocated. We went everywhere together: the hardware store, the grocery store, the bank. I had security but no sparkle. Romance was a chore since I had lost my attraction for him.

Eventually, my husband took a job in a different state. While I was selling the house, I also started plans to leave the marriage. We didn't have a dramatic ending; having no children made it easier.

Today I have a medical degree in using MRI machines and CT scans. I am with people all day long and have lots of friends with my sister as my best. I take chances and do many things out of my comfort zone. If I ever feel stuck, I hop on a plane or a train and go someplace I have never been.

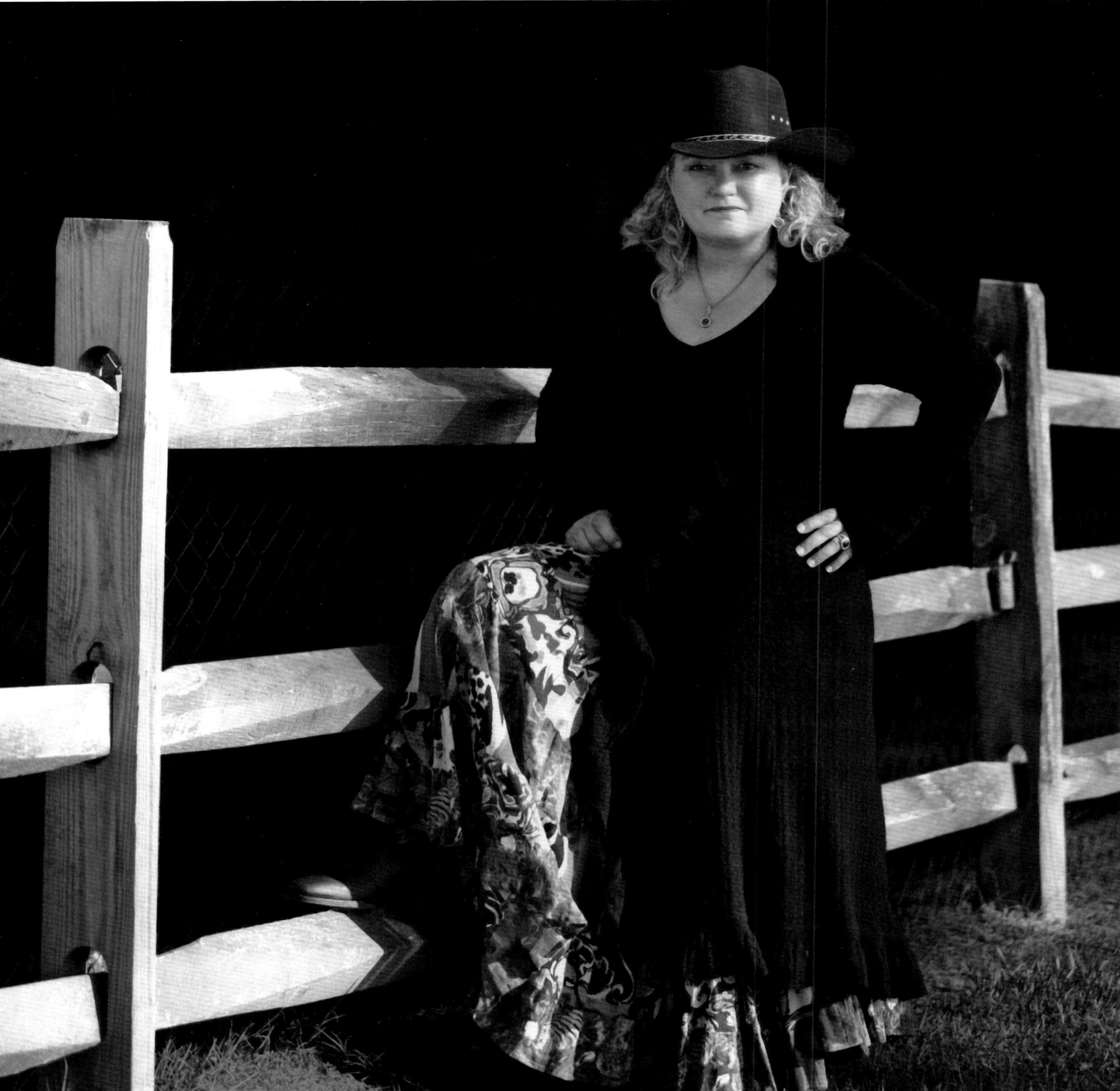

Gloria King

"No nonsense" are the words I would use to describe my family. I remember telling my father I was thinking of becoming a practical nurse. He told me if I was going for a nursing degree, it would have to be registered or nothing. Getting a C was like getting an F, and it was instilled in all of us children early on that we could achieve anything with hard work. When I was leaving for college, the only piece of advice I received was, "Don't come back with a husband."

My mother was fearless. Dad owned a drive-through ice cream store, and one night a man stuck a gun through the window and demanded the contents of the cash register. Mom grabbed the gun away from him by the nozzle and told him what he could do with his plans. He must have thought she was one crazy woman because he took off as though his pants were on fire.

After college, I got married to a man I thought was perfect. He was an entrepreneur and I was a nurse. I worked at home as well, doing the cooking, cleaning, gardening, and odd jobs that a handyman might have done. It was during this time that we had two children. As busy as I was, something was missing. I decided to go back to school and get a degree in business administration. My husband had not gone to college and was not happy about my decision. I wanted to do it while my children were young, thinking they'd need me more as they got older.

With this decision, my world expanded and I loved it. Once I had that degree, I wanted to get my master's. I remember a friend telling me that if I did, I would lose my husband. But I wasn't educating myself to hurt him; I was following my dreams and living the way I was brought up to live.

I did not grow up with people who got divorced, so the concept was foreign to me. Eventually, anything I said to my husband, even that it was a beautiful day, would turn into an argument. Our marriage was now about power and control of insignificant things. My mother encouraged me to get an education, so I could have independence no matter what happened in my life.

Eventually, as society changed and divorce became more commonplace, I decided to leave my marriage. The fear of the future was not as daunting as the day-to-day reality.

I regret that I didn't make it happen more quickly. It was a way-too-long death scene, and my husband sued me for alimony and child support. We were still living together in a kind of War of the Roses environment. It was unfair to our children, and it hurt them deeply. If I could change anything, it would be that.

Eventually, I got a job running a United Way chapter. I worked there for many years, raising more money than any of the other offices. I wanted to retire and received a fair compensation package from the board. The amount given to me was released to the press, and a backlash ensued. As a woman, and a black woman, I was an easy target. Who did I think I was? The public wanted me to return my compensation package for a lesser one. But remember how my mother grabbed the nozzle of the gun? Well, the public didn't realize that I was her daughter. It was a long battle, but in the end justice prevailed, and I kept the original settlement.

Today I am retired and live alone. I play golf, do Zumba, and tap dance. I have no intention of stopping or of looking my age. The only time I miss being married is when I am out with couples. I usually find out ahead of time and ask my daughter to accompany me. I don't need a man for that.

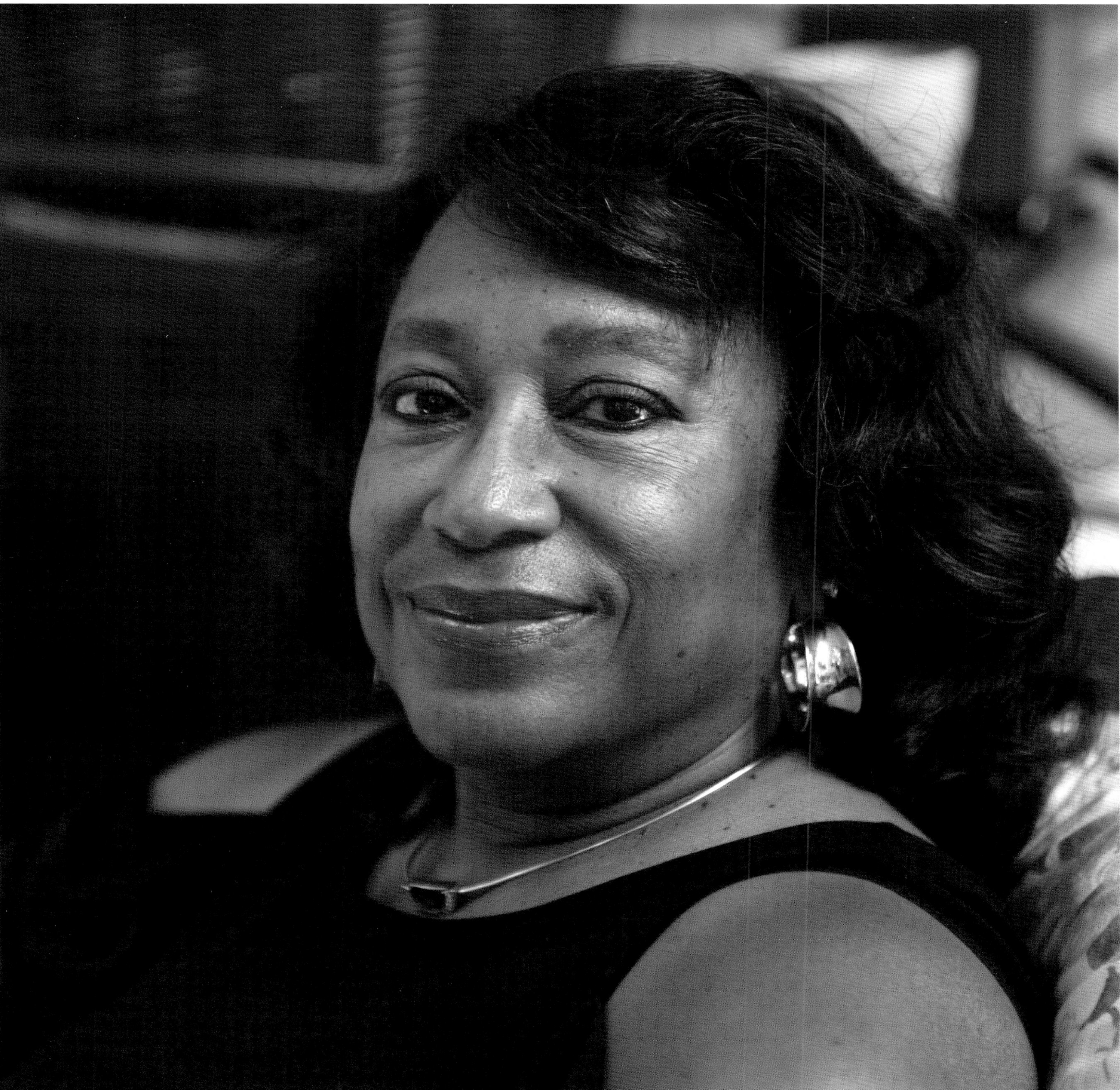

Paula Darlington

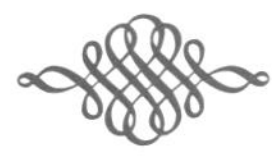

As a child I remember not being able to sit still and being distracted a lot. I should have been listening and paying attention, but I was so restless. Back then, there was little knowledge about kids who thought or acted differently. My behavior made me a target for bullies. My mother was a former schoolteacher who had the smarts to sit me down and tell me that the bullies didn't like themselves and that was why they picked on other children. She made me believe that they were the ones who had the problem. Today, when I come in contact with difficult people, I thank my mother for the early life lesson. Adults who continue to bully are no different than those kids I grew up with.

Before my father passed, we moved around quite a bit. I loved the idea of starting over again. There is the anticipation of a new adventure, but sometimes unfortunately, it does not always pan out. I love meeting new people and visiting new places. I find that I am highly adaptable and can make the best out of terrible circumstances.

In my twenties, I was hit by a drunk driver. According to the odds, I should not have survived. I was found pinned under my car. They put fifty stitches in my face alone. It taught me not to complain about a rainy day or a bad haircut. I can't say that I am glad it happened, but I know how to find gratitude for even the simplest things.

I married a man who was wrong for me. I think being trapped with no way out is terrifying. I had beautiful kids who I was responsible for and loved dearly, and it was really important to take small steps to leave my husband. I had no support system and had to learn to take on a huge amount of responsibility. Finally, we agreed to share custody and have worked it out so that the boys felt safe and secure in our two homes.

After my marriage ended, I had to reinvent myself. I became a student at the New York Film Academy. After graduating, I started a business doing videography and video editing. I am passionate about what I do and I really give it my all. Even during a struggling economy, I managed to keep the business afloat and enjoyed the process at the same time.

I am dating. That too is a process. Everybody has their ups and downs and particular baggage. As we get older, both men and women get set in their ways and it just becomes a question of what you can or can't live with.

I have found that just staying busy is a powerful antidepressant. I power-walk and exercise as much as I can. I also sing in a gospel group that is multi-denominational. The inspirational music lifts us all up and spreads joy to others. Singing with the choir makes me connected to my mother again, too. I like passing on this feeling of connectedness and helping others to find spiritual meaning in their lives.

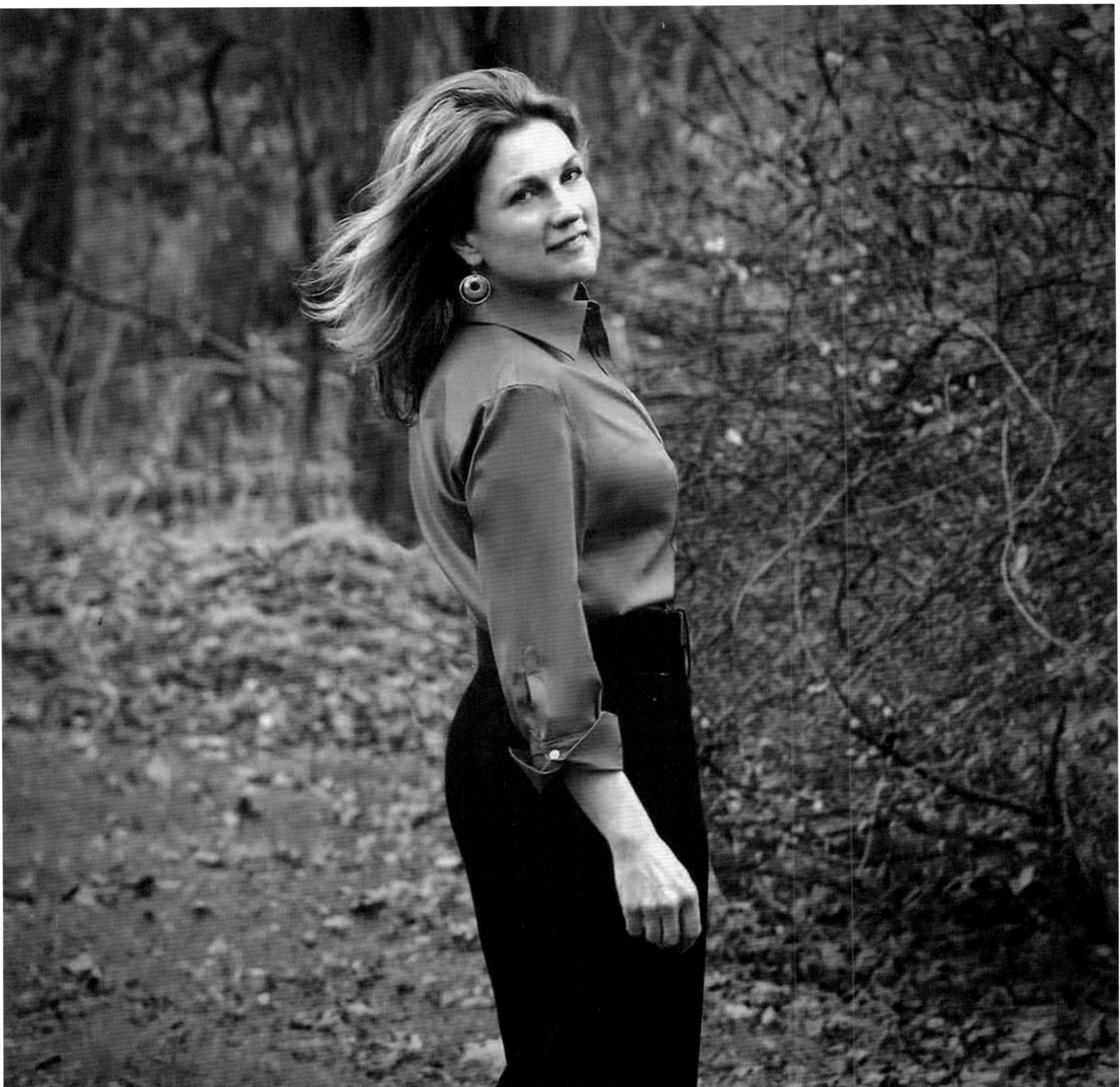

Jayne Kline

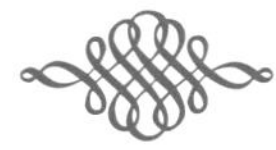

I grew up in West Virginia right next to Pittsburgh. My father was mayor of the town we lived in and I have five sisters. My dad was the butt of many jokes about having six daughters. It was a "salt of the earth" upbringing, with both parents not practicing prejudice to anyone or anything except maybe "The Steelers." One of my favorite stories about my father was when I missed the cheerleading tryouts and ended up on the basketball team by default. I didn't know it, but I was really good. I ended up with "all state honors" on the team that won the state championship. My father would go to his old buddies and ask them what their sons had won lately. I was proud that he was so proud of me.

I was a born athlete and sports came naturally to me. I am committed and competitive, but I play to have fun. I am a 4.5 tennis player and my handicap is 8 in golf. I love watching sports as well as playing. I always knew that as a girl, I was still a bit of a "Tom." I got my degree in mechanical engineering and worked for IBM for many years. Today, I am into flipping properties, which is lots of fun.

I married a man who loved sports as well, and he used to say that "we had more fun together by accident than most people do by trying." I wanted to have a big family, but that did not happen for us. Accepting it was the hardest thing I have ever done. Today, I am lucky to be the greatest aunt imaginable! I get to love my nieces and nephews and not worry about discipline, like a grandparent. It's a great place to be. For close to twenty years, I lived with, and eventually married my husband. We had an active social life and for many years a wonderful marriage.

When my husband and I were building our dream house, we took our time making plans. Right before the building was starting, we sold our big house on the lake and got a small rental near the land we were building on. It was a happy time, although the intimacy in our marriage had disappeared. I believed that it was due to my husband having minor health problems. The day before the ground was being broken, I got a text saying he was coming home unexpectedly.

I remember I was eating a turkey sandwich when time stood still. I thought he was going to tell me he had cancer, and I was terrified. When he came through the door, he told me that he couldn't be with me anymore. He needed time to think and be by himself. I felt like it was my husband's voice speaking another language. I couldn't comprehend what he was telling me. Or I should say, not telling me. He left and I was paralyzed. I called family members and friends and no one could believe what I was saying. It took at least a year for me to accept the reality of what many people suspected all along. He had been, for quite a while, having an affair with one of my girlfriends. The word "betrayal" seems a weak word for how I felt. I was blindsided by someone I loved dearly, and a friend who I had trusted. Obviously I had not known at all and I felt foolish for missing it. But I could not begin to believe what I couldn't conceive.

Time moved on, and I learned to hold my head up high in our small community. It was a bit freeing knowing that although I had been publicly humiliated, I was loved and embraced by many people who showed me kindness and compassion. Other women felt safe to tell me their stories, knowing my life was not as perfect as it may have appeared.

It took some time for me to realize I was not guilty of anything. I needed to understand I was as damaged as if I was in a fatal emotional car crash. It takes time to heal and I am learning to not just survive but thrive. I believe with enough practice we can all learn to choose our emotions and choose not to be bitter. My sisters and girlfriends have been my sanity, when I had none. I have met a man who is without a doubt one of the kindest, most compassionate men I have ever met. We have lots in common and are enjoying every moment while taking it slowly.

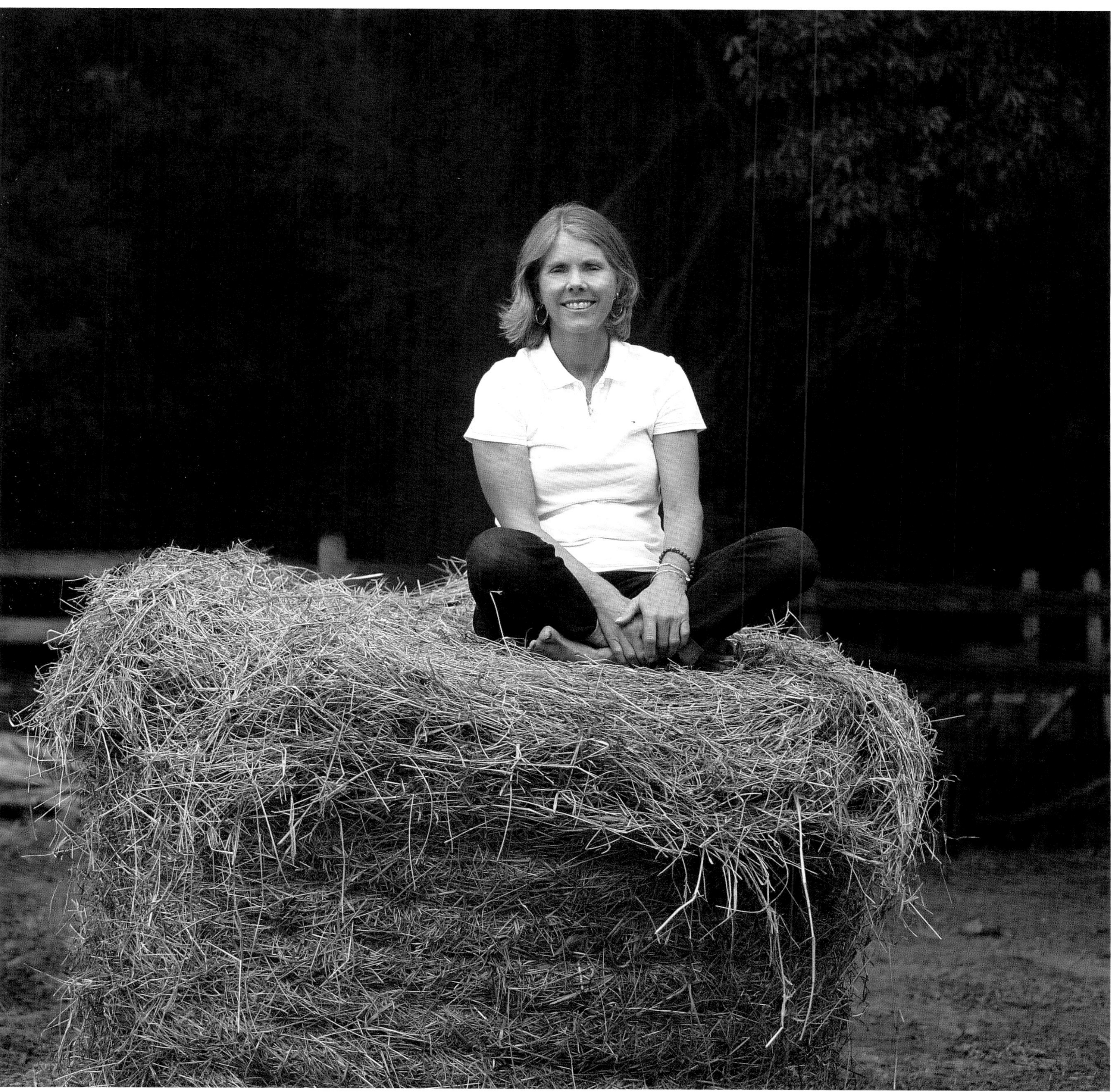

Jill Jayson

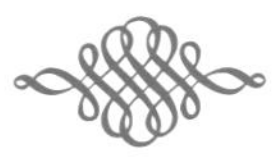

My parents were Joyce and Jack. Aside from sharing the letter J, they couldn't have been more diametrically opposed. Joyce was a risk-taker who believed in endless possibilities, and Jack was a cynic who referred to himself as a realist. Each time I would embark on a new adventure, Joyce would enthusiastically encourage me to go for it! Jack, on the other hand, was brought up during the Depression and played devil's advocate. He always steered me to the more secure path and pressed me to devise a game-plan. Joyce saw fairies circling my head and Jack saw fire-breathing dragons. Having parents who constantly disagreed with each other was confusing to me as a child. I remember crying in my room, thinking they would be happier if they lived apart.

Despite my parents bickering, they loved each other deeply. They were married for 64 years and lived into their 90s. They died within a week of each other. My marriage was not as fortunate. I had all the external things: a successful career, a Manhattan brownstone, two beautiful children, a vacation home and an adorable dog. Fifteen years later, it all fell apart. I was really unhappy. My only sister was gravely ill with cancer and there was a lot of stress. My husband and I were just too different from each other and I realized we should just be friends. I moved into a condo in the suburbs and got a cat. After that, I had some semi-fulfilling relationships and some semi-dysfunctional ones too, but no Prince Charming in sight.

When my sister passed away, it was a wake-up call to me to live my life fully. I did not want to waste another moment being numb. I threw myself into my business. At the time, I ran a corporate communications company that specialized in coaching adults for public speaking. One day, I was in the supermarket and ran into a neighbor who asked if I would coach her daughter for a theater audition. I agreed, and afterward I remember her saying that her daughter learned more from me in one hour than from three years in theater school. A light bulb went off, and I thought I could blend everything I offered in my corporate business to my audition consulting, creating a "theater for life" approach.

Within a month, my theater company was born. I love working with both adults and children, helping people to shape their inner and outer voices.

One of my proudest accomplishments is a play called, *Ever Happily After*, about a woman who falls in love with her own qualities of which she was previously unaware. My musicals and plays are always threaded with strong, positive messages culminating in self-belief and self-expression. My mantra is "Dream Big." I encourage everyone to take huge leaps with an underlying strategic net of support.

I am grateful and humble for every day of my life. I've found true happiness and fulfillment with two beautiful children, doing what I love, good health, and amazing family and friends. Who knows, as life continues to "happen" (even though Prince Charming doesn't exist), maybe I'll meet a wonderful, perfect partner along the way.

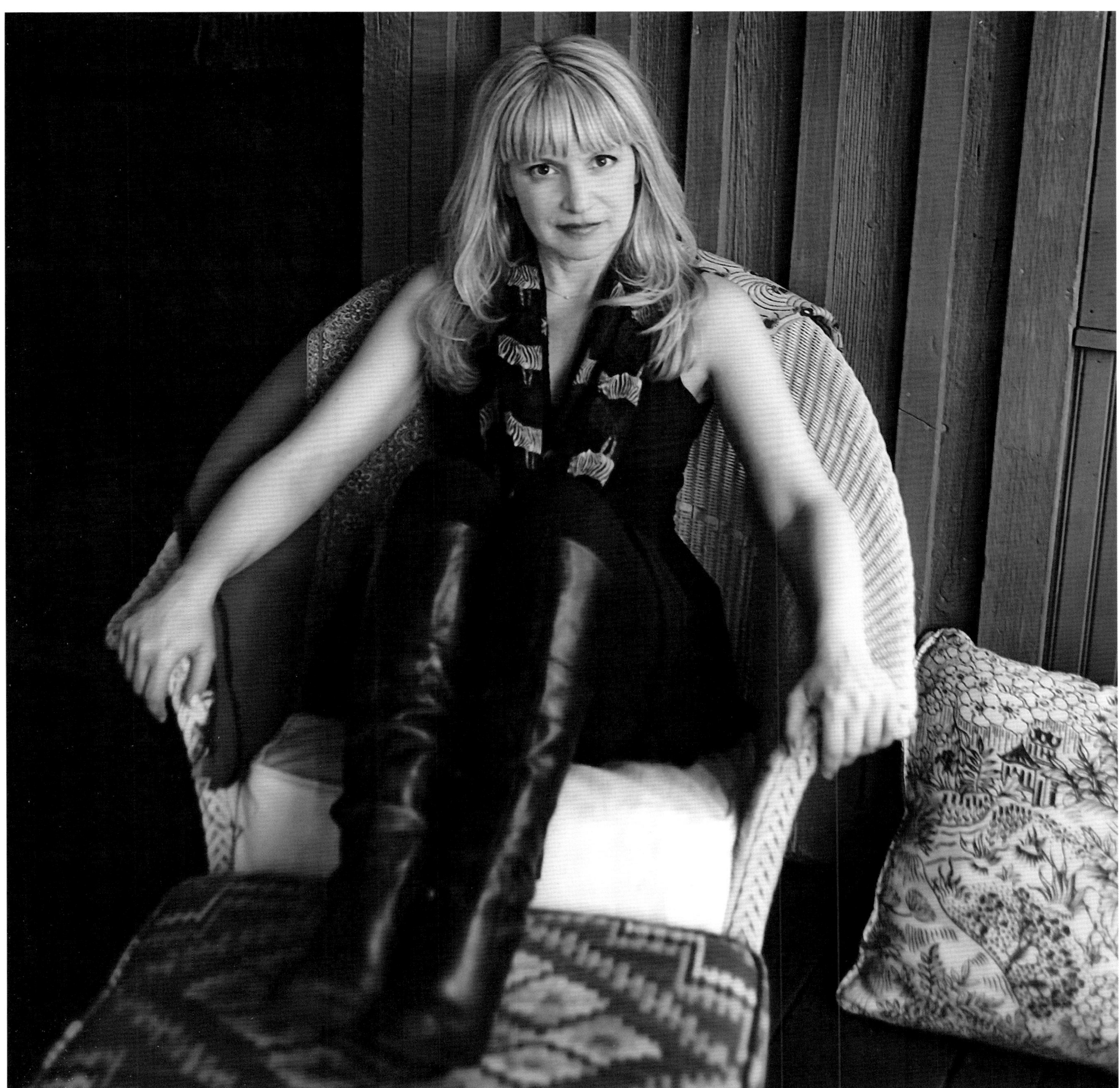

Laura Ring

I had great parents. My mother was a stay-at-home mom, baking cookies, and putting laundry on the line. Yet, I would see my friends' mothers going to work and wanted to do the same. The idea of dressing up and being part of something was appealing.

In my early twenties, I had a serious boyfriend and suddenly many of our friends were getting engaged and married. We got caught up in the excitement of the moment and decided to join the crowd.

I knew it was a mistake early on because I had no desire to have a partner. I'm a strong and determined personality. I have my own ideas, right or wrong. I find it amazing that people think if you're not married, something is lacking in your life. We had a daughter early on, and neither one of us wanted her growing up with parents who did not bring happiness to one another. One of the things we agreed on was that our love for her allowed us to end our marriage after two years without acrimony.

I found everything to be easier when I was by myself. There were no negotiations and I did what I wanted to financially. The only person responsible for giving me permission was myself. I went back to school for my master's degree in taxation.

I believe most people are able to focus on three things and do them well. I am an involved mother, a hard worker at a job I love, and have a thriving social life. No one can do twenty things well. I think it's important to figure out what you love doing the most and do them wonderfully. Today, family has taken on so many more connotations than it had when I was a child. I often see groups of friends having Thanksgiving dinner or spending Christmas together. The mother, father, and children stereotype will always continue to thrive. That said, it is wonderful other family options are now normal and acceptable.

My daughter is like me in many ways, but the opposite when it comes to family. She wants a husband, a houseful of children and dinner on the table every night.

I am the happiest single woman I know. For a long time, where I lived and owning a house was important to me. Not anymore. I've learned to simplify everything. I rarely give my daughter advice. I do however tell her often that no man is better than a bad man.

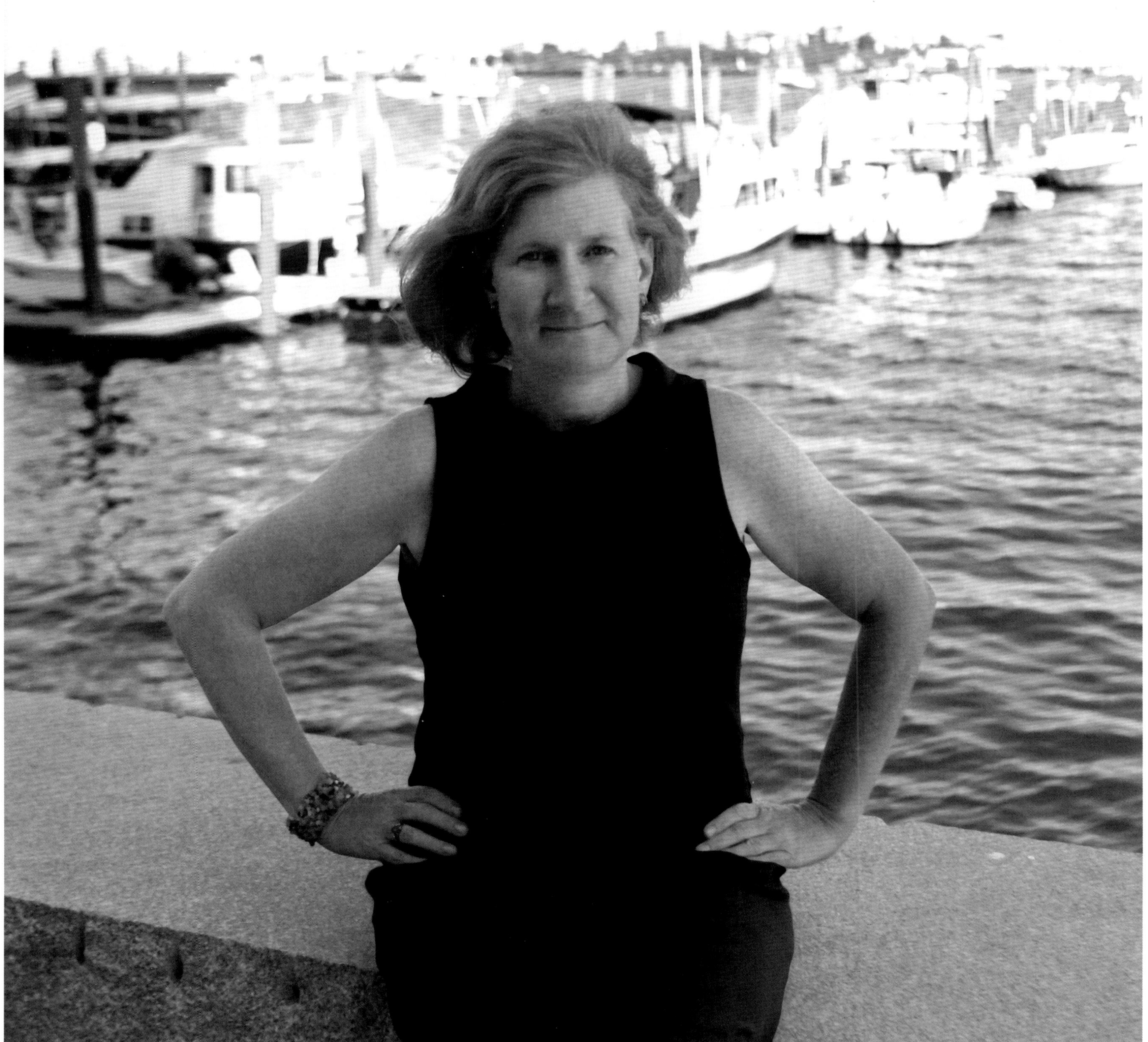

Pat Clark

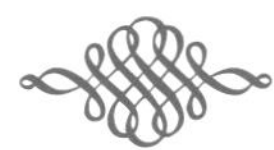

Growing up in the 1950s, I am envious of young women today. Title IX has given them so many more opportunities than women my age had. I believe that playing team sports leads to good team skills, which are important in the business world.

Like most women, I assumed I would get married. Young girls were traditionally given bride dolls. As a young girl I waited for that doll to arrive, but birthdays and Christmas would come and go, and no doll. Years later, I remembered that time and wondered if it was a foreboding of life to come. I knew my family assumed I would follow in my father's footsteps and go to college.

I got my degree in business as I watched my friends get married and start families. I loved being around them and felt vicariously as though I actually had a family, without all the responsibility. I just didn't have that biological clock in me.

I started out as a secretary, working for a senator in Washington. I loved being on Capitol Hill. My life was more exciting than I had ever imagined. What I didn't imagine was that I would fall in love with a married man. He was legally separated, but his religion, Catholicism, didn't allow divorce. For a price, you can get an annulment, but that's another story.

We were a couple for twenty years but never lived together. As time went on, the senator's chief of staff was retiring and Watergate was beginning. I was offered his position. Like everyone else, I had assumed the position would go to a man. I took the job. After all my years of conditioning, women's liberation was just starting, and it felt as if it was starting with me.

Eventually, I ended up taking a job with R.J.Reynolds, as one of the first female vice presidents. I loved my work and the many responsibilities. I ended up funding educational programs.

I mentored many women whom I am proud to know today. I was aware that many of the same people we meet on the way up are the same ones we might meet on the way down and was careful how I treated everyone.

I was happy in my job and shocked when I was diagnosed with rectal cancer. They caught it quickly, and I was lucky. Unfortunately, I took quite a bit of time off from work, and when I returned I saw that most of my responsibilities had been taken away. I realized immediately I had been handed the golden handcuffs.

At fifty, I got married to the only love in my life. We had the happiest marriage, laughing all the time, with great conversations, and we loved many of the same things. Maybe because we did not have children, we became best friends. We did not have many couple friends because we enjoyed being on our own. After fifteen years together, Jim passed away, and I have no interest in getting married again. I got struck by lightning once. I don't expect it to happen twice.

My mother died a year after my husband and I knew that if I wanted a new life, I was going to have to start building it. I know if you sit at home and wait for the phone to ring, you can drive yourself crazy. I have learned not to take it personally when people don't call me right back. Today people have complicated lives, and I usually find out that there is a good reason. I don't wait. I pick up the phone.

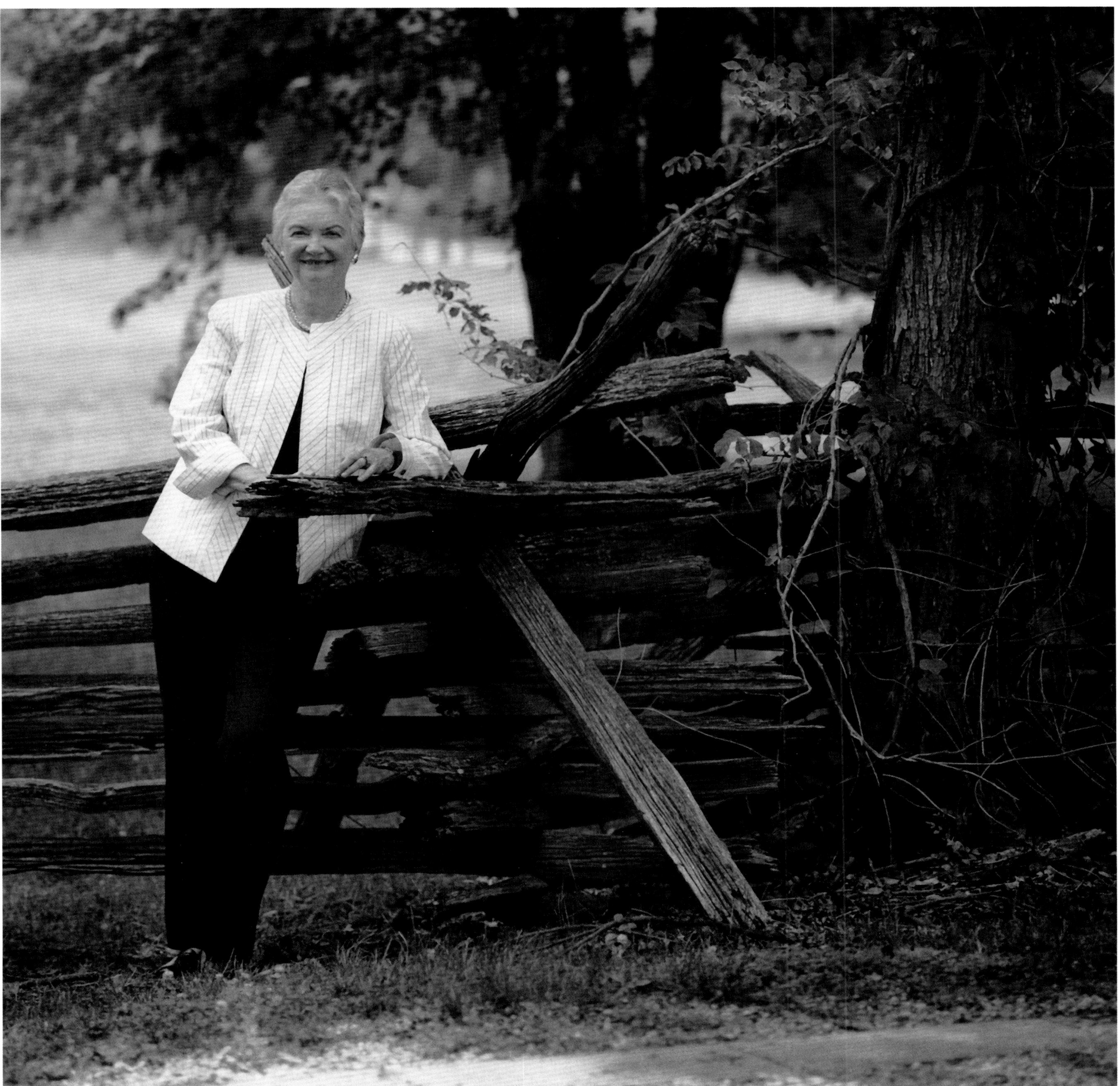

Sheila Callihan

I am the youngest of four children, and in many respects, I feel like an only child. I was born years after my siblings and was the only one living at home when my father developed ALS. Seeing him in pain developed my compassion for others.

After college, I took a job on Wall Street. I worked obsessively as I climbed to the top of the ladder. I wanted financial security, and I love a challenge. It was the perfect combination for me at that time of my life. I am a fighter and feel as though I can do anything… that is, anything except dating. I have no patience and dislike the game of it. I would love to be in a relationship, if the perfect person would just show up.

I was in a serious relationship once. He was from Ireland and loved nothing more than to sit in the pub all day, chatting with everyone, while I wanted to climb mountains. He did introduce me to the artsy side of the world. He also taught me that you can't change yourself or anyone else that much. So much of who we are, we are born with.

My female friends are my lifelines and I have many who share my interests, while others are now in a different world, with husbands and children. We have shared memories that can never be taken away, but I often have a hard time relating to their world.

After several years, I realized I was successful at what I was doing, but unhappy. I had stopped laughing, stopped dreaming, and was walking around like a robot. I made the decision to leave the enormous bonuses and sleepless nights for a journey into the unknown.

Today, I spend time taking care of my elderly mother, which is a joy for me. Nothing can beat walking in the door and seeing her face. I clean the house, do the laundry, shop, and sort the pills. I can see myself working in the geriatric field one day. I dislike the way this society ignores its senior citizens while spoiling its children.

I don't watch television and do my best to stay away from depressing news. I think silence is often a gift that goes unrecognized. We form our thoughts in silence. I read often and love jazz. If I want to see a concert, I buy myself a ticket. I have done Outward Bound twice and will no doubt do it again. I love my work at Habitat for Humanity. What a joy knowing what I do every day is helping people see their dreams come true.

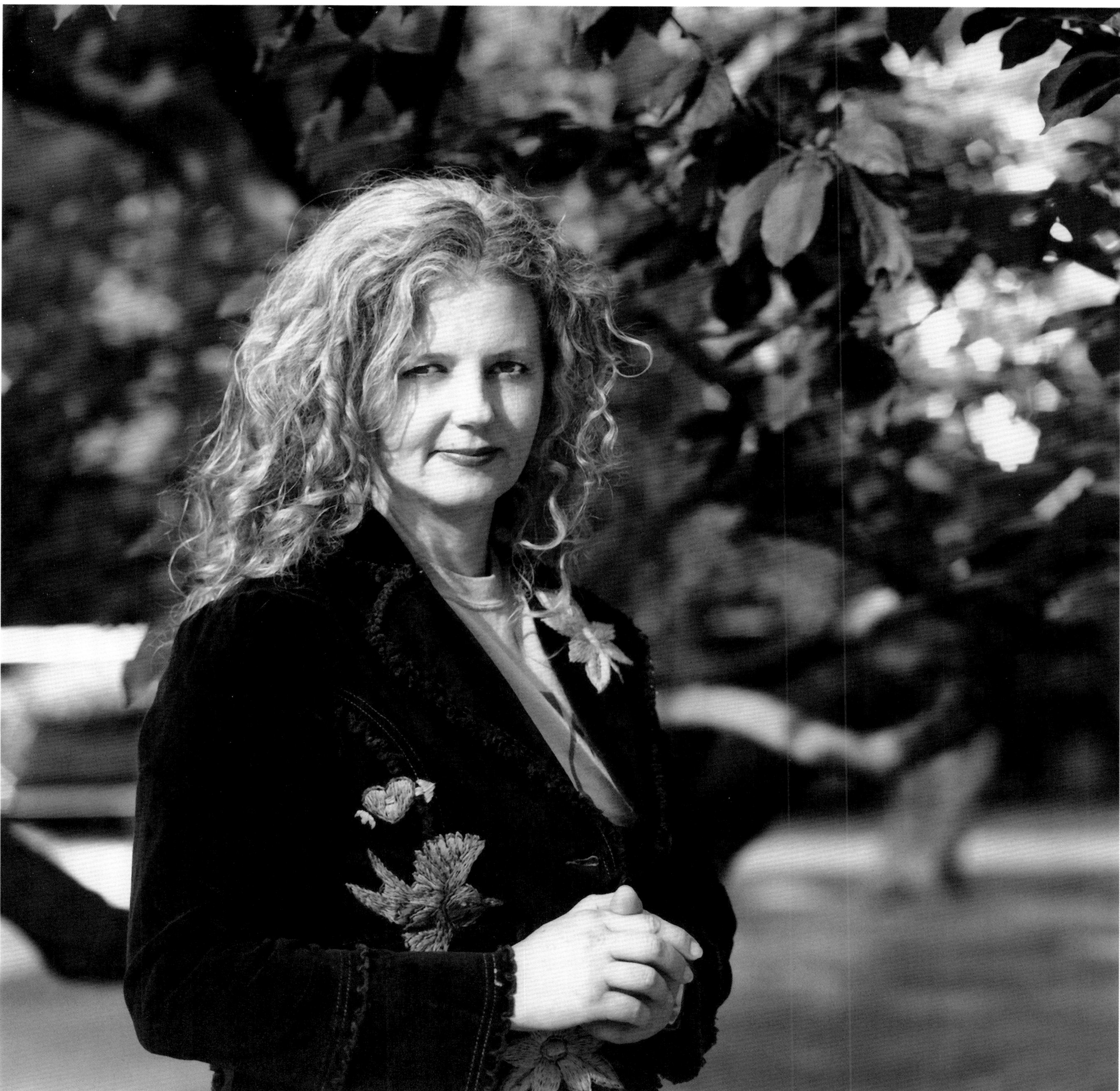

Ciska Weber

I came from a stable, happy family that lived on an island close to Holland. I adored my father, but he was sick from the time I can remember, and he passed away young. In a small town, everyone knew everyone else's business, which could be a good thing, but I was drawn to a bigger world from a young age.

I met an American man who was twelve years older than me. He was also movie-star handsome. I fell madly in love at sixteen and moved back with him to his home in the United States. Eventually we married. At the beginning, it was lovely and we had a daughter. We owned a restaurant together. My job was doing the work, and his was to complain about how I did it. People would comment on his attitude, but I had a hard time making decisions and sticking up for myself. It took me awhile to realize that if something is not working no matter what you do, it's ridiculous to work harder at fixing it. My husband had a way of making me look small, so he could look big. Eventually a friend told me that her husband said I lacked the courage to leave him, and those were the words that switched the emotions in my brain and enabled me to walk away.

For many years I fell for the wrong men. I don't like boring men, so I'm often attracted to men with an edge. My second husband was charming and successful. I felt lucky and loved. We dated for a few years and had a wonderful love life, but after we married, he lost his attraction to me. There was no sex and little affection when we were alone. I didn't change at all, but he had. I did learn a lesson from my first marriage and that was to not waste time. After counseling, writing letters and many conversations to no avail, I decided to leave him and the big beautiful house we shared for a small three-room apartment. It's a paradox that I dislike drama, yet I get so much of it. I must admit I was proud that I did not allow myself to be bought with material things.

I have my own business on the same street as my apartment. It is a gelato shop that also sells espresso and wine. I have many customers who come over and tell me their life stories, and I get to give a little advice now and again. It's a gift to myself to make people happy. I'm quite comfortable having very little; life is less complicated with simplicity. I love getting a bargain, so I am happiest at flea markets, farmers' markets and the beach.

My mother has been living with a wonderful man for many years. In Holland, it's financially complicated to get married and split the assets. She is my role model, and I don't feel the need to be married anymore. I am not saying I don't want love in my life because I do. I also have an amazing daughter and maybe someday I will be a grandmother. I hope that she has learned from me not to fall in love with someone who loves himself more than her.

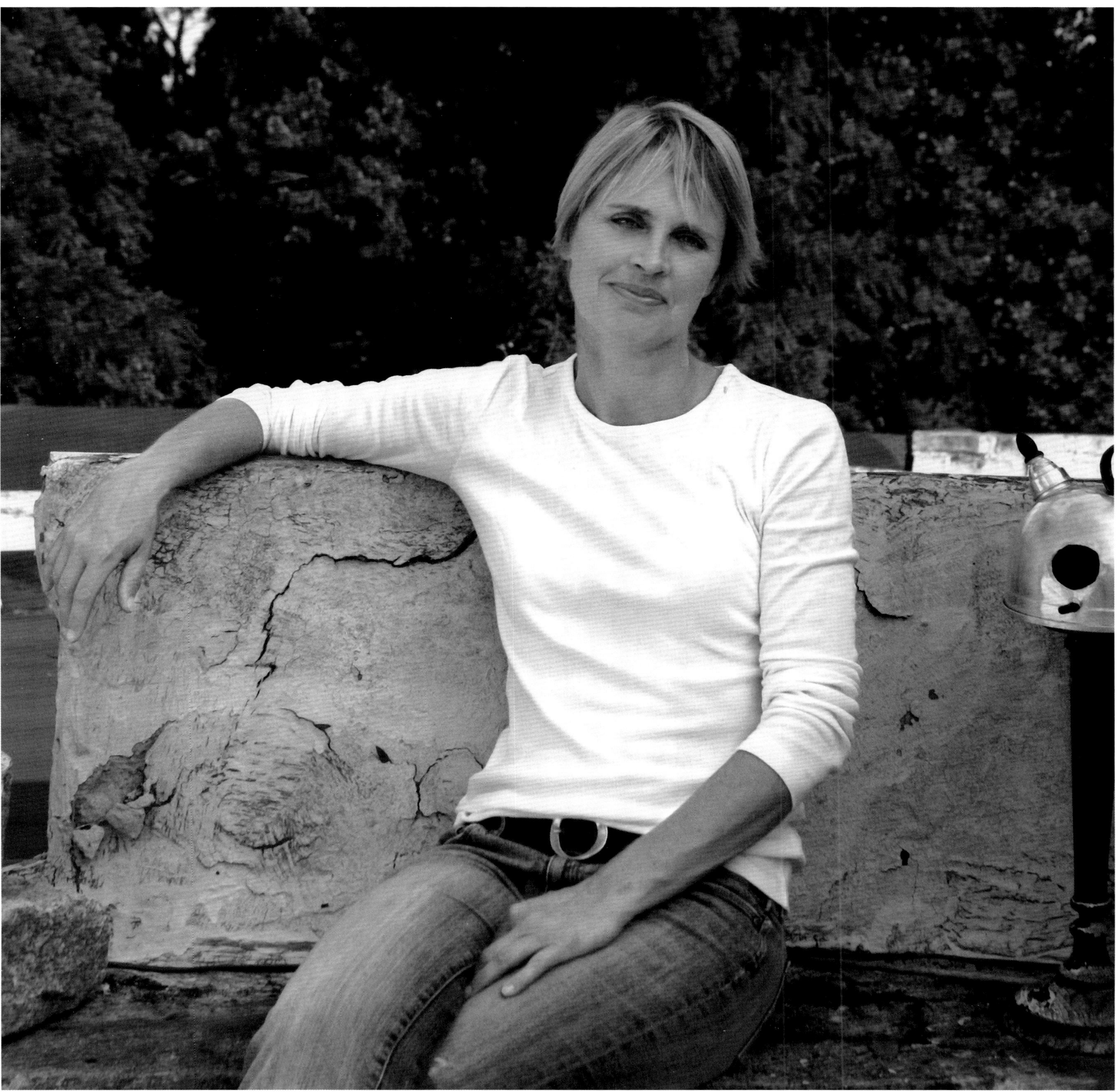

Paulette Chapple

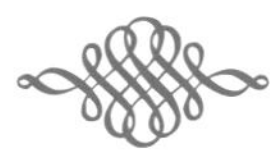

When I was young, I was shy and introverted. I dreamt about being a clothing designer. I spent days looking through fashion magazines and sketching designs of outfits I hoped other people would someday wear. My mother was a nurse and children's caretaker, but all I wanted was a glamorous life.

Mom was the Pied Piper of the neighborhood. Everyone wanted to be with her. She was so much fun and spread happiness everywhere she went. On any given day there could be up to twenty children in our house. It was not a daycare center, more like a play care center. There were times, however, that I resented the attention the other children received. I wanted her all to myself. Our family was biracial, but it was not a subject that was openly discussed. I knew nothing about social injustice because my parents protected me from our history. My father was from Burma and could pass for white, while my mother was African American.

As time went on, I went to school for design and got my degree. I was in between jobs and a bit disillusioned when I decided to try a temp agency. When they asked me what kind of job I would like, I surprised myself by saying I wanted to work with children. Without consciously realizing it, I had inherited the caretaker gene that was the core of my mother. I was offered work as a recreational therapist to help three young girls who had physical and developmental disabilities. I fell in love with those girls. I poured all the skills and techniques I had seen my mother utilize into them. The manager could see how happy I was and that the girls were thriving. I remember her telling me she saw something special in me from the beginning. She said she would be sure I received formal training and certification. She kept her word and that was the beginning of my career.

Eventually, I ended up at Catholic Charities, managing a group home. I worked there for many years. Now, I run a small group home for young men between seventeen and twenty-four who have emotional and social difficulties. I try to help them acclimate into society by teaching them etiquette, healthy eating habits and how to get along with one another and the outside world. I find I have to be tough on them sometimes but kind as well. I cook every night, but they clean up. I know it's far from the glamorous life I imagined when I was young, but those men make me feel like the queen of the castle! I don't see myself ever retiring.

I did get married more than once. I hate to admit this, but I married my problems. It took me awhile, but I did come to the realization that I should not bring my work home. From those marriages, I have two wonderful loving daughters and two grandsons who melt my heart. They are the loves of my life and whatever it took to get them was worth it.

As I look at the lives of women today, I feel we have come a long way. Although, there is still more we need to accomplish. The young women of today have a resilience we did not have. I know some people think the women's movement did not go far enough. Well, in my not-so-distant past, there were never women politicians, lawyers or banking executives. It was a man's world. Today, we have so many opportunities. Now we need to learn to become each other's cheerleaders. Once that starts to happen, the sky's the limit.

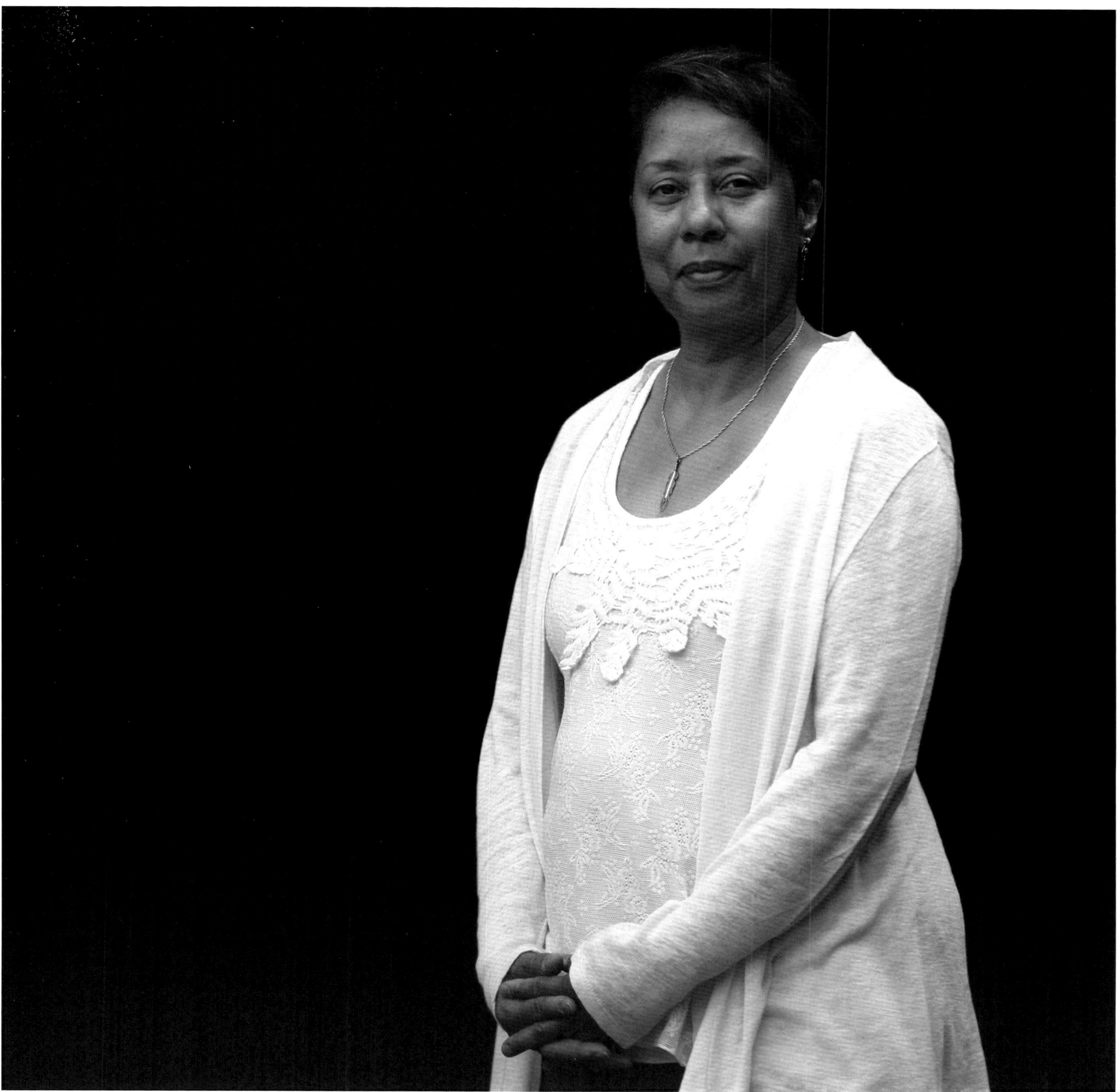

Linda Ruggiero

I was never a girly girl. From the time I can remember, I was more interested in what the men were doing. I love going into the basement and hearing the sound of a saw cutting wood, rather than aromas coming from the kitchen. I had quite the spunky personality as a kid. My neighborhood nickname was, "Thunderbolt." My parents put the quash on that and made sure I was well behaved and respectful.

I was married at nineteen and had two children. While raising my kids, I waitressed and attended college. I loved learning and being out of the house. My husband was jealous and wanted me to be at home. If I was five minutes late returning from the grocery store, he would be furious. Despite his behavior, I carried on, eventually getting my master's degree. Thankfully, I got a great job at a sheet metal business. I was a sales engineer, which meant that I sold prototypes to businesses and taught them how to use our product. The business was mostly working with men. I was successful and loved going to work every day. With my increased confidence, I was brave enough to finally leave my marriage. I finally knew no one was responsible for my happiness but me.

In time, I met a wonderful man who was smart, kind, and charismatic. He had a great sense of humor and we brought out the best in one another. He gave me a beautiful engagement ring and we planned on getting married. As time went on, we were having such fun together and life was perfect as it was. We did not feel the need to actually tie the knot. My kids were crazy about him, too! When my daughter was getting married, she asked him to walk her down the aisle.

During this time, I suddenly became ill. I could barely lift my head off the pillow or even walk without a cane. My sweetheart supported me through the crippling pain and helped me out on my most difficult days. It took four years to finally get a diagnosis. I had ankylosing spondylitis. It's similar to fibromyalgia, only more debilitating. I resisted treatment for a time, as I feared the possible side effects of the drug treatment. Finally, my rheumatologist convinced me to try it. The drug was miraculous, and I found relief almost immediately. Soon enough I was walking, hiking and even dancing.

Then the tables turned. My love had been a soldier in Vietnam. Like other brave men, he had been exposed to Agent Orange. Unfortunately, that led to lung cancer. He was diagnosed late and given a grim prognosis. He decided to live fully in the moment and we never discussed the unimaginable situation. After his passing, I missed him so much. We were together for 23 years. I ended up in grief counseling, which saved my sanity. It was life-changing to be with people who had been through a similar loss. We talked for hours every week. This allowed the healing to begin.

I am surprised by how little I knew about single life today. Being a naturally outgoing person, group activities appealed to me. I moved to the South to be near my daughter and granddaughter. At 67, I am biking, kayaking and doing anything I can outdoors. Staying healthy, making new friends and creating my own independent identity is my new job.

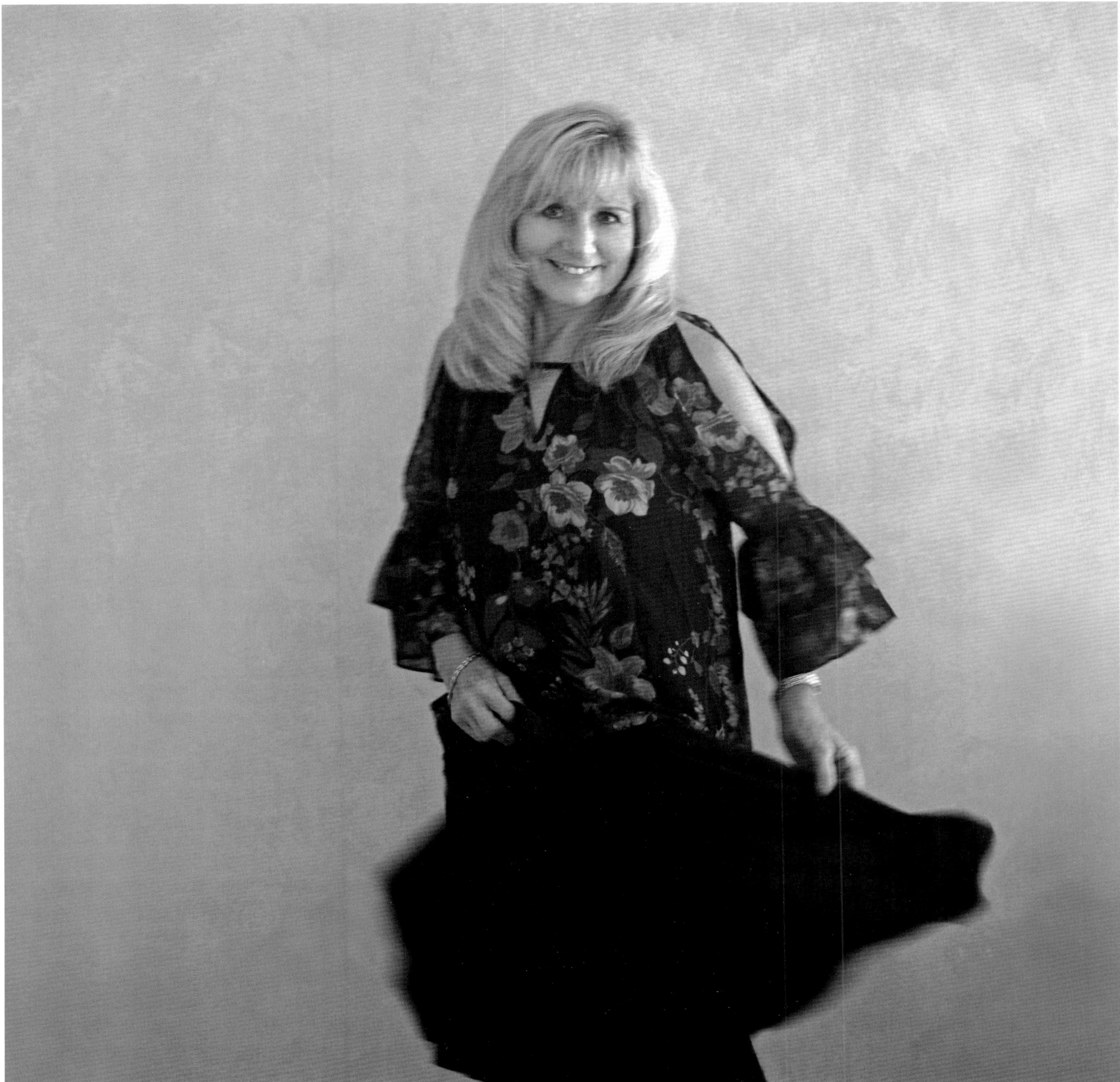

Jennifer Sendral

My childhood gave me a sense of adventure; I was the only girl with two fun-loving brothers. When we weren't living at the pool, and it was a holiday weekend, my parents would pack us in the car and we would visit a state park. We hiked, climbed and swam all over the United States. With Dad behind the wheel, we learned early on if any of us had to go to the bathroom, we had to tell him thirty minutes before it was true. He didn't like to stop the first time we asked. We had more than a few Chevy Chase moments over the years. Before any of us got our license, we had to know how to read a map, drive both stick and automatic, and be able to drive on the highway long distance, with Dad in the front seat. My parents had a strong work ethic, both having served in the Air Force for twenty plus years before retiring although still continuing to work.

I grew up on auto-pilot, thinking you went to school, then to college, then got a job, met someone who loved you, then got married and had babies. I was not preparing to be a bridesmaid ten times.

Where I live now it is unlikely that a woman of my age would share my lack of marital status. If you're not married in your early twenties, they want to know what is wrong with you. I often say with a laugh, "It's not like Price Charming comes falling out of the sky."

I graduated from the University of Alabama with an undergraduate in child development; I followed up by completing my internship at a navy base in Japan. I was a people person and I absolutely adored children. I taught preschool but was offered the opportunity to work with one of the royal families in Abu Dhabi. I was to not only be their teacher but coordinate the children's schedules and attend meetings and functions at school. I was a chaperone for the younger girls at parties and social events. I traveled abroad with the family and organized outings and activities in different foreign countries. I never had the same workday twice, which kept me on my toes. I was told a while ago that planning was God's way of laughing at you, and boy, did He have some good laughs.

I learn so much from people of different cultures and backgrounds. I never really knew what it was like to be in someone's shoes until moving overseas. We are all human beings no matter where we are from or what we look like. I'm a happy person and I believe there is never too great a problem in life that can't be solved. It may not be the outcome you're looking for, but again that points to the perspective you have in life as well.

I love to make people laugh. I tell everyone that I'm a little kid in a big kid's body. I often get the, "When are you going to grow up?" Or, "Act your age. This is why you are still single." I don't want to act my age when I don't feel that old. I love to have fun. I am working on my health. My boyfriends are Dr. Pepper and his sidekick, "Cookie two-scoop" ice cream. I know I should let them go, but they really want to stick with me.

Years ago, I struggled with worry. I would worry about the unknown bringing on stress when it was not needed or helpful. How often does what we worry about happen? A friend said to me, "Divorce it, walk away from it, and don't open the door again."

I often wonder if I have really learned the lessons I think I have, when I find myself repeating the same mistakes. Overall, I have done very well divorcing the worry, anxiety, and fear from my life. I would love to have someone to share my life with. I'm just saying if it doesn't happen for me, I won't be devastated. I firmly believe God has a plan for all of us, and His plan is so much better than the one in my head.

My biggest challenge is yet to come. Traveling the world has been amazing. Hearing people's life stories have been fascinating and addicting. I don't want to leave, yet the pull to come home is getting stronger. So, I will pray for discernment and knowledge of when the time is right to pack up and find out what my next adventure will be back home.

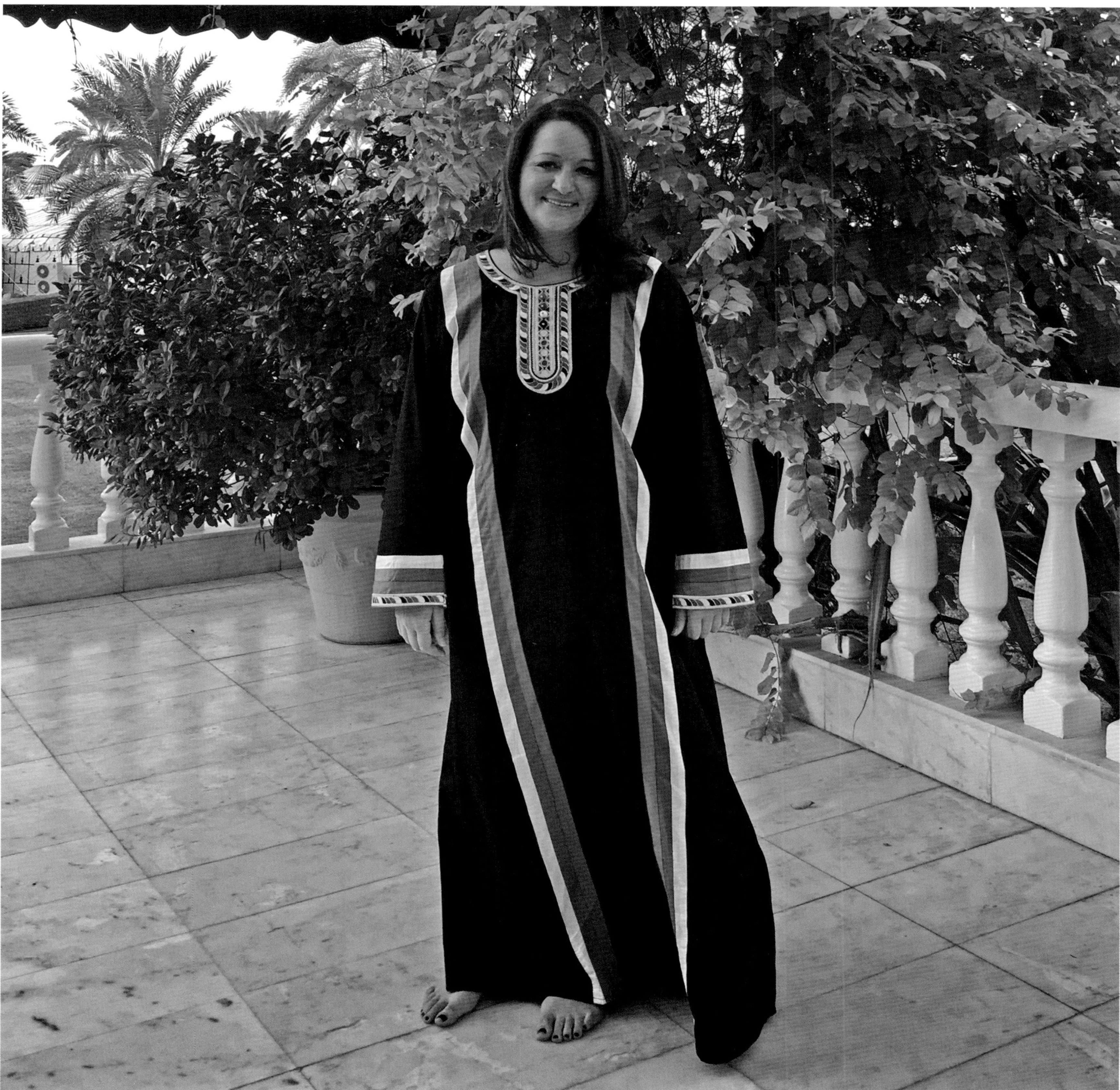

Patricia Meade

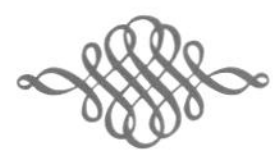

Like most people, my early childhood had a powerful impact on my life. Both my parents were alcoholics. My grandparents raised my siblings while I wound up in the foster care system from birth to age twelve. Those years of profound neglect and sadness carried over into my early twenties and thirties.

To shape myself, I took the qualities in others that I admired and incorporated them into my life. I am an exceptional listener. It is an art form and provides an education as well. Silence can be deafening if one wishes to get her point across. I perfected patience later in life. There was a time I truly believed I had to be liked by everyone and I would feel crushed when that didn't happen. As I grew older and wiser, I realized it was an exercise in futility. I also realized feeling sorry for myself for having alcoholic parents and suffering physical and sexual abuse was not productive. I was an "innocent child victim" of cruel and mentally disturbed adults. Thanks to therapy, I no longer victimize myself.

Today, I am both a divorcee and widow. My daughter is from my first marriage, which ended after a decade. My husband was unable to pass the bar exam after graduating from law school and was unwilling to seek another job. We had critical money issues. I worked at night to keep us afloat while he stayed home with our daughter. Eventually, I lost both respect and love for him. Shortly after the collapse of my marriage, I was diagnosed with breast cancer. It was a very hard, sad time and I had little support. I did what I could to keep my daughter and me safe and sound. We came through it together and that was over two decades ago.

I met my second husband five years later. He was kind and gentle. He was a successful senior producer with *ABC News – 20/20*, and we traveled the world. For the first time in my life, I was financially secure. I managed everything so he could dedicate his life to his career. We had a fun, happy marriage. It was a bit unconventional because of the traveling, but it worked for us. At sixty-six he was diagnosed with pancreatic cancer. We were lucky that he lived a few years longer than most. Not a day goes by that I don't think of him and feel gratitude for what we had.

Today, at seventy-two, I am happy to be alive, watching my sports-oriented grandsons (ten-year-old twins and a thirteen-year-old brother) grow into beautiful young boys. I moved to live closer to them. I love golf and play often. I love most sports and am an enthusiastic fan. Recently, I joined a dating site. I never thought I would and I don't know how it will turn out. I know many women my age are now doing it, and some have actually met gentlemen instead of cavemen. However for me, it might be an issue, because while my heart and mind are open to finding a companion, my legs are closed.

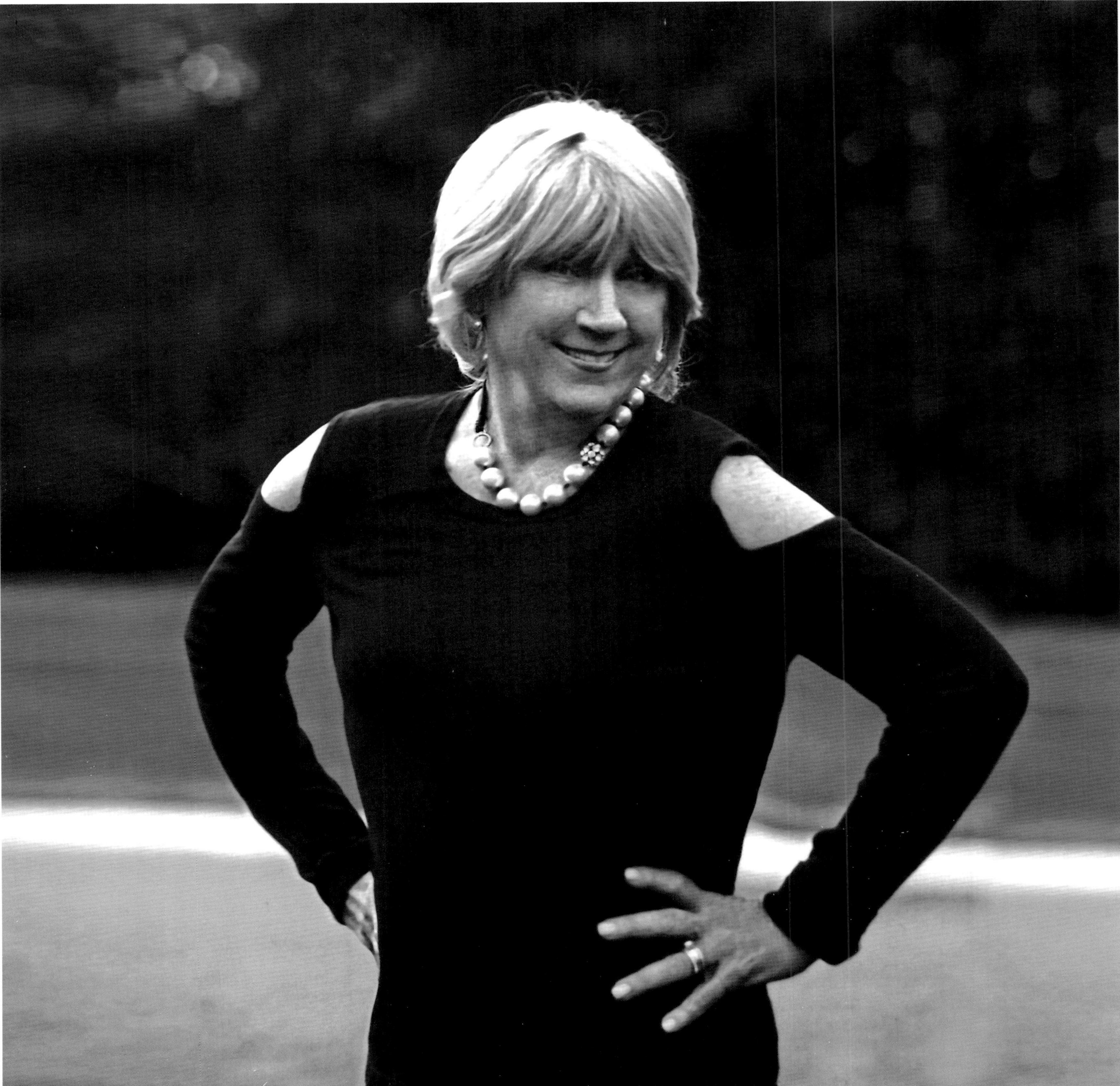

Kelly Fillnow

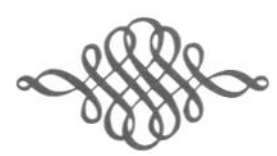

I am an identical twin who grew up in Pittsburgh. My brother was a star athlete who set a high standard for me and my sister. We tried desperately to keep up with his level of excellence. He had a perfect score on his math SATs and was invited to train at a tennis academy in Hilton Head, South Carolina. We moved, but my dad kept his job in Pittsburgh and commuted every other week to be with us. My mom was taking care of Grandma, who had an alcohol addiction, and my other Grandma who had cancer. During those hard times, I saw my parents never give up on one another. Their relationship taught me that no matter what life throws my way, I will keep fighting and never give up

No one likes trials. But the messiest chapters of my life, filled with pain, brokenness, and unmet expectations, are my defining moments. I accepted the unanswered prayers, stopped running from fear, and growth happened. I expected comfort and ease without struggle and success without failure. I am a professional triathlete. I love the thrill of pushing my body so hard when my mind just wants to quit. I learned the value of grit, self-efficacy and never giving up from my childhood.

To be honest, I struggled with perfectionism. I had to be the best in everything I did. I wanted to be the fastest person with multifurcation-timed tests. In high school, I would not settle for less than being valedictorian. In college, I wanted to not just be the best tennis player but the best athlete. Accolades, recognition, and success drove me. Second best was not enough. I look back and wish I had spent my time laughing with friends at the lake instead of studying for an exam two weeks away. Although, I don't regret my athletic persistence, the best times from my childhood and college years are the laughs with my teammates, not our victories or defeats.

A defining moment in my life was my third year as an amateur triathlete. I stood on a gorgeous mountain top in Switzerland, after just setting the American Amateur Ironman record in a time I never dreamed to achieve. As I sat there in this magical place, I knew I was looking for fulfillment in all the wrong places. I knew happiness did not come from striving for a never-attainable level of perfection. I knew I wanted to help others, and as I sat there and prayed to Jesus for help, I didn't want my life to be just about me.

Soon after, I started a coaching company. We work with athletes all over the United States and help them discover their best selves. We work with triathletes, runners, and lifestyle athletes, as well as giving corporate educational talks and health challenges. We personalize daily training programs and keep the athletes accountable. It is a joy to see people challenge themselves and accomplish what once may have been a faraway dream.

I was always so consumed with sports and studying that I never made time for guys. I never would have thought I would be unmarried at my age. I just expected it to eventually happen. Being an identical twin makes dating that much more difficult. My twin sister has desired marriage for the last decade. I cannot imagine being married before she gets married. She does not want me to wait for her to move on with my life. In fact, the very idea infuriates her. But the bond between twin sisters is indescribable. Once she is married, I feel like my heart will be open.

Right now my dreams are simple. I want to continue helping others. I want to make the most of every moment. I love cathartic runs with my shoes crushing the fallen leaves. I love deep conversations with my closest friends. I love challenge in all areas of life. I love being so exhausted from training, I falter getting off the couch. I love finishing something I never thought was possible. I love exploring nature with people. I love and dipping my toes into sand while reading a captivating book. I love singing praise and worship songs at my church. While I wait for the bigger dreams to come true, these small, yet big things sustain me.

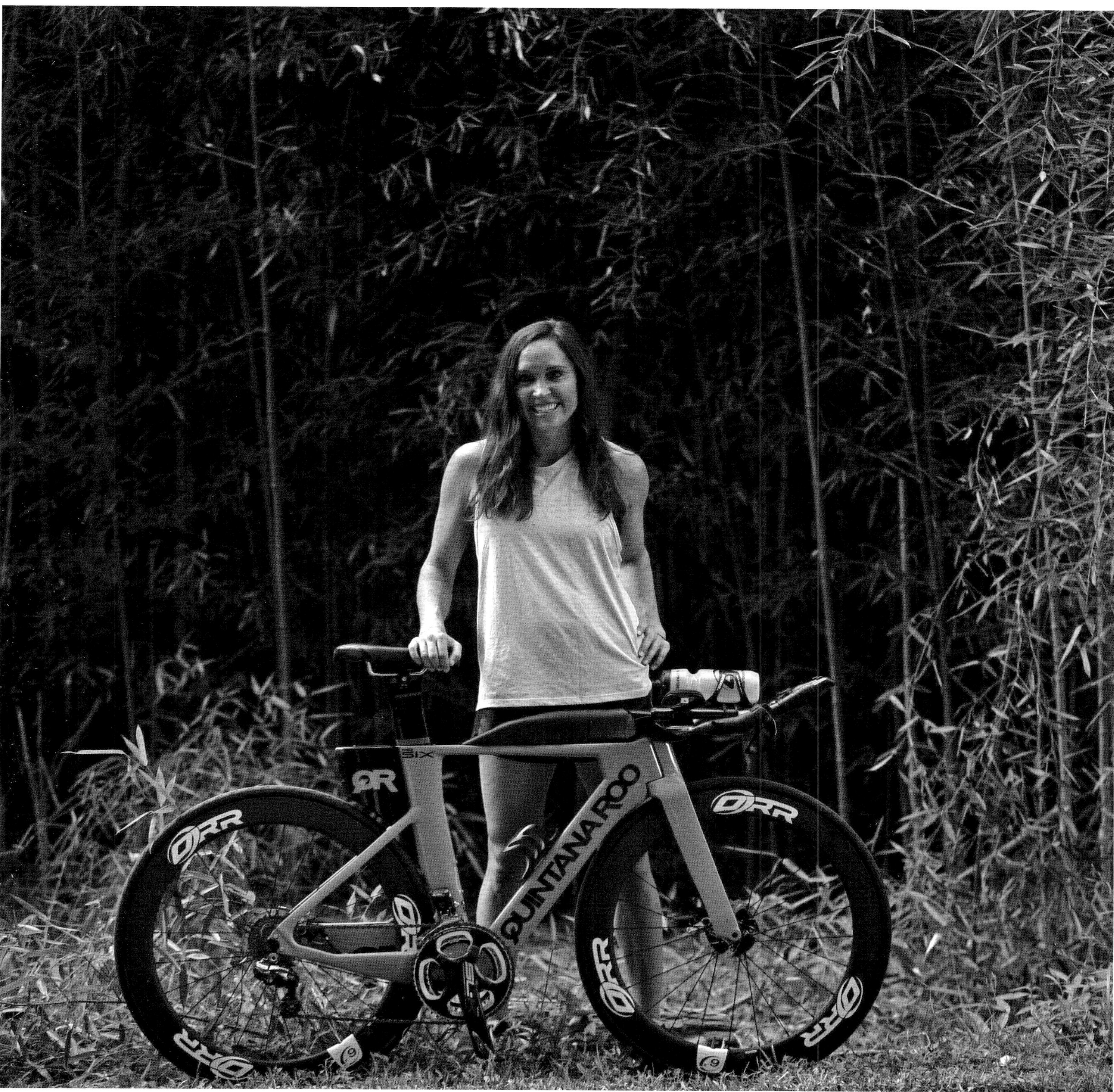
QUINTANA ROO

Beth Latshaw

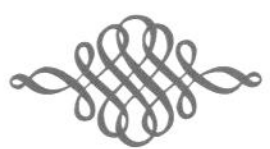

I was born in Charlotte, NC, in a stable, kind and conservative home. I was the eldest of three children. I loved all kinds of sports: swimming, biking, water skiing and anything with a ball. My favorite childhood memory was on Sunday night after church, my parents would drive to Krispy Kreme to get a box of hot doughnuts and then drive to the designated parking area to watch the airplanes take off and land. I was fascinated by all the different color lights and found the experience thrilling.

My father was a WW2 US Navy veteran who was drafted before finishing high school. When the war was over, he got his GED. Years later, he married my mother who was an RN and ten years younger than he. Soon, they had three children and he was stuck in his job as a claims adjuster. It was a decent job financially and walking away would have been difficult. (I can see him today, ranting about how he hated his job.) Looking back, that was one of the greatest lessons I learned from my dad, because I knew I never would stay in a job I hated. College was encouraged in case I ever needed to support myself. I ended up with a BS in elementary education.

In the summer of 1980, my parents paid for me to take flying lessons. They gave me $500, which was enough for me to learn to solo an airplane. I definitely wanted to pursue flying as a career but had no idea if it was possible. I was a track runner at my university and that year was the second fastest 1500-meter runner in the state of Indiana. I wanted to letter all four years, and for that reason, I was reluctant to transfer to a university with a flying program. I ended up teaching school but never got flying out of my mind.

Eventually I got a job in an airport loading planes and in station operations. It was there I started meeting pilots and learned what I needed to do to acquire my flight certificate and ratings. In a couple of years, I became a flight instructor and went to a commuter airline. After working for American Eagle for two years and becoming captain, I got hired by United Airlines. I have been there for twenty-five years, currently a B767 captain mostly flying to Europe.

In my thirties, I was a new-hire pilot at United and got pregnant with my son during my first year of employment. All pilots are on probation their first year at a major airline. There were some older pilots who make it clear they did not think the cockpit was a place for a female, no less a pregnant one. Some tried to make my life miserable. Seven years later, when I was upgrading to a B737 captain, one of the senior captains, who was particularly mean to me years earlier, actually apologized and told me how proud he was of me.

I am passionate about "excellence." Laziness drives me crazy. I love helping those who make an honest effort. I tell young people, "You don't have to be the smartest one in the class, just outlast everyone else."

I have a personal philosophy regarding relationships that has brought me enormous happiness. I have older friends whose lives are rich with valuable life lessons, and I have learned from them. I have close relationships with my peers, which is filled with laughter over shared experiences that we have had over the years, and I mentor young people. Every summer I take my Piper Cub airplane to a "Brigade Air" camp and talk about aviation with the teenagers. I always tell them that life is too short to not love your work... and if you love it, it's not work.

I have been on my own for over three years now, having been in a marriage that was abusive. I honestly don't get lonely. I have a close relationship with my son and his wife. My neighborhood is unusual in that every household has at least one pilot. The camaraderie is unique and wonderful... we are like family. I love that now my identity and happiness is not dependent on another person.

The past decades have been a wonderful adventure that I could never have imagined in my younger years. Through it all, kindness, justice and a humble spirit are characteristics I appreciated when shown to me. Now that is exactly what I consider important to convey to the ones I influence in my journeys.

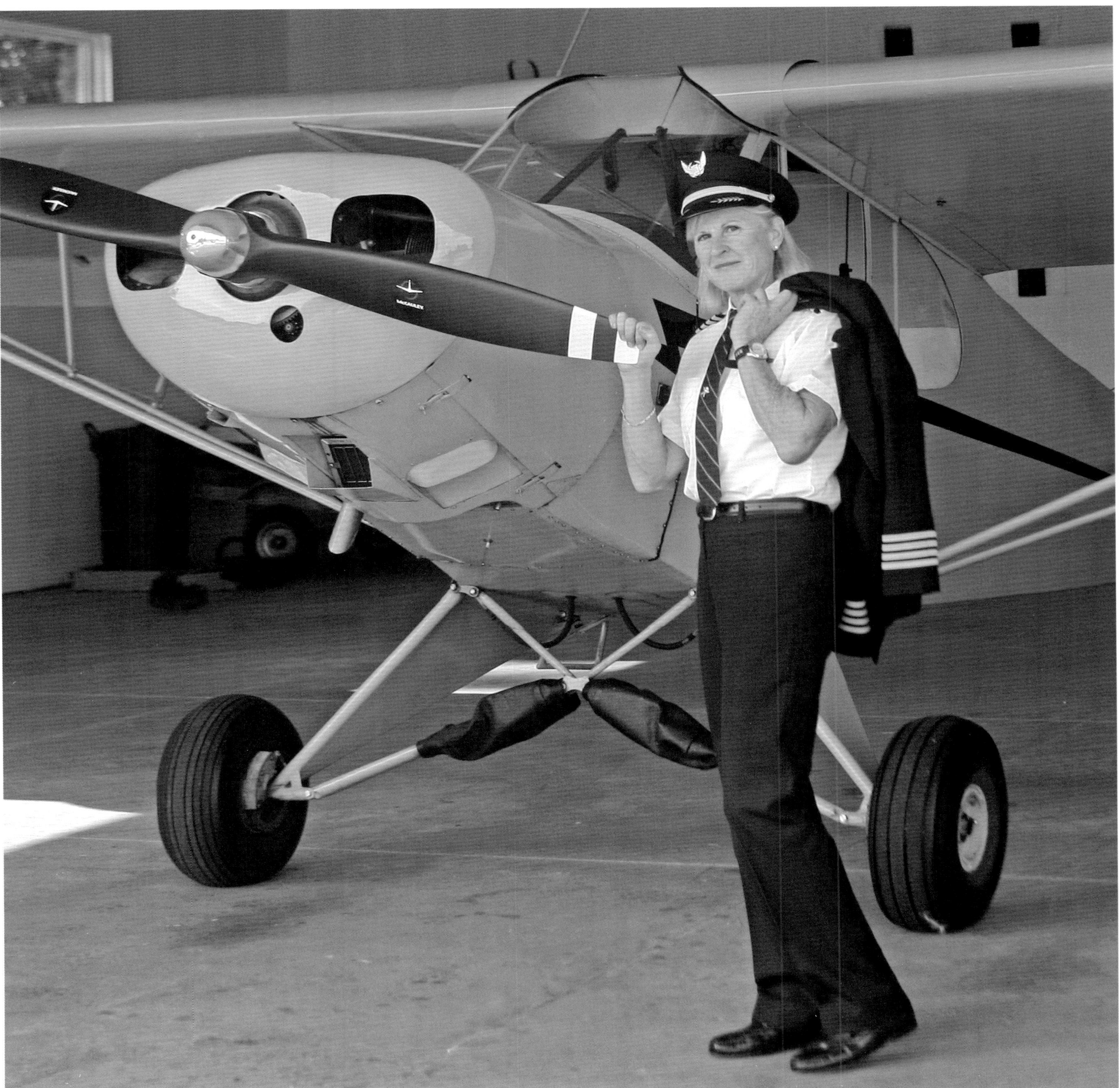

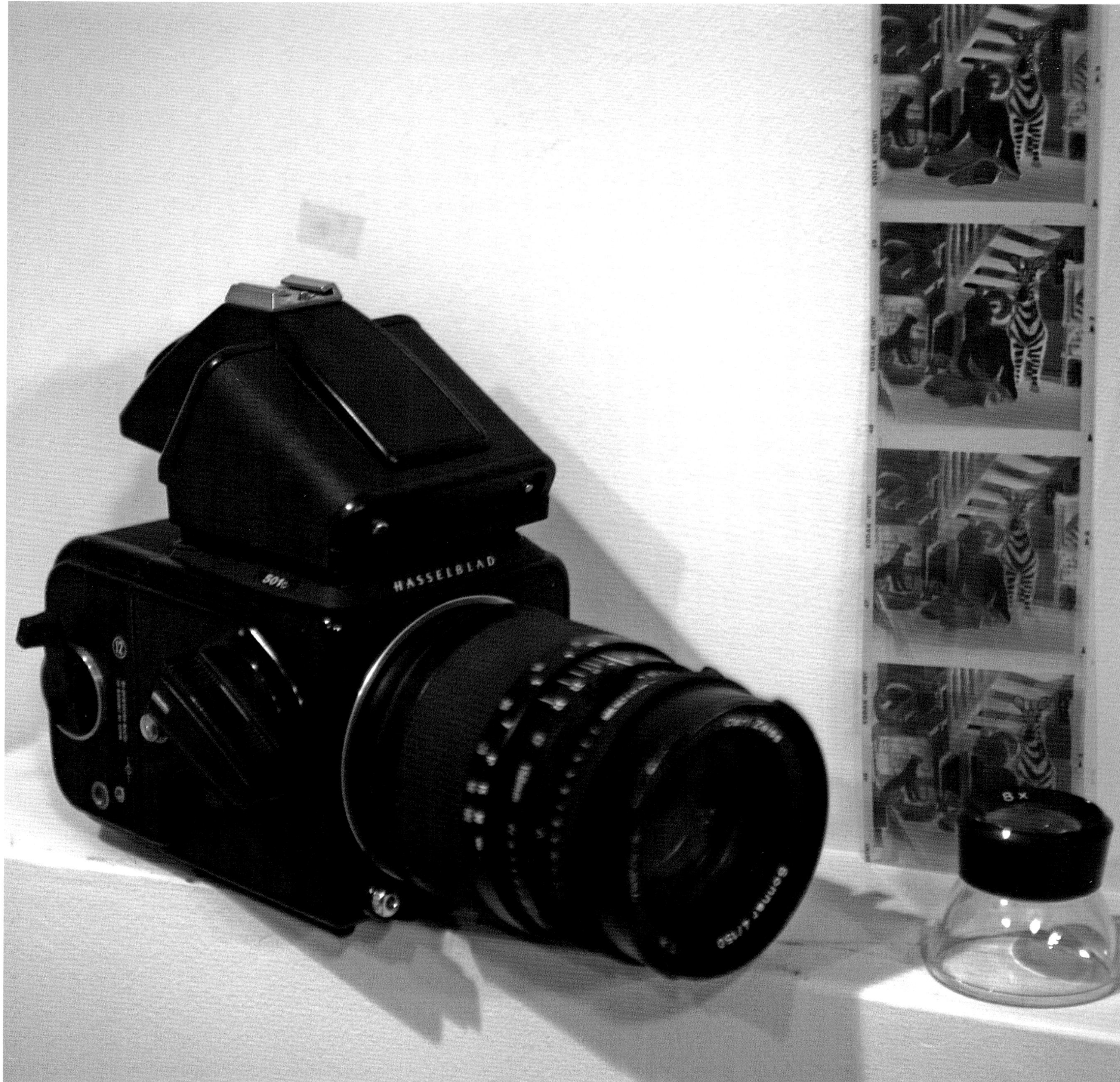
501c
HASSELBLAD
8 x

A NOTE ABOUT THE CREATIVE PROCESS

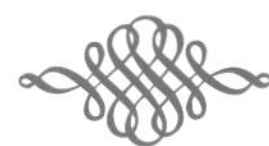

The photography for this book blends old and new technologies. Some photos were shot with a classic Hasselblad camera. As technology changed, I reluctantly changed with it. I had a hard time giving up film, especially since being in the darkroom and being a bit of an alchemist was magical for me. I decided to purchase a Canon D5 and quickly fell in love with the miracle of immediate gratification. I was also enormously impressed with the reproduction quality of the photos. I used natural light and reflectors while working outdoors and traveled with a black velvet background, which I used often.

The women in this project came from referrals from people I know and trust. Once in a while I would meet someone on my own and knew she was perfect for the book. The ladies came from New England to California, from Florida to Maine. For the most part, I did the photo shoot and interview on the same day. I asked them to wear what best represented them and made them feel comfortable. When circumstances or timing did not permit for an in-person interview, the women emailed me, phoned, or used a tape recorder. They revealed their personal background, life experiences and lessons learned. There was alot of follow-up and many of these women have now become my friends.

I have been asked why I created a book on "solo" women. It's a good question, since I have been married 49 years. My prior books, *Divas, Dames & Dolls,* honoring fabulous older women, and *Soaring Spirits*, showcasing women at the Senior Olympics, featured close to eighty women who were living by themselves. I found them to be very inspiring, so doing a book of solo women felt like a natural next step.